A Community of Writers

EDITED BY ROBERT DANA

A Community of Writers

Paul Engle and the Iowa Writers' Workshop

UNIVERSITY OF IOWA PRESS Ψ Iowa City

University of Iowa Press, Iowa City 52242

Printed in the United States of America

Design by Richard Hendel

http://www.uiowa.edu/~uipress

Printed on acid-free paper

Library of Congress Cataloging-in-Publication Data

A community of writers: Paul Engle and the Iowa Writers'
   Workshop / edited by Robert Dana.

        p.   cm.

    ISBN 0-87745-668-2

    1. Engle, Paul, 1908–1991—Friends and associates.
  2. Creative writing—Study and teaching (Higher)—Iowa—
History—20th century.   3. American literature—20th
century—History and criticism.   4. Authors, American—
20th century—Biography.   5. Authorship—Social aspects—
Iowa.   6. Iowa Writers' Workshop.   I. Dana, Robert, 1929–
PS3509.N44Z53   1999
811'.52—dc21   98-48369
99   00   01   02   03   P   5   4   3   2   1

CONTENTS

Preface, vii

The Writer and the Place, *Paul Engle*, 1

PAUL ENGLE, IMPRESARIO

Recollections of the Iowa Writers' Workshop, *James B. Hall*, 13

Some Recollections, *Warren Carrier*, 18

Paul at Stone City, *R. V. Cassill*, 24

A Miranda's World, *Donald Justice*, 27

My Time, *Constance Urdang*, 34

When Literary Life Was Still Piled Up in a Few Places,
        Robert Bly, 37

A Crisis of Sorts, *Curtis Harnack*, 45

Dear Hualing, *Vance Bourjaily*, 52

"I'll Make Your Career," *Kiyohiro Miura*, 57

Engle's Workshop, *Lewis Turco*, 63

He Made It Possible, *Marvin Bell*, 72

Every Shut-Eye Ain't Asleep, *Michael S. Harper*, 78

A Tale of Two Fathers, *Bharati Mukherjee*, 89

The Fellowship, *Philip F. O'Connor*, 93

Thank You, Paul, *Wai-lim Yip*, 107

"Next Year You Can See for Yourself," *Michael Dennis
        Browne*, 109

New World Symphony, *Kurt Vonnegut*, 113

MENTORS, FOMENTERS, AND TORMENTORS

Mentors, Fomenters, and Tormentors, *W. D. Snodgrass*, 119

Far from the Ocean: Robert Lowell at Iowa, 1953,
    Robert Dana, 147

Mine Own John Berryman, *Philip Levine*, 160

Improvisations on Donald Justice, *Charles Wright*, 186

R. V. Cassill, *Jean Wylder*, 193

Ray B. West, Jr., *Richard Stern*, 196

Marguerite Young: Trying on a Style,
    William Cotter Murray, 201

Vance Bourjaily, *Eugene Garber*, 206

Kurt Vonnegut: Waltzing with the Black Crayon,
    Gail Godwin, 213

MYTHS AND TEXTS

The Emergence of the Writers' Workshop, *John C. Gerber*, 225

Flannery O'Connor in the Writers' Workshop,
    Jean Wylder, 229

Chicken à la King, *Oakley Hall*, 235

Snapshots of Paul, *Kay Cassill*, 237

Dylan Thomas at Iowa, *Ray B. West, Jr.*, 241

So Began the Happiest Years of My Life, *Henri Coulette*, 260

Fair Days and Fowl, *Steven D. Salinger*, 262

Afterword, *Hualing Nieh Engle*, 273

Notes on Contributors, 281

Acknowledgments, 293

Preface

"We do not pretend to have produced the writers included in this book. Their talent was inevitably shaped by the genes rattling in ancestral closets. We did give them a community in which to try out the quality of their gift."

These words were written by a wise teacher in an era when the number of writing programs in the world numbered exactly two, a world fewer and fewer people remember ever existed, a world fading but, at the same time, folding into the "gold enamelling" of myth. No matter. Paul Engle's words are as good now as they were when he wrote them, long before his University of Iowa Writers' Workshop became world famous, much imitated, and academically rich.

". . . to the young writer, with his uneasiness about writing as an honorable career, or with his excess of ego about calling himself a writer," he went on in his 1961 preface to *Midlands*, an anthology of poetry and prose spanning twenty-five years of writing from the Iowa workshops, "to them, we offer hard criticism and decent sympathy."

And that is, indeed what we got.

Paul Engle was not on the scene when I arrived at the University of Iowa Writers' Workshop in 1952. He was on Averill Harriman's estate in upstate New York. Doing what, I don't, to this day, exactly know. Writing poetry, making the kinds of contacts he needed to make outside the state of Iowa to keep the dream of the workshop going? He was as distant from my immediate situation as Moses on the mountain, a rumor, a possibility.

My immediate situation was a corrugated metal hut on the Iowa River. Here sat Karl Shapiro, then editor of *Poetry* magazine, and fifteen to twenty young men and women much like me, a little awed to be in the classroom with a Pulitzer Prize—winning poet, the famous editor of a historically famous magazine, one that had published work by Yeats, Eliot, and Pound, Wallace Stevens and Marianne Moore, at a time when it very much mattered. And it was still publishing much of the best poetry being written. Shapiro took the train from Chicago to Iowa City once a week to meet his workshop and conduct personal conferences. Here was one of the powers of poetry, a man who could be thought to know what he was talking about.

Paul Engle never did things by halves. He staffed the fiction workshop with gifted writers and teachers like R. V. Cassill and Ray B. West, Jr.; and whenever he was absent as the guiding power of the workshop, he replaced himself with exceptionally talented poets: Shapiro, Wallace Fowlie, Robert Lowell, and John Berryman, to mention only the stars of my own time in the workshop. And he left them alone to run things their own way. Which of us, under such tutelage, could have failed to learn some important lessons about our craft?

And Paul saw to it that that was what the workshop was about: craft. The craft of fiction and, in my case, of poetry. The writing of the poem. What one needed to know about metaphor, about diction, about forms: the elegy, the ode, the sestina, the villanelle, the sonnet. Who wrote best in these forms, and so on. (Even if we were not, in fact, going to continue to emulate the past, we had a duty to know its work thoroughly.) I still remember clearly Paul quoting Rilke's *Letters to a Young Poet* or reciting his favorite passage from Stevens about poetry—"an abstraction blooded, as a man by thought." Or passing on Frost's observation that "a poem is what begins in delight and ends in wisdom." And he would recite these passages with relish and complete conviction. You knew he loved the words. You knew he believed them to embody enduring truths. You knew he cared about poetry and poets and the writing of poems.

It may be worth mentioning here that I don't think I ever heard anyone speak of a literary "career" back then. That was not what the workshop was about in the 1950s and 1960s. Most of us hoped we'd be lucky enough to find a job teaching literature somewhere. We'd write poetry or stories as part of our work, and maybe we'd get good enough to achieve something noteworthy. There was a certain modesty that presided over our occasional dreaming, a modesty born of the conviction that writing is hard work, that it requires sacrifice and self-effacement. It was part of the mood Paul Engle created.

Like any great impresario, however, and that's what Paul Engle was certain days of the week, he could be enigmatic and contradictory and hard. He could pass you by in the university library without so much as a nod. Was he preoccupied with some poem of his own, or some promotional scheme to bring in scholarship money (he once tapped an ice-cream manufacturer in Chicago to help bankroll a festival honoring Baudelaire!), or was it that you hadn't turned in any good work lately or published it anywhere? You never knew, and you'd never ask.

On the other hand, a letter might turn up in your mailbox, as it once did in mine a year or two after I'd left the workshop. Someone from Doubleday saying a poem of mine had been selected for use in one of their forthcoming anthologies. I was completely baffled as to how they had gotten hold of the poem. Only a few friends had copies. I'd thought the piece too slight to bother doing anything more to it and had discarded it. Weeks later, I found out in casual conversation with him that Paul had given copies of a couple of my poems to the editor of the anthology and had simply forgotten to mention it.

Another time, again after I'd graduated from the university and was living and teaching nearby, I got a call from Paul. "Bob, what are you doing tomorrow? I need someone to pick up William Carlos Williams and Flossie at the Jefferson Hotel and drive them to the Amanas to meet some people for lunch. Could you do it for me?" I was stunned. Could I do it? I wouldn't sleep a nod that night with the excitement of the prospect. And I wasn't disappointed. For a good half hour, while we drove, Williams sat next to me doing his best to try to clarify for me his idea of the triadic or relative foot, the new American metric he believed we badly needed.

Paul Engle was very complex, needless to say. He was sometimes the shrewd and hardheaded horsetrader he claimed his forebears had been. But he was also the scholar of literature who had won a Rhodes and crewed for Oxford, and who, at twenty-six, had been a poet of promise and of some achievement. And he was, above all, the genius behind the Iowa Writers' Workshop, a role that required all the qualities of the horsetrader, the scholar, and the poet.

Many of the fine essays in this collection testify to the generosity of impulse at the core of Paul's character. Indeed, isn't it, I wonder, at the core of his vision of the workshop? "In America," he was fond of saying, "we don't have any sidewalk cafes as they do in Paris, where younger writers meet with older writers and talk about their craft. The workshop is our version of the sidewalk cafe." Generosity. The masters of the craft.sharing with the young and aspiring their knowledge, hard and sometimes bitterly won, and their love of the art.

Today, of course, there are literally hundreds of writers' workshops in colleges and universities all over America. They are as common as Paul Engle's beloved corn. Indeed, they can be found in Europe and Asia and elsewhere around the world, many of them founded and directed by graduates of the original Iowa Writers' Workshop. In turn, these communities of talent have given birth to what is undoubtedly the greatest writing binge in the history of literature. So it is strange, as Kurt Vonnegut notes here, that more than half a century after Paul Engle's passion has spread worldwide, he remains little honored by his home state and by his university. There is no marker, there by the river, next to the Memorial Union, to indicate the spot where the old corrugated steel sheds stood that housed the original workshop office and classes. After those buildings were torn down, the area went to parking lots. And now a Frank Gehry designed technology lab stands there blank as a sphinx. Nor is there any bust of Paul Engle in stone or bronze to be found in the little grassy mall there that leads to the footbridge where many a young writer stood and looked down into the muddy waters of the fast-moving Iowa River, wondering. The elegant old house on Clinton Street that now serves the Writers' Workshop, in fact, bears someone else's name.

So, many thanks to Hualing Nieh Engle, whose idea it was to put together this collection of essays as a memorial to Paul and to the early mentors of the University of Iowa Writers' Workshop. It was Hualing who originally invited and gathered much of the material included here. Without her diligence, her faith in the project, and her urging, I would never have undertaken to edit and shape this book. Its structure is simple and, I think, reasonably direct: a section given over to memories of Paul Engle in his heyday; a second section focusing especially on those teachers, aside from Paul, who made the workshop hum on a day-to-day basis; and a final section mingling a little history and some good yarns. In fact, of course, these categories are not absolutely exclusive. Myth and history mingle to a greater or lesser degree in each writer's recollections. Within each of the three sections of the book the work of each writer is presented by decade — the 1940s, the 1950s, the 1960s — although the essays are not dated. No attempt has been made to airbrush the pictures that emerge, although some essays had to be edited to conserve space. Each writer has said what he or she wanted to say, recording both gripes and glories. Paul wouldn't have had it any other way.

Thanks also to Fritz and Kenneth Maytag, trustees of the Maytag Family Foundation; and to William and Teddy Shuttleworth for their financial support, which bought time, secretarial and research assistance, office supplies, and much more.

A great debt of gratitude is owed, of course, to each of the writers who contributed their work to this book, without remuneration, as a gift to the memory of a man and a time.

Special thanks to Donald Justice and William Cotter Murray for their many invaluable suggestions, and to K. K. Merker, who plundered his archives for photographs.

Julie Neff deserves special mention for her technical expertise in the production of the manuscript and her unfailing skill in coming up with time-saving solutions to textual problems. Also Havilah Meinel for her "bits"—the results of her library researches, as well as for her filing and word-processing afternoons.

And finally, thanks to my wife, the indomitable Peg Dana, for her unfailing sense of tact, her wise advice, and her hours spent reading and proofreading and discussing this text after a full day's work of her own.

A Community of Writers

The Writer and the Place

It was a vision.

By vision, I do not mean the abrupt and ecstatic experience of Saul on the road to Damascus, blinded by a light "above the brightness of the sun," and startled by a voice speaking from heaven.

By vision, I mean the steady development at the University of Iowa of the conviction that the creative imagination in all of the arts is as important, as congenial, and as necessary, as the historical study of all the arts. How simple, and yet how reckless.

This gradual revelation was quite as astonishing as a sudden idea seen, for the first time, in a flash of light. It took imagination, some years ago, for an educational institution to put its trust in the imaginative arts.

Universities are not famous for taking chances, but the University of Iowa took one. There were doubts at the start. Could the writer keep his native frenzy in an academic air? Would not the place be overrun with aesthetes who come not to work but to dabble their delicate fingers in the Iowa River, which flows through the campus? (The answer to this was an easy "No!" for the river is frozen hard all winter and it is too muddy all summer, although with the finest mud in the world.) Would there not be fire, violence in the streets, and, most criminal of all, loafing in the classroom? If you gave young writers enough rope, would they hang decency and honor instead of, as might be hoped, hanging each other?

The French novelist Gustave Flaubert said, "The sight of a nude woman makes me think of her skeleton." Similarly, the university looked beyond the superficial image of these doubts and thought of the solid talent beneath, although perhaps not with Flaubert's analytical enthusiasm. By doing so, it recognized a powerful new direction in this country's culture, the writer everywhere on the campus, the older as teacher, the younger as student. For the first time in the sad and enchanting history of literature, for the first time in the glorious and dreadful history of the world, the writer was welcome in the academic place. If the mind could be honored there, why not the imagination?

One can understand why European universities would find this distasteful, with their ancient and rigid structures, although young writers are increasingly found at English institutions today. It was the flexibility of the American university, with its effort to roam over all areas of human activity, which made possible, if not easy, the addition of the creative person to the campus. If it is proper to teach children chicken-sexing, which calls for extreme acuteness of eye, and weaving, which can be a matter of the most gracious taste in design, then why is it not appropriate to teach originality in writing? To say that the creative has no part in education is to argue that a university should not be universal.

There is still a question to be asked — however pleasant this may sound, will it really work in practice? Here are a few facts from the University of Iowa in the last couple of years. In the anthology *New Poets of England and America* (edited by Hall, Pack, and Simpson), one-third of the whole American section consisted of poets who were then, or had recently been, at the poetry workshop, surpassing in number those at any university in this country or in England. In 1959 the Lamont Poetry Award given by the Academy of American Poets was won by Donald Justice for *The Summer Anniversaries*. In 1960 it was won by Robert Mezey for *The Lovemakers*. In 1960 the Pulitzer Prize for poetry was given to W. D. Snodgrass for *Heart's Needle*. The Yale Series of Younger Poets volume for 1959 was William Dickey's *Of the Festivity*. Winner of the first University of Nebraska Press First-Book publication prize for a new manuscript of American verses was Bruce Cutler's *The Year of the Green Wave*. The Scribner's annual series, *Poets of Today*, has included five Iowa workshop poets in the first six volumes: Harry Duncan, Murray Noss, Joseph Langland, Theodore Holmes,

Donald Finkel. The National Book Award for fiction, 1959, went to Philip Roth, now teaching at the fiction workshop, for his book of stories *Goodbye, Columbus*; in 1960 the National Book Award for poetry went to Robert Lowell, a former teacher in the poetry workshop, for his *Life Studies*. The *Esquire Reader*, a collection of ten new writers of fiction, 1960, includes five who are either students or teachers at the fiction workshop.

These are works from the middle of the imagination by people who have been part of this creative effort in the middle of the country. They represent only the most recent of the scores of books of fiction and poetry published by members of the writing program, and hardly a fraction of the hundreds of poems and stories which have appeared in every magazine of consequence in this country, and in some from Europe. I would rather not resort to this sort of obvious cataloging of successes, but they are unassailable facts proving objectively that the university today is an honest and helpful place for the writer to be.

When President Lincoln was ill one time he said, "Now let the office-seekers come, for at last I have something I can give all of them." The writing program at the University of Iowa, more modest and less infectious than the president, does not offer something to all seekers. We believe that you can only teach where something in a mind is waiting to be taught. We do not pretend to grow blonde curls on an autumn pumpkin (alas, for what a triumph that would be in a farm state; when this happens, Iowa will be first). When Shelley wrote Keats, after reading some of his early and unrestrained poetry, that he should load every rift with ore, he was engaged in the sort of teaching we try to do; that is, he was identifying talent, and then saying what he could to make it better. Indeed, if Shelley turned up at the University of Iowa today, as English poets now do, his talent would be recognized and encouraged, and it is inconceivable that he would be thrown out as he was at Oxford. Maxwell Perkins editing the massive manuscripts of Thomas Wolfe into presentable shape is the sort of teaching we believe can be done.

After all, has the painter not always gone to an art school, or at least to an established master, for instruction? And the composer, the sculptor, the architect? Then why not the writer? Good poets, like good hybrid corn, are both born and made. Right criticism can speed up the maturing of a poet by years. More than that, tough and detailed criticism of a young writer can help him become his own shrewd critic so that, when he publishes, the critics will not have to be tough on him. In the process of original writing, every word and every attitude is subject to a constant scrutiny, or should be, and much of what we do is to heighten the sense of awareness which this requires. We knock, or persuade, or terrify, the false tenderness toward his own work out of the beginning writer. This is the beginning of wisdom.

As so often, Flaubert has said it wisely, "Beware of that intellectual overheating called inspiration," he wrote, and this is our warning too. Learn that it is not the intensity of emotion in the writer that matters, but the intensity of the shaped language (to paraphrase T. S. Eliot). Unless the writer keeps his aesthetic distance from the object he is creating, it may well overwhelm him in an excess of self-commitment. Flaubert said it: "You can depict wine, love, and women on the condition that you are not a drunkard, a lover, or a husband. If you are involved in life, you see it badly; your sight is affected either by suffering or enjoyment." This is not to argue for coldness in the writer, but only for that minimum level of calmness without which the work will not have the control necessary to achieve form, without which the moving cry becomes only screaming.

Flaubert knew the emotional risks of the writer, and only urged an objective stare at the subjective scene because he was so greatly in danger of drowning in his own subjectivity. "When I was describing the poisoning of Emma Bovary," he commented, "I had such a taste of arsenic in my mouth and was poisoned so effectively myself, that I had two attacks, for I vomited my entire dinner." What young writer could be harmed by discovering such an example? He is more likely to be harmed by looking at writing as the spontaneous outpouring of immediate feeling, like a patient on the psychiatrist's couch, the sodium amytal in his blood dissolving his inhibitions. The typewriter seems to act as the hypodermic syringe, releasing his babble of language. This writing then goes to the printer unrevised, lively perhaps, with the immediacy of its memories, but turgid in its unshaped prose. This delusion, that writing is not a formed art, but that it falls naturally onto the page like sudden rain, we try to persuade out of any heads which have it thundering and raging inside.

In a country with so ranging a landscape, with its concentration of culture so widely diffused, the problem of where a young writer is to feel at home becomes far more urgent than in England, where London is in easy reach. There must be an alternative between Hollywood and New York, between those places psychically as well as geographically. The University of Iowa tries to offer such a community, congenial to the young writer, with his uneasiness about writing as an honorable career, or with his excess of ego about calling himself a writer. To them, we offer hard criticism and decent sympathy. More than that, our way of mimeographing poetry and fiction for the workshops offers everyone a hearing. To have your work read by all the members of the workshop, and publicly criticized and praised by your instructors in the weekly meetings, represents a helpful and at the same time less hazardous form of publication.

The system offers proof that writing can be seriously regarded, and that it is a difficult art not only worth an absolute commitment of faith, time, and energy, but demanding it. The writer finds that the students around him are alert to his faults and quick to praise his virtues. In brief, he is, while practicing a completely private art, reassured by a sense of belonging to a group which gives him decent regard. For as long as he is part of this community, he has a useful competition with those around him, and at the same time is freed from the imperatives of the marketplace, as he may never be again. He can have a manner of publication without losing too much blood.

This matter of place is of tremendous importance to the writer in the U.S.A. We do not have that intense concentration of talent in one city, as certainly exists in Paris, London, and Rome, where writers either know each other or know a good deal about each other. Our plan gives the writer a place where he can be himself, confronting the hazards and hopes of his own talent, and at the same time he can measure his capacity against a variety of others, some better, some worse. He grows up rapidly. He becomes his own self-critic. He discovers that learning to write is not a mere acquiring of "techniques," as if he were learning to be a laboratory assistant or an appliance repairman, but in part a learning of his own nature. The criticism of a manuscript may be directed less to the prose than to the personality who wrote it. Sometime the young writer must understand that writing is a hard and solitary occupation, accomplished only by the old and bitter way of sitting down in fear and trembling to confront the most terrifying thing in the world — a blank sheet of paper. It is heartening to be able to do this in a place where you know that others are facing the same ordeal.

Place does not mean simply the boundaries of the United States. We have found that the creative imagination is wonderfully alert in breaking down the barriers of nationality and language. The workshops have heard the voices of poets and fiction writers speaking English (and writing it) in a charming and original way, which varied according to whether the speakers were from Japan, Taiwan, South Korea, the Philippines, Ireland, England, Canada, Sweden, India. A former officer in the Imperial Japanese Navy has heard his poems on the fall of Japan criticized by a former yeoman in the American Navy. A girl from India, looking as if she had stepped down from her usual job of holding up the corner of a temple roof just to attend this class for an hour, has heard with shock the story of an American boy's anxieties and bafflement in his relationship with women. "But why all of this fuss about sex?" she asked in a voice British in enunciation but gently, beautifully songlike.

The man who wrote the story, a former Marine sergeant with shoulders which looked as if they could have held up the temple alone, glared at her and demanded with a luminous suspicion, "OK, so what's wrong with sex?"

"Oh, nothing," she replied, dropping the words into the air as if they were carved in stone, "but why do so much worrying about it? We settled all of that thousands of years ago."

For a moment all discussion stopped while the calm-out-of-violence of ancient India hung in the troubled atmosphere of a hot

August afternoon in a modest-sized Iowa town just about to become one hundred years old.

The strength of this international quality in the workshops is an example to us all of the power which the creative impetus has. Kim Yong Ik, probably the leading South Korean fiction writer in English, describes his widowed mother diving far down in the freezing waters of a Korean island to gather edible plants to feed her family. The place is strange to us, the customs are stranger, the language spoken by the family is strangest of all. Yet in a plain room in Iowa City, with the closest salt water over one thousand miles away, in the presence of young writers from the red earth hills of Georgia, the green counties of the English Midlands, the brown width of Texas, the granite-gouged valleys of New Hampshire, the deep Minnesota woods, the shallow Louisiana swamps, the California coast sun-brilliant below Los Angeles, the northern fog of Dublin, and the southern jungle of Negros Island in the Philippines, the story of that diving woman and her family was as close as the air they breathed. Reason: it was told with imagination.

For such a community, home is not the place where, when you have to go there, they have to take you in, as the Frost poem accurately says of its people. Home is the one place where the creative energy finds that, once it has come there, they are glad to take it in. The benefit to the whole United States of giving these articulate people from the far islands and continents of the earth a conviction that this country cherishes their talent (as their own countries often do not) is beyond measuring. For those seeking a true image of America, it is lucky that they come not to a seacoast city but to an interior town in the midst of the fat land that feeds the nation. Here they have a direct look at the daily life of the U.S.A. in its most typical manner.

Of course there are those in the academic life of the U.S.A. who either suspect us, deplore us, or hate us. In certain cases, we are proud to have them as enemies. In other cases, we regret the misunderstandings spoken about our beliefs or intentions. Let us be definite about this. There seems to us no reason for hostility between the study of literature and its creation. There are those who feel that writing is better done by the inspired ignoramus, uncorrupted by the weakening influences of the university. To us, it makes no difference what grows on the wall outside the writer's house, whether it is English ivy, poison ivy, hops, morning glories, or gourd vines. F. Scott Fitzgerald said once that there are no second chapters in American lives. Too often there are no second books, or at least there are second books no better (often worse) than the first. We think that the critical study of past literature will give the writer a maturity and an awareness of all the infinite variety of forms and attitudes, and that this will give bone and tendon to the soft flesh of his feelings.

A very important help here is that scholarship has never been so congenial to the writers as today. In much of their work, many scholars make literary insights which sometimes equal in perception the insights contained in the text they are studying. There has been a good deal of criticism today which surpasses in imaginative texture some of what is taken for literature. . . .

It would be folly to deny that there are often reasons for hostility. Never in the world's cultural history has the study of literature been so minutely organized into departments of English, with numbered courses and named degrees. How can this immense apparatus really find enough fresh material to equal its massive arrangements? Will there not be several scholars converging through the tall grass of the library's meadow, all aiming for the one poor little rabbit-fact? New interpretations there will always be, but as of now the scholarly pattern is set up as if there really would be a place for the textual scholar as there had been in the past, when we needed a definitive text of Shakespeare and Chaucer. Here is where the writer becomes useful. Why should he not be a small, indeed a very small, part of this academic intelligence. But it has its value, wanting to teach the writers of the past from the writer's point of view, as imaginative expressions of his agony and delight, rather than as historical instances. If the creative writer is a menace to scholarship, then take a cold look at what that scholarship truly is. All too often it lacks the substance and power, not to mention the decent prose, of even minor writing.

. . . We do not pretend to have produced the included writers in this book. Their talent was inevitably shaped by the genes rattling in ancestral closets. We did give them a community in which to try out the quality of their gift, as New Englanders used to speak of trying out the oil from whale blubber. Much of this writing was done in Iowa City and received our criticism. Some of it was written far away. In either case, the writer was for a while part of the community we have made here where the university has stood in the position of friend and, to a lighter degree than we would wish, of patron. It is conceivable that by the end of the twentieth century the American university will have proved a more understanding and helpful aid to literature than ever the old families of Europe. That sort of patronage had its doubtful aspects too. Franz Joseph Haydn, radiant in his talent, was counted in the lower ranks of the domestics by the great Esterhazy family of Hungary. He wore a blue uniform and ate down at the end of the table. He composed much of his sunlit music while living with that family, whose idea of fun was to have in the music room a big chair which, when sat in, played a cheerful flute solo.

We believe in the solitary genius, not in the agreeable average. Art may turn out to be the last refuge of the individual in our time. The one man raging in his terrible talent may be worth more than the sum of one hundred thousand bland mediocrities. When Flaubert wrote the word "hysterics," he says that he was so swept away, was bellowing so loudly and feeling so deeply what his little Bovary was going through, that he was afraid of having hysterics himself. This is seldom, I would guess, the way of scholarship. The bellowing of scholars I have been happy enough to observe was not out of sympathy with the characters they were studying. Such conduct indicates a different disposition in the sort of people coming to a writing program. To our delight and astonishment, they can adapt, they can be at home, they can find a heartening help.

Of course there are risks. The mild frost of a university air can kill the tender plant. Excess of self-consciousness can slow down a talent which has little momentum. An English novelist, V. S. Pritchett, laments that the American university may induce "an unnatural hostility to vulgarity" in the writer. I have seen twenty-five years of American writers at a university. Have no fear. They will not lose their vulgarity.

For some, the university will never be the right place, and this is right. They should remain on the road or on the beach or up in the attic or down in the cellar. It's a big country, mister. There's a place for everybody, in or out of the university, in or out of the house, in or out of jail. . . .

The curious extraordinary devices which made this writing program possible in a state university are a part of the lavish variety of the American way of doing everything, including education and literature. It is proper, then, to express our thanks to a country which has given freedom of voice to its own young talent, and to that of many other nations. We have been allowed to run, stumble, and jump over the lovely landscape of the imagination. How can writers praise a country more than by saying: Look! In this place we have been free.

Paul Engle, Impresario

Recollections of the
Iowa Writers' Workshop

At war's end and a few years after, an unusually talented group of new writers began to hear of Iowa City and the Writers' Workshop. More often than not we were referrals from other regional colleges and universities where we had met local competition, or we had published something (my case), or we were here on faith, because we were "interesting." The Graduate Record Exam was not required for admission.

No matter, the workshop was an exciting idea, said to have been the brainchild of Professor Wilbur Schramm—he who once played trumpet in Sousa's band, and "invented" the word "communication" as we now know it, and who went on to other things.

An exciting idea because the workshops were closely aligned with an influential intellectual movement centered in the Iowa English Department: The New Humanism. Under that scheme, among other things, learning and creativity were highly valued in that order of importance; to turn loose an ill-educated writer on the world was not in the best interest of the university. Therefore, early on, one was expected to do a variety of things and do them to a certain level of competence: the history of criticism, the rudiments of scholarship, and knowledge of the other arts. The creative work was to be of high literary quality.

Put another way, we were expected to please, to pass the kindly scrutiny of a variety of masters, Humanists all; on the creative side, we were expected to write and to react with local staff and a whole series of visiting writers, in residence either for weeks or, for some, years on end.

The unique nature of the Iowa program claims early mention. Post–World War II, in all of the U.S., there were but about five places where creative writing was offered in some programmatic way at the graduate levels. To be sure a place like Harvard or Stanford might offer the odd course, usually under the tutelage of an academically based writer or poet; certain programs were under schools of journalism where an immediate market-orientation was the rule. By contrast, in 1996 there are more than four hundred creative writing programs of degree-granting intent. In addition there are a great many nonacademic programs in creative writing, usually by correspondence, all of which in some way or other use the "workshop" concept, the essence of which is an apprentice-master relationship of some duration.

We were pioneers, but did not know it.

Because so many of us were fresh from combat (or merely "service"), admission to the program was informal: a manuscript or two, a publication, a telephone call, GI papers, and any past transcripts might well come along later. In my case I telephoned Paul Engle one Sunday morning (much too early, apparently) and said I had published a story in *Story* magazine, and was calling because Walter Havighurst (Miami University of Ohio) said I should do so. "Sounds interesting," Paul said. "Why don't you just come on out?"

At that moment I was on terminal leave from the army, newly married, had only four years of the GI Bill benefits, and no idea where Iowa City might be. I went west by train, and as I bought tickets our local station master said only, "Have to route you through Chicago."

And we were "interesting."

R. V. Cassill was a painter, a former Chicago Art School instructor, and of late a Medical Corps hospital administrator in the Pacific. W. D. Snodgrass was from Pennsylvania and in the navy had decided to become a symphony conductor. The first of the cool men, Warren Miller, was pale, addicted to Graham Greene. Oakley Hall was from California and the marines; Wirt Williams hit from New Orleans, no longer either a journalist or the skipper of a sub chaser. I was a former Ohio farm boy, once of the 82nd Airborne and Military Government in Germany. There were also Herb Knipson (later the distinguished editor of *Ebony*), Ed McGuire, and a former professor, late of the navy, Hollis Summers. Others, men and gifted women, from the South, the eastern seaboard.

And, of course, not everyone had a service background. Flannery O'Connor had earned a scholarship to the Iowa School of Journalism, but had crossed over to do "shom storrowies." Two poets suggest the range of personalities in those early days. William Stafford was a deceptively sunny conscientious objector from Kansas who had a will of iron. By contrast, in my opinion, one of the most gifted students I knew briefly in the early days at Iowa was Anthony Hecht. Even then his poetry was clearly promising; he played classical piano, and knew a great deal about art and music. A cultivated young man.

Beyond talents for imaginative writing, this early group had a renaissance flair. Flannery had illustrated children's books; Charles Ruff was also a gifted jazz pianist and had been on the road with big bands; Charles Embree had studied painting with Thomas Hart Benton; one poet did the book and music for a musical comedy that was produced locally. So we could fly airplanes, navigate at sea, pack a parachute, repair your car, wire your house, address a Cedar Rapids ladies club, or handle explosives.

Nor were our teachers on the scholarly side always narrow specialists. For years Engle handled both the fiction and poetry workshops, did a large part of the administrative work, published his own work and many, many reviews of the work of others. Andrew Lytle was a demanding, affectionate man, and saw no conflict in his own career as writer, sometimes farmer, and one-time professional actor.

Most of the resident scholars and critics were eager to "look at some work." Austin Warren was a scholar, critic, and musician who did a great deal to form a workshop student's taste in modern poetry. The ranking Medievalist was a fine practical critic. For some years, at the end of tutorial conferences, Curt Zimansky and Seymour Pitcher — learned men, indeed — always suggested or gave me something I should read; I'd read it, and then they gave me something else I had never heard of. I still remember some of those books — and their kindness.

The visiting writers were of another order. Nearly always they lived by their work. Paul Horgan stayed both semesters; James T. Farrell arrived with his workingman's lunch box; Robert Penn Warren came through and might "borrow" an apartment for an evening and then invite all his friends. He, too, had been a faculty member at Iowa. Then there was the British delegation: Dylan Thomas, who rolled all the way down three flights of hotel stairs, but seemed not to understand how he got to the bottom; Ruthven Todd also drank in about the same league and one day a U.S. immigration agent came to his office and took him away. Though only "visiting" the U.S., he had thoughtlessly signed a contract to teach at Iowa. Back in London it was said he stayed aboard the plane and went on to Paris.

And then there was Spender, Auden, the off New York literary agent looking for talent, and eminent painters who gave articulate gallery lectures on their current work. The writers were a vital part of the allied-arts audience, especially for the painters and musicians. In their various ways, visiting writers read our work in manuscript, spoke with us in conference, and tried to improve the work.

As to the purpose, the larger intent of the new writer's poetry, short fiction, and novels, I think there was an understandable ambivalence. On the one hand, one's work was not to be rushed, and we worked to the highest literary standards — or believed this was so. On the other hand publication brought a kind of luminous distinction to the program, and most of us understood a student publication in a good place was powerful medicine in the Dean's Council House.

One incident illustrates the conflict. In a graduate fiction workshop one student in fact published a novel with a then-famous New York publisher. He received the grade of C — in graduate school, a failing mark. I was one of the delegation who called on the instructor to protest. He heard us out, then said, "Well, you know, it really is not a very good novel."

We walked out, accepted his judgment without further protest. At Iowa at that time literary and artistic standards prevailed over mere commercial publication. Along this line another short story writer had work published by the *Saturday Evening Post*; thereafter, some people would not speak to him, and he began to drink, and finally departed.

All that now seems long ago, and very far away: we were the pioneers who did not know it, and better it should be that way.

In retrospect, it is clear the workshop program must have had its thin spots, its faults of concept. Otherwise, the exercise would not have been so easy for other institutions to copy.

Possibly the university — or Paul Engle, who did so much for me — tried to accomplish too much with too few assets. There was a nice, American optimism about the operation; expansion was a way to prove worth and obtain more program money. As a joke, with some truth to it, it was said the budget was in the dean's side pocket and the plans were in Engle's head. Academic programs that by policy expand do so often over stretched bodies.

Life in Iowa City was at once terribly high minded, demanding, and — always — no end in sight. Each spring there was a sensational murder of some kind; the divorce rate was too high to be exemplary. The period vice was drink, with no upper level stated on consumption, either.

Then there was the time five or six new writers brawled in Davenport, and everyone ended up in jail. Two o'clock in the morning, cold as hell, and the only man to call was Paul Engle.

"Why, Ed? Where are you . . . ?"

Some Recollections

In 1949, after receiving my A.M. in comparative literature from Harvard, I decided to postpone getting a Ph.D. I had been studying full time at Harvard and teaching Spanish language and literature full time at Boston University (neither Harvard nor Boston University knew of my double academic life). I had married and had a brand new son; I wanted to finish a novel I had started (it was published three years later); and I wanted to teach in a less hectic way to support my family. I informed my major professors, Harry Levin and Albert Guerard, of my intentions and began negotiating with Bard College.

A few days after I announced my intentions, I received a telegram from a Baldwin Maxwell at the University of Iowa that read approximately as follows: Don't take Bard job. Letter follows.

Needless to say, I was dumbfounded. I had not applied to Iowa and had never heard of Baldwin Maxwell. When, with some suspicion, I showed the telegram to Albert Guerard, he smiled and said — and this I remember exactly: "We need to keep you in the big league so we can bring you back to Harvard."

Though I was flattered by Guerard's regard, I thought the whole idea a bit extravagant. A letter, however, as promised, did arrive from Maxwell. It offered me a position as assistant professor of English and suggested I consult with Paul Engle.

I then received a letter from Paul, saying he was spending the summer on Cape Ann, and inviting me to drive up from Cambridge to visit with him. I had heard of Paul Engle. He was the poet who had the courage to publish a volume of poetry entitled *Corn*, and who was director of a highly regarded writers' workshop.

After a couple of Paul's arid Martinis, I relaxed and began to enjoy his sly style of quizzing his guests, his wry sense of humor, his shrewdness, his midwestern charm (never mind Oxford and Columbia, his travels, the breadth of his reading, the ever extending reach of his connections, he was unequivocally Iowan). He wanted me to teach modern literary criticism (the New Criticism) and courses in the European novel and poetry in translation. He thought that creative writers should be exposed not only to British and American writers but to Dostoevsky, Chekhov, Mann, Rilke, Gide, Baudelaire, Mallarmé, and Lorca.

The prospect of teaching courses in the broad areas of my own field instead of being centered in Spanish and of being connected to the Writers' Workshop was even more intoxicating than an Engle Martini. I was happy to accept the conspiracies of Guerard and Engle (with the collaboration of Maxwell) that put me somewhere I now wanted very much to be.

My first actual workshop session was an eye-opener. I read carefully the stories the students had submitted and which were to be discussed in class. The faculty — Paul, Verlin Cassill, Hansford Martin, and I — met half an hour or so in advance of the class meeting. Paul asked for our opinions of the stories. Tyro that I was, and eager to demonstrate my critical acumen, I offered an extensive critique of the stories. Verlin and Hansford made a few cogent comments. We entered the classroom in a barracks by the river and sat in the front, facing the students.

Paul opened the session. His comments consisted substantially of his version of the critique I had offered in the preclass meeting! I now understood why Cassill and Martin had said so little. They had a good deal to say to the class while I was left to scrounge for ideas. While I was pleased that Paul liked my criticism, I took care on future occasions to keep some of my gems for myself.

Sometime in the fall of 1950, the English department decided that assistant professors could teach only one advanced or graduate course, and that the remainder of the course load should be at the freshman or sophomore level. At that time my schedule was precisely the reverse. I was teaching only one lower level course, The Greeks and the Bible; the rest of my teaching was at the upper or graduate level. These were the courses in modern literary criticism and European literature Paul wanted for his creative writers, and which he had specifically recruited me to teach.

I was aware that there were conflicts between the "scholarly" members of the department ("the hill") and the writing program, but other than being ignored by "the hill" members, I had suffered no offense. The new rule was another matter. Paul saw the rule as an attack on his program, and on one of his faculty members, and mounted a blistering response. He made the case for his courses and pointed out that I was the only member of the department who was qualified to teach European literature. He then went on to note that I had just published a book of translations, had a novel accepted for publication, and was reading a paper at the December meeting of the MLA. Which other department members could claim an equal record of a year's productivity?

I wanted to crawl into the book rack below my seat.

The department was ultimately persuaded to make an exception for workshop faculty. It had become clear to me that Paul would defend his programs with whatever weapons might be required. Faculty generally were aware that President Hancher supported Paul and his workshop. It was, after all, putting Iowa on at least one kind of national map.

And so the courses survived; and I, of necessity, with them.

Paul had ambitions for a literary review to be attached to the workshop. These were heydays of the *Kenyon Review*, the *Southern Review*, the *Hudson Review*, the *Sewanee Review*, edited often by the then ascendant Southern Agrarians, John Crowe Ransom, Allen Tate, etc., and full of New Critical articles, poems, and stories by those same writers and their disciples.

Moving in that direction, Paul recruited Ray B. West, Jr., and, of course, his major asset, the *Western Review*. Paul promised support for the magazine, which, while hardly of the same caliber, might provide at least a basis on which to build. Ray was probably aware of Paul's aspiration; the degree to which he was aware that Paul did not necessarily believe he was the one to lift it to a level of renown, I suspect, was not clear in the beginning. I think it became clear.

Paul persuaded Ray to take on Robie Macauley and me to read manuscripts. I was given the title of associate editor. I don't remember whether Robie was given a similar title or not. I had been the founder and original editor of the *Quarterly Review of Literature* (still being published from Princeton after fifty some years!). I don't remember now, if I knew then, what editorial experience Robie had before coming to Iowa, but it was obvious to me that his perceptions were keen and his judgments well founded. (His later success as editor of the *Kenyon Review*, and senior editor in the more diverting but rigorous environs of *Playboy*—on his way to becoming executive editor at Houghton Mifflin—surely confirmed his gift.)

It became apparent to Ray that Robie and I had fairly high standards for what we were prepared to accept for the magazine, and that we were not particularly influenced by friendly connections. It should be said that neither of us was explicitly engaged in any Engle intention to "absorb" the review, but it is my surmise that Paul counted on our editorial judgments to help point the way beyond Ray's Western directions.

Exemplum: Caroline Gordon, in those days a fairly well known writer of short stories for literary magazines (and, incidentally, the wife of Allen Tate), submitted a story that Robie and I agreed was not good enough for the magazine, and one that she probably shouldn't publish anywhere. Our recommendation put Ray in something of a dither. Turn down a story from his friend Caroline Gordon, wife of his friend, the distinguished poet? But he felt forced in the end to accept our decision. Gordon was furious and wrote Ray a nasty letter, and later, when the story was published somewhere else, a gloating one.

Other associate and assistant editors followed. Suspicious of Paul's long-range motives, I would guess, and fearful of losing immediate editorial control, Ray eventually packed up his *Western Review* and fled to San Francisco.

I don't know whether Paul approached the textbook publisher Scott, Foresman, or Scott, Foresman approached Paul about doing a textbook anthology of modern poetry, but Paul did approach me about coediting such a book. We discussed several possible structures for the book and came up with the notion of a critical anthology that would take advantage of the existence of the explications of many modern poems by prominent critics and, in some cases, by the authors themselves.

These were the days, after all, of the New Criticism, which stressed the reading of the actual text as opposed to the emphasis on the biographical and historical context that had prevailed in criticism and scholarship before (and long before the advent of those who set out to "deconstruct" the text and the author and replace them with the critic).

The poems would be arranged from those more available to the usual college student to those more difficult. About every seventh poem would be accompanied by an analysis by the author of the poem (usually, an account of the occasion and process of writing the poem) or by a well-known critic. On the premise that though teachers and scholars were frequently limited by the constraints of being specialists in English or American literature, the poets themselves had not been, an appendix of translations of European poets who had influenced modern poetry in English was to be included.

I put together a list of poets and chose poems to be included. Paul modified it. I scrounged periodicals and books for applicable exegetical material to be excerpted, and collected translations.

It was the Very Model of a Modern Poetry Textbook. It went through three editions, original, paper, and revised. It was a standard college text for a decade, but never a big seller because, I think, modern poetry was not a big market; the arrangement from easier to more difficult went against the grain of teaching — which is basically historical; and because, I think, teachers preferred to keep the book to themselves, using it with all its critical explications as a teacher's handbook.

Working with Paul, I realize now (having done other collaborative editing), was comparatively easy. We each had our biases, but we compromised on most of our differences. And I had by then been chastised by something I read in a letter from Hansford Martin to Paul. The letter had been left open, face up (intentionally?), on Paul's desk at Stone City. "I like Warren Carrier better now that

I realize his arrogance is not about himself but about the writers he admires."

I thought Hansford along with Verlin Cassill among the best critical minds teaching in the fiction workshop during my tenure at Iowa. While I don't think I was born again as a result of my accidental snooping into Hansford's letter, I did accept Paul's preferences with respect, and with all the grace I could muster.

It has been argued that writers' workshops do not make writers, and I agree. If would-be writers do not have the talent, even a good program will not give it to them. But a good program does provide an opportunity for critical analysis, self-assessment, improving skills, for recognition and encouragement, for associations with other writers. All of this support may be unnecessary for some; for others it is essential. The workshop at Iowa did all of that, and, further, provided financial support for many, and for some freedom from the tyranny of homelands.

As a faculty member, I also learned a good deal about writing from associating with writing students, resident colleagues, and visiting nabobs from the beer-drenched and sonorous Dylan Thomas to the aristocratic and diffident Cal Lowell. The student with whom I learned the most was Robert Shelley. My course in modern literary criticism often turned into a dialogue with Shelley as we explored the intricacies and limits of criticism. And Shelley, had he lived, would, I am convinced, have ranked with Justice and Snodgrass and Stafford as a poet. His inability to cope with reality and especially with his homosexuality led him to suicide, a sad event for which all of us who knew him felt guilty.

And I learned from Paul — not so much about writing as about the importance, as an administrator, of cutting through the bureaucratic bumf and focusing on the encouragement, support, and welfare of students and faculty. He built an extraordinary program. His example, for which I am grateful, stayed with me throughout my career as an administrator.

Paul at Stone City

I

For a poet lucky as Paul believed himself to be, the pinnacle of his luck is to place himself simultaneously at the center of his world and at the center of his imagination. It seemed to me I saw him at these coinciding centers in the summers of 1949–1952 when he spent the hot months with his family in Stone City and drove in to Iowa City once a week to meet his classes and hold conferences with students and useful faculty colleagues.

The mansion at Stone City had never been much better than dowdy, I thought, and in its decadence it sat among elms on the hill above the river with a frumpish charm. It cannot have been a comfortable place in the dazzle of Iowa summers. But its air of tattered finery made a picture in which Paul saw himself as the character he intended to be—at the same time alien and entirely at home amid the cornfields. He genuinely liked the farmers who were his Stone City neighbors, enjoyed their condescending to him as a poet as he condescended to them as farmers.

The frumpy mansion was a good place to hide away in and from which to sally forth, a masquerade and a frank avowal that he was a farmer among farmer friends, and a bird of far different feathers than his neighbors. A bit of utterly solid make-believe, suited to the make-believe of his vocation.

There was a bit of a tower in the yard. Paul fitted up the second story of the tower as the kind of office he always kept, untidy and richly laden with books and correspondence.

Arriving in the blaze of midafternoon at his office in the rickety building by the Iowa River, Paul's first meeting was usually with Mike Martin and me, his assistants in the fiction workshop. Mike and I discreetly believed that Paul came to town without having read the manuscript in fiction to be discussed in a short while by the fiction writers. No matter. He sat listening to us in his swivel chair, swinging his knee and agitating his eyebrows in a judicious and eloquent manner while we gave him the pith and gist and the details of what was to be discussed, throwing in a good bit of personal information about the writer. I will say it was somehow the best preparation in the world for Paul. Beneath the nimble brows he was composing a kind of super-fiction. When, at the appointed hour, he took his place at the head of the sweltering room and faced the writers, when Mike had squatted on a desktop and begun to chain smoke from alternating packs of Kools and Camels, and I glowered from a rear corner, Paul swung into his presentation and inquisition.

He was a very quick study, let us say, one of the very best leaders of classroom discussion I have ever heard in my long listening at this classroom or that. He somehow knew that all stories are the same, but that is not enough of an explanation. A very special and personal mixture of sympathy and aloofness made his presentations convincing however much or however little time he had spent working them up. And then he had Mike and me to help him, and I will say after all these years, amid Mike's smoke and Paul's mirrors we made high drama out of the art of fiction as we enacted it there by the river.

When our act was finished after an hour or two, Paul went to meet his poets in the other workshop. The rest of us streamed diagonally up across the shadowed campus green to our favored beer joint on the street facing the main university buildings, talking as we went, talking as we ordered suds, creating new strings of the story in which we had so deeply participated. The circus animals had been with us under Paul's direction and somehow would never desert us in the long years that led up over the hills of other land-scapes, campus and rural.

Mansion and tower and the bovine dignity of the landscape that Grant Wood trivialized were Paul's hideaway from those who wished him ill, but also his playing field for his teams who came year after year to join in the Great Game he proposed. Among the farmers of the community he was among friends, bound to them with the reciprocal sympathy that must exist between poets and those who do useful work. Intellectual friends from Cedar Rapids and Chicago stopped there for a night or a week, carrying on the conversation begun long ago.

Once each summer he and Mary put on a barbecue for students from the poetry and fiction workshops. And the picture of cars arriving from Iowa City and spilling out young couples waving their own bottles and racing toward drunkenness under a mottled Iowa sky and the cathedral elms is the one my passing eye chose to keep.

IV

Once a friend from the East had sent Paul a barrel of iced oysters. He broke them out to serve us as we arrived. There was something wildly exotic about oysters under the homely elms of Iowa and about the shells glittering in the sullen grass beyond the tires of the parked cars. It was for that exorcism and for the familiar that we had come to share Paul's hospitality. I said we raced in upon him to get drunk. You bet. No one can now estimate how much drunkenness there was in those days nor how much Paul incited it, because it was certainly not liquor alone that made us drunk. It was that, as well, but it was the stage he gave us, the incredible elms, the unthinkable darkness of the trampled grass, and thunderheads folding their majestic colors away into the deepening closet of the night. We knew, all of us, what we saw, the spectacle and the pointing signpost, exemplary signs that would shape our lives.

A Miranda's World

We arrived on a bleak Saturday afternoon in late January of 1952, my wife Jean and I; arrived at the bus station downtown, for we had just completed an epic journey by cross-country bus from the winter sunshine of my hometown, Miami, Florida, to this midwestern wasteland—and, indeed, I remember that bleak and rather forbidding first impression the town made on us as the bus cruised past the first scattering of ugly midwestern houses, bits of lawn patchy with smudged snow, and on into the old-fashioned town center. We were very tired and we knew no one. Paul Engle had put in a letter that we should phone him on arrival, and we did, a little doubtfully, expecting little.

When he pulled up at the bus station, spotting us no doubt by our beat and battered look, two polite small girls were riding with him, his daughters, and he had first to drop them off for the matinee at the Englert Theater before he could drive us and our bags on to the apartment he had already made arrangements for us to rent. (Mrs. Bristol's, $60 a month, in one of the oldest houses in Iowa City, out on Bowery Street. The downstairs smelled of the thick cigar smoke of Mr. Bristol, a teacher of business; fortunately, we were lodged upstairs, in an apartment already broken in for writers.) Paul made sure through his wide connections with the local people that there were a number of these apartments passed down from hand to hand, like items of clothing in large families. The Bristol apartment had already housed James B. Hall, Robie Macauley, and Herb Wilner before us, among writers I know of. Later, it would be John Berryman's unlucky apartment, the one he tumbled down the back stairs of, breaking an arm.

That first impression of Paul was of a man in the midst of a busy life that was pulling at him from all sides, a man tireless and virtually unflappable, joyful and proud in his duties, which included helping and defending others, especially writers. This impression lasted all the years I was to know him. In the course of the next week or so Paul—apparently aware of my interest in music—took me to a string quartet recital at Macbride Hall. During a snowstorm this was, and Paul had no trouble at all negotiating the snow-piled streets, even without snow tires, a skill that impressed a Floridian like me greatly. It seemed to say that this was his territory; he knew his way around.

Even as we were getting settled in, Paul asked us to invite to dinner another newcomer from the South—a would-be writer of stories who had recently worked for the *Greensboro Daily News*. This may have been intended to give both of us, as recent arrivals from the South, some sense that we were not alone in alien territory. Paul had evidently told this newspaperman (whose name I have forgotten) that I too had worked for the Greensboro paper. Peter Taylor, my brother-in-law, then teaching at Greensboro, had put me in touch with Paul in the first place, only a few weeks before, and that may have led to the confusion. (Not that it much matters — as so much that I am remembering doesn't really matter except that by now it has all, even the trivial, begun to seem a part of the Lost Good Time one doesn't quite yet want to let go of.) In any case, I believe that over the next forty years I was to know Paul he remained convinced that I had been a reporter in Greensboro. I never asked him about it, but there would be little references from time to time that made sense understood in that light. Paul seemed to have a comprehensive filing system in his head for all the writers who were just then beginning to migrate through the workshop at Iowa, and it is not surprising that he now and then got a detail wrong; for him the details, right or wrong, seemed to be fixed for good, but the most important fact was always a judgment, mysteriously arrived at but seldom wrong, about how good the newcomer was likely to turn out to be as a writer.

A week or two into the semester Paul gave a small informal dinner party in his house on Friendly Avenue (aptly named) so that

Jean and I could become acquainted with other young poets and their wives. There were the Bill Belvins, the Jack Meades, the Don Petersens, and, as I remember it, the W. D. Snodgrasses. (I had come to Iowa ostensibly to teach an undergraduate course in fiction writing; funny how Paul knew from the start that I would end up a poet.) Paul whispered to me that the best of the young poets were Petersen and Snodgrass; I understood him to be pointing out the competition — a very friendly and happy competition, it was to turn out. In the same way he tried to steer me and the other new student writers into courses at the university taught by professors more or less sympathetic with the workshop, for there were more of his colleagues than there should have been who were not at all sympathetic and who were, not to mince words, Paul's enemies — and, by extension, ours. It was told of one of Paul's colleagues that, Paul's house lying on this professor's way home from the Saturday afternoon football games, the unhappy man would stop in the street, emboldened by drink, and shout out taunts and curses at the writers' workshop. I am sorry to say that I never witnessed this performance myself, but I am sure that any writer who heard the tale would have considered it plausible enough.

One final instance of Paul's great kindness should complete the picture. I had arrived in the dead of winter with few warm clothes; my overcoat was an uncle's GI overcoat, which did not fit. Paul asked if I might have any use for a winter suit, and took me out to Friendly Avenue to try on one of his that he claimed to have outworn. It was still a fine suit, heavy green tweed, warm enough for the Iowa winters, and though it did not really fit me, I was very glad to have it and to wear it right through till spring. That it had been Paul's gave it, to my mind, a certain distinction that more than made up for the poor fit.

I hope it is obvious that Paul was a generous man. He gave Jean and me a warmer and richer welcome than we were ever to receive anywhere else, even at those schools where, later, my presence had been somewhat zealously sought.

A few years later Paul was to rescue me from the wilderness of teaching in barren little schools that did not appreciate me and that I did not appreciate. I have always felt that Paul was the first person in a position of authority able to appraise me with a pure eye and to want to give me a proper chance to prove myself. For Paul was never one to be prejudiced by any of the ordinary preconceptions: what he liked in others was talent, as he saw and registered it, and in this he had an extraordinarily quick eye. (Such prejudices as he had, so far as I was ever able to detect any, were two. He seemed to be remarkably fond of bringing to these shores young British writers — it was easy to theorize that this was due to his years at Oxford [his Oxford oar was mounted above the door of his famed hog-house study] — and other foreign writers, especially from Asia or from behind the Iron Curtain [a preview of his founding, some years later, the International Writing Program, which was to institutionalize these interests of his]. The second prejudice was simply that he did not in those years — not for long anyhow — tolerate people who drank too much.)

My rescue came about in this way. In 1957 Paul conceived the very odd idea of celebrating the centennial of the publication of *Les Fleurs du Mal* in Iowa City, of all unlikely places. The bizarreness of the idea was surely part of the charm of it for Paul. The upshot was that a number of scholarly papers on the subject of Baudelaire — including mine, dashed off on the train the night before — came to be delivered one warm day in the senate chamber of Old Capitol, an appropriately handsome setting; Harry Duncan — master printer — printed not only a handsome program for the occasion but also a pamphlet of poems by young workshop poets as a tribute to the great French poet; and best of all — the climax of the whole thing — was the banquet that evening at the Amanas. Paul had planned most of it. Before dining we stood around the lawn outside Bill Zuber's restaurant with drinks in our hands, basking in the late spring heat, entertained by a men's glee club from some nearby volunteer fire department and a glittering blond cheerleader prancing and twirling her baton. (Paul had not planned this part; at least I don't think he had.) Our spirits were high; we kept exclaiming about how *decadent* it all was. But it wasn't really; it was very American, very midwestern, very Engle, one could say. At the banquet Paul got around to asking for suggestions for someone who could take his place teaching the poetry workshop in the fall, since he would be away on a Guggenheim. W. S. Merwin had been asked but did not want to teach. The poet Henri Coulette's wife, Jackie, surely no more than half seriously, suggested to Paul that I be invited instead, since I knew something of how the workshop operated. At the time I did not have a book out and the idea, even to me, seemed outlandish. I don't think bold Jackie would have had the nerve to propose it if the rhubarb wine of the Amanas had not been flowing. Nothing came of it that evening, but a few weeks later I had a letter from Paul offering me a job. I felt like one who had been sprung from jail — from a life sentence at that.

Thus began years of working together, all good ones. It may have been hard for some people to get along with Paul, who had such definite and novel ideas and a will of iron, but never did Paul and I have the slightest problem with one another. We were in it together; we wanted the same things and, despite what I can now see, looking back, as grounds for certain doubts, we were convinced then that these were good things to want.

The first years, for some reason, remain the most vivid for me, perhaps because they seemed so new, so filled with possibility, and not just for me but for the other young writers too. Possibility filled the air, filled our talk, kept us awake nights, made us work very hard at what we liked working hard at, what we had come to Paul's workshop for, what we were hoping to live the rest of our lives for. Whatever it was, it was all Paul's doing, most of us felt, even those who complained, and there were plenty of those, too. Paul had what you really would have to call a vision, and if the future did not wholly live up to what Paul's vision called for — and in my view it was destined not to do so — it was certainly not his fault.

Even then, before it had become common to have a poet or two around your college for show, Paul liked bringing the best young poets he could find to teach a semester or two in the workshop. In my days as a student that meant having classes with Karl Shapiro, Robert Lowell, and John Berryman as well as Paul himself, meant getting to know them, too. It was Paul's example that set the tone for the informal style of the workshop and from the start the visiting poets all came to us on a first-name basis — Karl, Cal, John.

I had the idea that one ought to schedule a conference or two about one's poems with these poets we thought so much of and indeed, later, my students always seemed to expect conferences with me. But it did not prove easy then. I finally got an appointment with busy Paul. What it amounted to was that he invited me out to Friendly Avenue, we adjourned to the hog-house, had a couple of Martinis, and he glanced through two or three recent poems of mine, none of them much good except perhaps for one Baudelaire translation. He shuffled the papers. Coming on a certain line in the translation, he gently questioned the meter. "The impotent angels would damn themselves for me"— that was the line. Perfectly good, if you took into account the elisions, I explained. He saw the point and agreed readily. We finished our Martinis. Despite the pleasure Paul had seen to it that the occasion brought, I was a little disappointed, disappointed because I had not come any closer to learning the secrets I still half suspected someone knew and could tell me.

I was to come not much closer with any of the gifted teachers who followed. I remember no conferences with Shapiro — he was commuting weekly from his job in Chicago as editor of *Poetry* and had little spare time — but I do remember that in class one afternoon, obviously thinking of a current poem of mine about Hamlet but considerately not singling it out for special condemnation, he issued a kind of general anathema against all literary poems — and perhaps I should have listened more mindfully, for the literariness of some of my poems is one of the chief complaints reviewers (who don't seem to care much for literature) like to make against them. At my one conference with Lowell, he sat brooding silently for some minutes over the incomplete draft of "On a Painting by Patient B" that I handed him. I broke the silence at last by remarking that I was afraid it showed a little too much the influence of Auden. He briefly considered that possibility before mumbling, with what appeared to be embarrassment, the one word, *Yes*. I suppose I should have been glad that he agreed with me. It was a period when Lowell did not seem able to summon up much interest in student work, though he was always perfectly kind about it. As for Berryman, I recall no conferences at all, but he treated my poems so generously, so sympathetically in class meetings that I must have concluded I would be wasting his time to ask for a private session; besides, I probably enjoyed the more public attention, though I don't remember thinking of it that way at the time.

The workshop was the center of our lives, but the social life coming out of that center none of us who knew it then is likely to forget. And one of the high points of those first years was always the annual summer picnic out at the Engle house on the edge of Stone City, thirty or so miles from Iowa City itself. As I remember, it was a mansion of a farmhouse, three stories high, very grand despite the lack of indoor plumbing, and with a stone tower some yards off from the house, which Paul was said to use as a study, a midwestern Robinson Jeffers. Impossible to check now my memory of the place, for, sadly, it was to burn down a decade or so later. There would be food and drink those afternoons and evenings; there was at least one summer when the poetry workshop held a session while the party swirled around us in the other rooms. And one moonlit night a few of us climbed to the top floor and out through a trap door to the roof, precariously aslant and bright with the moon, where poems began inevitably to be recited. It was all very well at the beginning but once Robert Bly began on Yeats there was no stopping him, and for the first twenty or so minutes no one even wanted him to stop. The very extravagance of course in the end came to endear the evening to us.

Workshops are commonplace now, for better or worse — workshops, almost all of them, on the Iowa or Engle model. But back then? Back then they were rare. Ours was a Miranda's world — brave and new.

My Time

A native New Yorker, when I came to Iowa at the urging of Ver-lin Cassill in 1954, I had never spent any time in the Midwest. On the train from Chicago I was delighted to hear the conductor sing out "Ioway City!" just the way they said it in the movies.

There were only four women, including myself, in the poetry workshop, and I'm not sure if Gertrude Buckman (ex-wife of Del-more Schwartz) and Emma Swan were actually enrolled in the class. I think Julia Maria Morrison was. The men I remember from that year were Augie Kadow, Bob Dana, Henri Coulette, Bill Dickey, De Snodgrass, Don Petersen, Knute Skinner, Robert Bly, Paul Petrie, Peter Everwine, and the Irish poet John Montague. At the time I believe only Kadow had published to any extent.

I was so ignorant of the procedures of academe that it had not occurred to me to apply for any kind of financial aid — I'd never heard of assistantships. During my first semester I got a job in the University Hospital, transporting patients from place to place on gurneys (at what now seems to me the incredible wage of eighty cents an hour -- as I recall, men were paid $1.20). I can't remem-ber if it was that semester or in the spring that Paul turned up in my apartment kitchen one day and handed me $100, saying, "Don't ask where this comes from — just take it." Needless to say, I was to-tally surprised, and have been grateful ever since.

Shortly thereafter he somehow wangled a nonteaching assis-tantship for me out of the university, and introduced me to Satoru Sato, a young Japanese poet. At the time, modern and contempo-rary Japanese poetry was totally unknown in this country. Sato and

I worked on translating what he felt were representative poems from a group of pre- and postwar poets in Japan. Sato's English was good, but not perfect, and I knew no Japanese. A selection of these poems was published during the editorship of Henry Rago in a special issue of *Poetry* devoted entirely to them in May 1956.

Ray B. West was away in 1954, and the fall semester began with John Berryman teaching Ray's course, "The Form and Theory of the Novel." Berryman, who pointedly omits any mention of his Iowa City sojourn in his memoirs, stayed only for a few weeks and left under a cloud of scandalous rumors that became part of workshop folklore.

During my second year in the workshop Paul suggested that my assistantship apply to working with him on Prize Stories 1957: The O. Henry Awards. For me this meant reading the hundreds of short stories published in U.S. magazines during the year and coming up with a group from which Paul would choose about twenty for publication, awarding prizes to three of them.

That year (1955–56) was when I met my husband, Don Finkel. Earlier, he had rejected a batch of poems I had submitted to *Accent*, published at the University of Illinois, where he was a graduate student on the editorial board, so I was already prepared for a confrontation. In the poetry workshop that year, in addition to Don Finkel, were Phil Levine, Bob Mezey, Ted Holmes, Martha Grimes, Bob Sward, John Taylor, Kim Merker, and the Irish poet John Montague. Don Justice was a once and future poetry workshop member and instructor all through my years in Iowa.

During the summer of 1956 I got my M.F.A. and Don Finkel and I were married and went to live in Mexico for a year. When we returned in 1957 Don became a half-time instructor in the English department, and once more I worked with Paul and also, this time, with Curt Harnack, on *Prize Stories 1959: The O. Henry Awards*.

I really didn't know many people in the fiction workshops, which were taught by Marguerite Young and, at various times during those years, by Robert O. Bowen and Hortense Calisher.

My time in the Iowa workshops certainly affected the rest of my life in many ways — whatever literary success I've had, and even the course of my personal life changed markedly thereafter. I will always be grateful to Paul for his support, both literary and financial, and for his encouragement in pursuit of my talent.

When Literary Life Was Still
Piled Up in a Few Places

I first came to Iowa City in 1954, driving an old '42 Dodge which I had bought from a German exile in Boston for $65. I spent a couple of weeks on the way at the famous literary summer school in Bloomington, Indiana. John Crowe Ransom gave a talk on "A Litany in Time of Plague" by Thomas Nashe. One stanza reads:

> Beauty is but a flower
> Which wrinkles will devour;
> Brightness falls from the air,
> Queens have died young and fair,
> Dust hath closed Helen's eye.
> I am sick, I must die.
>> Lord have mercy on us!

He noted that most teachers describe this poem as iambic, but if you speak the poem passionately, your voice will tell you the meter is not iambic at all. Powerful beats come in at the start of each line, so the meter is an imitation of the old Greek and Roman rhythms.

> Strength stoops unto the grave,
> Worms feed on Hector brave,
> Swords may not fight with fate,
> Earth still holds ope her gate.
> Come! the bells do cry.
> I am sick, I must die.
>> Lord have mercy on us!

This marvelous lecture gave hints of new possibilities beyond the iambic mode I had been taught. I also saw William Empson with his long beard riding down the street on a bicycle. I mention these details only to give a sense of what high or elegant literary life was like in those days. It wasn't spread all over the country, so to speak, to a depth of one or two inches as it is now. Instead it piled up in separate places such as Gambier, Ohio, or Bloomington, Indiana, or even Iowa City, at a height of six or seven feet. I remember hearing that Robert Lowell, on his first honeymoon, pitched his tent on Allen Tate's lawn. He had a fine instinct for where the water was high. Jean Stafford later complained that he kept leaving her alone in the tent; he was always inside talking with the Tates.

When my $65 car finally approached the center of Iowa City, I was astounded. The buildings were two stories high only. I guess I must have had in mind some sort of image as that I've just given, an image that associates literary intensity with physical heights, which may have translated itself into high buildings. I felt dismayed. I knew Robert Lowell had been teaching in Iowa City, and I said to myself, "What kind of country is this in which a poet that great is teaching in a town with two-story buildings?" There's a lot wrong with my perception, but I was so self-centered and full of fantasies that there's not much use going into the inaccuracies. One could say that it wasn't as if Lowell had been exiled. Paul Engle, with his useful and intelligent impulse toward concentration of literary intensity, had called him there, and Lowell understood. Lowell's acceptance was a compliment to Paul's grasp of the way literature proceeds. A year or two later Engle brought in John Berryman; and Phil Levine's marvelous essay about Berryman's teaching in *The Bread of Time* suggests perfectly the way the physical presence of one superb writer, in this case Berryman, can change the life, and restructure the body cells, so to speak, of a younger writer ready to be made more intense.

I had come to Iowa hoping for a writing grant from the Rockefeller Foundation, but when I arrived, I heard it had gone to another, and so there I was in Iowa City with no money and no life. I went to see Paul Engle, and after some conversations with Ray West, and the head of freshman English, I was allowed to come into the workshop and was given two classes to teach, one in freshman English and one called The Greeks and the Bible. The salary was $100 a month for each, as I recall, so there I was. I could get by on $200 a month, living in a tiny room and eating at a boarding house. Paul was generous, straightforward; he loved poetry, knew good poetry when he saw it, and was no slouch at building a program.

My only other workshop had been at Harvard with Archibald MacLeish. Among the participants were John Hawkes, Kenneth Koch, Don Hall, Mit Hughes, Bob Crichton, Bill Emerson. Most were World War II veterans, just now back in college, and all we did was attack Archibald MacLeish and belittle his friends such as Ezra Pound and Ernest Hemingway. We rarely discussed our own work. Our behavior was outrageous, and it took MacLeish a long time to get over it. So when I sat down in Paul Engle's workshop, it was the first time I had ever seen that strange thing, blue dittoed poems. I was amazed. It seemed beneath the dignity of art to mimeograph poems. We didn't attack the teacher this time; in general, the aggression went against each other. Everyone knew that W. D. Snodgrass, the graduate of an earlier workshop and still hovering in the neighborhood somewhere, had done something introspective and important in poems later called *Heart's Needle*. But he had to be careful if he turned up, because knives seemed to be out for him. That's the way I recall it. I don't recall being aggressive myself, but perhaps my memory is bad. I do remember hearing around 1975 a story of my behavior in the Iowa workshop twenty years earlier. It seems that I regularly brought a snake to class with me in a gunnysack, and whenever someone began to criticize a poem of mine, I would take the snake out and lay it on the table. I was amazed to be imagined as a snake handler. But we can feel several kinds of fear in this story.

The workshop discussions were actually a little pedestrian; certain fads among the poets would dominate for a while. That's always the case with workshops. At the end Paul would come in and say rather sensible remarks. Given my history with MacLeish, whose lofty pronouncements floated down from some earlier heaven, this workshop was my first experience of literary democracy, even perhaps of that horizontal and envy-ridden culture which I later called sibling.

This piece will be more a memoir of the time than of Paul himself, but the literary excitement and dedication we all experienced was due to Paul's sagacity. The teaching most of us did made our lives rather hectic, and I commented in my diary, "In such a hectic life no large work can be conceived." I wrote in my diary one day, "I could work today only from 2:45, when I got back from a conference with Paul Engle, till 3:30, when I had to go to Muncie. Then I worked again from 5:30 to 5:45, hardly one hour altogether. I wrote the poem for Paul Engle, or rather attempted it. How wonderful it is to write poems for someone who cares about you!" So it was clear that I felt a lot of affection and support coming from him.

I also found notes from a conversation I had with Paul, in which I remarked, "Paul's greatest need is precisely to be needed." So he and I were much alike in that way. He gave me advice on a group of poems I showed him, poems full of Ideas for poems and Possibilities for inner life. To me he always talked straight; he warned me about my grandiosity and my tendency to live six lives at once. His advice was very good: "Do one thing, not many." These were warnings that didn't do much good.

Many lively events happened in our workshops, and many able writers came to speak, but I failed to notice most of them. One personality did become vivid to me, a Korean short story writer, Kim Yong Ik, whom Paul had recruited for the fiction workshop. He and I would walk out in the Iowa City cemetery and look at the black-winged angel and talk about art. He looked at the creation of art as a marvelous opportunity which in the course of human life, may arrive as a real possibility only once in every ninth or tenth generation. It had come to him. Dostoevsky was our hero, who would talk to himself in his room while he imagined some character in his fiction, and then he would weep over what had happened to that person. "Surely this is what writing really is — to give all," Kim said. And when we parted near dawn, he would say, "Tomorrow morning we must work very hard." He knew a lot. One day

I brought to him a poem that I had begun in New York, and it said something like:

I wander down the streets, not knowing
Who I am, and I am lost.

Kim said, "Oh no. If you say you're lost, that means you're already partly *found*. If someone is in the woods and truly lost, he doesn't even know that he's lost."

I was stunned. "Well, what do I do then?"

"You just take out the phrase 'I am lost.' Then you compose some images that seem not to belong exactly, rationally. Then when the reader experiences those images, he will say, 'This kid is lost!'" I've been grateful for that for years.

He didn't believe in Western competition. Sometimes when we walked in the cemetery, he'd say, looking at the large stones and the small ones, "You see, even after death they're still competing." I asked him about Korean graveyards. He mentioned a graveyard with wooden markers in his town that stood on a slope. After a few years, the markers and graves would all wash down the slope. I must mention that Kim who had lived for many years in Pittsburgh, writing well, died only a few months ago, during an emotional trip back to Korea.

I noted in my diary, "William Carlos Williams is coming next Monday." He read his poems in the Old Capitol Building on campus. The head of the English department introduced him and said, "Tonight we have William Carlos Williams, one of the finest poets now writing in English." Williams stood up and said, "Goddam it! How many times do I have to tell you, I write in American, not in English!" That's what he was like. I loved him, and had hitchhiked to see him when I was an undergraduate.

Later in the spring, Robert Lowell came back for a visit, though he wasn't teaching at the workshop while I was there. I heard that he was staying at Ray West's house, so I sent a manuscript and, calling, asked if I could talk to him. He replied that he had to leave for the airport at such and such a time, but I could come. Here's how I described the fast glimpse of him in my journal: "He stood there hunched, a weight behind his eyes — gentle, graceful, unburning — wise in adaptation. How I trembled to meet him. How odd a poet is in this lousy world, simply growing older among small things and small talk. What graceful hands draped questioningly at his chin . . . Marvelous is the word for him." I didn't describe our actual conversation in the diary. When I arrived, he was chatting with Ray West and Delmore Schwartz's first wife, getting ready to go to the airport. As they exchanged remarks, I was amazed to hear that the subject was William Carlos Williams, and his bad poems, ridiculous attitudes, his provincialism, etc. I began to burn. I knew that Williams had been and still was a sort of foster father to Lowell; Williams acted helpfully to balance the influence of Lowell's other, more conservative foster father, Allen Tate. Finally I spoke from my corner of the room and said this wasn't a true picture of William Carlos Williams or his poetry. All three turned and looked at me as people look at a cockroach. They went on talking, but moved on to another subject. I waited further. Finally Lowell said, looking at his watch, "All right, come on over." He had in his hand the little manuscript I'd given him; he had picked out a brief poem that I had written the year before while living in New York and virtually as a hobo. After being cooped up in the city for months, I drove with friends in someone else's car down through Maryland and felt amazed by the great trees. The poem goes:

With pale women in Maryland
Passing the proud and tragic pastures,
And stupefied with love
And the stupendous burdens of the foreign trees,
As all before us lived, dazed
With overabundant love in the reach of the Chesapeake,
Past the tobacco warehouse, through our dark lives
Like those before, we move to the death we love
With pale women in Maryland.

I was uncertain about the poem, uncertain about everything. What he said took me by surprise. He said, "Do you know which county you were passing through in Maryland?" "No," I said. "Well you could find that out," he said, "then go there; or go to a library and find out details of the history of that county. That's what

I do. In that situation, I look up all the historical facts I can, find who founded that county, what sort of crimes took place, who introduced the tobacco farming, and so on. Then as I rewrite I try to get as many of those facts as I can into the poem." He wasn't unkind. At least his advice was clear. But I slumped out and was depressed for two or three weeks, saying to myself, "Well, that's it. If that's how a genuine poem is done, I can't do it. I'm not a poet." I didn't look at the poem again for a long time. Six years later, when I was gathering poems for what was at last to be my first book, *Silence in the Snowy Fields*, I found the poem again and realized that Lowell had been wrong. Some poems don't have historical facts, they just float. This particular poem is a bit elevated and naively romantic in its juvenile love of death, but still it has its integrity like a haiku or a small Chinese lyric. If one puts extraneous, interesting facts into such a poem, it will sink to the bottom of the river. I recalled a poem of Tu Fu's that Kim had often recited to me in Iowa City, a kind of exile's poem:

At the end of the mountain gorge,
I hear dark monkeys wail.
In native land a white goose flies over.
Where are my sisters?
Where are my brothers?

This poem could use a few historical facts, perhaps, but if its aim is grief, it's best left as it is.

Paul and Mary would have big parties up at their stone house in Stone City, and I became fond of their children. In the spring of 1956, my wife Carol MacLean and I and Lew Harbison, a student of mine, and his wife went down to the Mississippi River bottoms a few miles southeast of Iowa City, all wet springiness and tall bare trees and flat ground recently abandoned by the river. High in a tree we saw two young great horned owls. Using a thin movable dead tree, we managed to push the owls along until they fell off the branch. Then we put them in a box and brought them back to Iowa City. I planned to bring the owls north to the Minnesota farm later that week. When Paul heard about the owls, he asked if I would bring them into his daughter's third-grade class for the children to see. I did, and the little owls were spectacular, full of feistiness, with huge, intense eyes, like novelists or generals. A few days later, I did drive them up to the farm in Minnesota and let them go, and they were both around there in the draw for years, hooting to each other and wondering what happened to the Mississippi River flats.

When I heard in 1975 or so the story about the gunnysack I would take to class with the snake in it, I realized that it was the same story: the human proclivities for envy, projection, and malice had altered the tale of two half-grown owls in a cardboard box in the third grade to a snake in a gunnysack in a graduate school classroom. So it is.

These adventures, these meetings with writers, this gathering place for people sick of small towns, all rose from Paul's sagacity. It was Paul who asked Marguerite Young, that amazing poet, essayist, raconteur, surrealist, fictionalist, to come to town. In my last dip into my diary, I'll put down a few sentences about her:

Tonight I met Marguerite Young and once more the real world returns. Words, vision, meditation, the incredible greatness and sweetness of those on the limb of words. It is all words, and how the whole world dissolves away and leaves in its place the love for those people, and these people, who so love and in return are loved by words. Look into your heart; disregard the world of classes and deadlines and the blue world crossed with red, that entices and takes all away, that one cannot love. Love those who love words, and restrict your friendship to those.

A Crisis of Sorts

If you believe yourself to be a writer but by age twenty-nine have nothing of literary merit to show for it, though you have been writing furiously for years, a crisis of sorts is upon you. While in my fourth year as instructor in English at Grinnell College, 1955–56, I was informed that I must finish my Ph.D. at Columbia University or elsewhere—there would be no further teaching job without it. And my then-wife delivered an ultimatum as well: wasn't it time to start a family, settle down, where were our lives heading?

Mine would be in the direction of the Writers' Workshop. Now the moment had come to put my art on the line, live more riskily, and as luck would have it, the distinguished international journal, *Botteghe Oscure*, accepted an Iowa farm story of mine, later incorporated into my first novel, *The Work of an Ancient Hand*.

Paul Engle and I had already met several times and he seemed to regard me as an up-and-coming fellow Iowa writer of promise. He had read my journalistic pieces in *The Iowan*; and the *Botteghe Oscure* acceptance, which I quickly told him about (actually, the magazine stopped publication before it ever appeared), was the imprimatur needed. He asked me to coedit with him Doubleday's *Prize Stories: The O. Henry Memorial Collection*, a selection of the year's best published stories. My modest stipend would come from an assistantship in the English department, therefore I was obliged to enroll in graduate school and participate in the Writers' Workshop. I was a bogus graduate student, having no interest in pursuing a Ph.D., but I needed a literary sounding board of some sort and professional criticism, which the workshop would provide.

Twice a week I commuted to Iowa City from Grinnell, where my wife taught modern dance, sometimes staying overnight in a seedy downtown hotel and hanging out at Kenney's Bar, where all of us writer-hopefuls created our very own Parisian Left Bank, and drank a good deal of beer.

Novelist Harvey Swados liked my novel manuscript concerning a Depression-era farmer uprising, mostly for its leftist political content I felt, since I was having trouble believing any of it and didn't know why I should be writing this tale merely because it really happened. Harvey was a politically engaged writer — in his novels often able to convey emotional power through ideas. One would have thought he'd be the perfect teacher for me then (though one doesn't really have a "teacher" in creative writing — more a friend or interested guide). But the ardor of his political beliefs made me see that I was lacking in this essential quality for the project I was embarked upon.

Marguerite Young, my other workshop instructor, who regarded herself as "on the side of the angels," was more interested in my Iowa Gothic short stories — which would eventually become chapters of my first novel. These two fiercely honest teachers were pulling me in opposite directions, and it was just what I needed, to wake up. R. V. Cassill, the third workshop lecturer who held forth on those Monday afternoons in the Quonset hut, discussing our mimeographed stories that had been distributed prior to the session, brought a different perspective, that of literary quarterly fiction, of which he was a master. At that time the Writers' Workshop experience (by Paul Engle's design) often involved hearing strongly different notions argued passionately. Where did the truth lie, who was right? That was for you to decide — could be anywhere — perhaps in your own errant views.

Marguerite was astonishing in the way she believed in her literary genius, which many critics and writers had proclaimed as well, but the whole world — not yet. She cosseted her dreams of eventual literary glory, for the day would come when she'd finish her long opus, *Miss MacIntosh, My Darling*. Then, she believed, she'd be showered with prizes, honored, and fussed over — plus rewarded with riches through royalties. Those of us listening to her fantasize found it rather pathetic; we doubted any such glories would happen. Eventually Marguerite did finish the book (Scribner's, 1965), which garnered considerable reviewer attention as an eccentric, intermittently brilliant work. But universal recognition eluded her.

Unfortunately, Marguerite encouraged a coterie to form around her, enjoyed having students imitate her embellished, fanciful writing style, and urged us all to extend our most far-fetched visions: we must put in more, reach for yet another striking image or beautiful phrase. The result, alas, was often unbearable preciosity. But for me, the right sort of stretching.

Marguerite loved the twisted-apples side of Sherwood Anderson and saw in my Iowa stories something of the same. I reveled in her encouragement — up to a point, but never went wholeheartedly into her credo. She taught me not to fear one's imagination or be too much confined by prosaic reality. She had a poetic gift for language but no ability to organize or shape her longer prose works, all of which suffer from circularity and self-indulgence — witty and astonishing though they are, line by line. Maxwell Perkins at Scribner's was her longtime editor, and had he not died when he did in 1947, she might have agreed to submit to pruning and editing (though I doubt it), as Thomas Wolfe had. Her work remains a curiosity, still in print, and in later years, living in Greenwich Village, her hair dyed purple, she became even more of a calculated eccentric. I was living in New York then too. She took a hate to me, for some reason. Although I hadn't seen her in years, at a Gotham Book Mart literary event, when I went up to her, she gave me a verbal tongue-lashing: said Hortense Calisher (my wife) had "stolen" her sentences, and clearly I was responsible. Upon her death at age eighty-seven in 1995, her unfinished book on Eugene V. Debs was reportedly over two thousand pages in manuscript. One might have expected that the cult of personality, so much a mark of our times, would have elevated Marguerite Young into the celebrity limelight, where she so much craved to be. But today the "high art" of which she was priestess has been pushed aside for "pop" in all its forms, and few readers seem to care what she was up to or appreciate her arcane references.

Meanwhile, Paul Engle expected me to do the initial screening for the O. Henry short story volume, and boxes of tear sheets from the leading magazines were at my disposal, plus every issue of the American literary quarterlies. During that year (and from then on) I hoped to support myself as a freelance writer on the side, reselling my regional journalistic articles to national magazines — anything rather than return to academia, which now seemed to suggest failure for any writer-hopeful. I realized that almost no serious literary author made a living from his work. But it was slim pickings in the freelance writing business — sales to *Ford Times, Earth Science Digest, Country Life* for paltry sums.

I felt comfortably based in the Midwest for my literary outpourings and wondered uneasily about my father-in-law's friend, Richard Bissell (*The Pajama Game*), formerly from Dubuque, who had since settled in Connecticut — abandoned his roots and "sold out," it seemed to me. And yet, Paul Engle's career also gave pause, much as I admired what he accomplished setting up the workshop. I had seen those glowing front page notices in book reviews when he first appeared in print in the early 1930s. This canny Rhodes Scholar from Cedar Rapids, who had been at Oxford with poets C. Day Lewis, W. H. Auden, and Stephen Spender, had returned to live in Iowa, where his considerable talents were expected to grow. But had they? He seemed nowhere near these poets in accomplishment, or was it fashion that had changed? And did he do too much well-paid journalism for major slick magazines like *Life*? Should I be learning something from his example? Had he possibly made a wrong career decision at some point? No writer can ever be sure what constitutes the true path — and that's what makes decisions so difficult, and self-blame later on so easy, for mistaken turns.

My classmates in the Writers' Workshop included some (Thomas Williams, Walter Tevis) who had already published novels, were in Iowa City for recharging, fresh worktime, and the informal interchange of new friendships, which developed on the softball field — poets against fiction writers — and in Kenney's Bar, where artists of all kinds mingled. A writer-loner discovered that there were others from all over America (and the world) who were hewing to this strange artistic course. It was exhilarating. We knew that Flannery

O'Connor had been present in this very Quonset hut near the Iowa River, only a few years before, as well as other writers who were now publishing and in the literary news. Which of us would emerge from the pack? One fellow writer (Louis Vaczec) said to me: "I'm falling through the air, waiting for God to catch me." I knew what he meant.

One important thing I learned during that freelance year: a clearer notion of my suitability for journalism, which I thought would replace teaching as an income source. It happened this way: I picked up the *Des Moines Register* and read that Otto Preminger, the Hollywood movie director, had chosen Jean Seberg from Marshalltown, Iowa, to be Joan of Arc in his forthcoming film. Here was a potential feature story practically thrust into my typewriter. I knew Grinnellians acquainted with the Seberg family and could easily do a piece on her for *Look* magazine, for a fee of a couple thousand dollars. I reached for the telephone to call *Look*, but my hand froze. I remember the moment clearly: *What am I doing this for? I don't give a damn about Jean Seberg or Otto Preminger's movie — so why am I wasting my time on this?*

Obviously, to make money. But this commercial venture wouldn't feed anything in my writing, might even poison what was there trying to come out. But if I wouldn't bestir myself to work up a magazine article that had come my way so easily, there was no point in kidding myself about earning a living as a journalist. What then? Paul suggested I teach the undergraduate courses in the workshop and put in a second year on the *O. Henry Prize Stories* collection. Harvey Swados urged me to spend the summer at Yaddo, in Saratoga Springs, N.Y., and he would happily sponsor me.

My life was taking another new, sharp turn: by the end of that school year my wife and I were divorcing. In late June I drove east, and at Yaddo wrote the entire first draft of what would become my second novel, *Love and Be Silent.* In September I settled into a little cottage on the edge of Iowa City, where my landlady insisted on calling me "Marcus," and I rather enjoyed the fresh identity. I put aside the new novel manuscript for ripening; devoted myself to finishing the mosaic of related stories arising out of my farm childhood, which would become my first published novel.

My being a native son was something of an anomaly in the Writers' Workshop; most were from elsewhere, often with exotic-sounding backgrounds. In contrast, mine seemed hopelessly mundane. That second year I did some of my work in a secluded room of the Quonset hut, and one day fellow workshop teacher Vance Bourjaily stopped by, greeting me with "And how's the Iowa writer today?" Was that label merely descriptive, or was it a put-down?

Though gaining in confidence, I never forgot the unnerving fact that many young writers in Iowa City (some not so young), felt equally convinced of their talents and sure of ultimate success. One of my students that year was a man in his thirties, with two children. He had pulled up stakes from somewhere in the South, his wife now working as a checkout clerk in the Piggly Wiggly grocery store to support them while he devoted himself to his "big chance." Alas, the stories he handed in for criticism were embarrassingly second-rate, cliché ridden, each one seemingly worse than the last. In my view this fellow possessed no literary gifts whatsoever; he was deluding himself, putting his family through a needless ordeal. I tried to be tactful but honest in my appraisal; he was not listening to me.

Indeed, how could one know for sure? I learned later from Hortense Calisher of a supposedly similarly talentless, dogged fiction writer, who had sent stories to a leading New York literary agent, Marion Ives (also Hortense's agent). Rejection after rejection, and Miss Ives had almost decided to go further and urge him to quit trying to write — she would say outright that his prospects were nil, it was hopeless. Probably he wouldn't have stopped scribbling anything. In any case, the writer had turned out to be J. D. Salinger.

That September of 1957 Paul Engle found me useful for various errands, since I was newly divorced and with time on my hands. I spent one frustrating afternoon in a pasture near town, trying to corral a couple of Paul's skittish riding horses, without success, never having been around horses much as a kid. Or he would send me on sorties not so much personal as workshop-related, such as my excursion to his barren country house in Stone City (Grant Wood's former establishment) to pick up barbecue equipment for a forthcoming workshop picnic. The school year was starting, with new faces arriving. Paul also delegated me to meet the train of the workshop's guest teacher for the fall term, short story writer Hortense Calisher. Paul and I had just given her second prize for "What a Thing — To Keep a Wolf in a Cage," which would be reprinted in the next *O. Henry* collection. Paul had insisted that Martha Gellhorn be awarded first prize, considering her long, honorable years of literary work, although I didn't think so highly of this particular Gellhorn story from the *Atlantic*.

Oddly enough, when I arrived at Yaddo July 1, I had noticed Hortense's name on the guest list for June — she had left the day before. She has often said it was a good thing, too, for she never would have paid me any attention — Yaddo offering a precious time for work, not to be interfered with. She was in the process of obtaining a divorce, had accepted the workshop teaching stint to get away from home and earn money (scheduled to teach at Stanford in the spring) — and I was in a similar unsettled state. Now we were well-met and our relationship began, all with perfect ease and naturalness. Given the times, Iowa City was surprisingly accommodating, with no comments or any awkward social complications — perfectly sophisticated

In 1959, now married, and me with a book soon to come out, we returned to teach for a year in the workshop, living in a pooky A-frame chalet on the edge of a valley, Mr. Black's house on Brown Street, where I learned to imitate the call of owls, enjoying my last year as an Iowa resident, connecting as usual to the landscape and its inhabitants. From then on in much of my work, I would live in Iowa only through my writing.

Dear Hualing

If I may, I'd like to put my words about Paul and the workshop in the form of this letter to you. This will let me ramble, free-associate, and generally commit disorganization.

If I were to try to put my recollections of twenty-two years at Iowa in any more formal way, it would be a major and lengthy effort, which is neither what you want nor what I could supply accurately.

The beginning of my association is clear, though. Paul asked me to come out from New York (to the place at Stone City) to interview for a visiting lectureship and, probably, make some sort of appearance before the students in Iowa City.

It's the Stone City visit that I remember — the ease with which Paul put me at ease, the warmth of his and Mary's hospitality, and, oddly enough, the striking affection and concern he had for his two daughters. That third element so strongly set the tone of my visit that I went off feeling that not only had I met an important, innovative educator and leader, but also that I'd met an extraordinary family man. The affection and concern must carry over to his students, I supposed, and I supposed right, embattled though he was with some of his faculty colleagues.

But nobody who could raise money for Iowa as Paul could would lose that kind of battle. My having been asked out to Iowa was due to the working of an old-boy network of former contributors to *Discovery*, a magazine I edited. Herb Gold had preceded me in 1955–56 by two years, Harvey Swados by one on Herb's recommendation, and then me on Harvey's (we were, in turn, replacing

Marguerite Young). Paul knew my stuff; he'd reviewed me in the *New Republic.*

When it came my turn to recommend, the network became coeducational (coeducationalist?) since my pick was Hortense Calisher. And, of course, I stayed on myself that second year (1958–59). As for Hortense, she met and married Curt Harnack—to mention something you already know, but other readers may not — who was then, if I'm not mistaken, still a graduate student.

Mistaken is something I'm quite likely to be, here and there, like all gossips.

One thing I'm sure I'm not mistaken about is that I appropriated the honor of designating the Iowa-old-school tie, a navy blue number from Brooks Brothers, embroidered with small, gold pigs. Mark Strand had one, and I recall trading one with John Cheever, much later on, for a similar tie with something else embroidered on it, though I can't recall what. Bulls? Trout?

Part of my eagerness to spend a second year in Iowa City had to do with the close friends I made there. The students, particularly those who were war veterans, were close to my own age and we had experiences in common. The first who comes to mind is the late Tom Williams, 1970s National Book Award winner. Because of Tom's strength of character, engaging personality, and the fact that he'd already published a novel before arriving at Iowa, he was pretty much the student leader.

Sometimes I think of one of the first things Tom told me about part of Paul's legend, something the students enjoyed discussing: "Did you know that Paul Engle is the only man who ever appeared on the Arthur Godfrey show and took Godfrey?" That is, dominated the other man's show by presence, charm, and quickness of wit.

Tom wasn't the only person Paul had recruited, when I started out, who had reached publication status. (I'm limiting myself to writers of fiction, students and faculty, since there are poets who can tell that part of the story — or spread that part of the gossip — better than I.) There was also Richard Kim, though I'm ashamed to say I don't remember whether he was Korean or Japanese, whose first novel was published as, I think, *The Martyred.* He was a quiet, attractive, diffident fellow, who seldom spoke up in class. Class was held in the temporary, wartime-built steel sheds north of the union, and that first year we all met together once a week, poets, fiction writers, and other rascals; the lead rascals, up at the front desk, were Paul, Don Justice, and myself, and all three of us had to deal with whatever manuscripts had been dittoed up, whether prose, poetry, or drama.

On the day when Richard Kim took charge, one of the manuscripts dealt in some way with suicide, and I may have said something about thinking suicide was too easy a solution for the problem in the story. It was at this point that Richard rose, looked to us for recognition, and on receiving it, said: "We have a rather different attitude towards suicide in my culture." He went on to describe people who thought of suicide as honorable, courageous, and ritually necessary in certain situations. I think most of us learned something from that small lecture. It was striking, through the years, how much I learned from my workshop students, and I used to recall that in Appalachian English the verb is used both in the customary way and as a synonym for *teach* (e.g., "She learned me my ABC's.").

I left Iowa after two good years with no particular thought of returning, and we spent much of 1960 in South America. Then, when my family and I reached San Francisco, I had occasion to phone Paul about another matter. He asked if I'd like to return. I found that I had missed the workshop and Iowa City far more than I realized and, after consultation, called again to say "Yes." In those years in Iowa City, we never locked our house or our cars; in fact we generally left the keys in the ignitions. That benign climate began to change in the later 1960s, but by then I'd said yes again several times, and continued to say it for the next twenty years.

In spite of the change in climate (because of the coming of the drug culture, among other things), the late 1960s and early 1970s were the most memorable. Based largely on the achievements of students who came out in response to Paul's extraordinary success in recruiting, we had students during that time like Gail Godwin, John Irving, Andre Dubus, John Yount, John Casey, and many others who wrote in Iowa and published soon thereafter.

We had faculties in fiction which included Verlin Cassill, Philip Roth, Kurt Vonnegut, George P. Elliott, Angus Wilson, Anthony Burgess, Jayne Anne Phillips, Fred Exley—all names listed neither in chronological nor alphabetical order, but as they pop into mind, and probably with important omissions—aforementioned Cheever, Ray Carver, Dick Yates. And Nelson Algren, whom Paul called "good company," though Nelson managed to avoid doing much teaching. The students were pleased to know him, anyway. I'll take responsibility for Nelson's having been there.

That brings me back, in my disorderly way, to another part of the Engle legend, which is how he went about the recruiting, of students in particular. It was done by correspondence, with letters tirelessly composed at night in an old, backyard chicken house, Paul's workplace in Iowa City, and we told one another that the lights were on there far past midnight constantly. Later, of course, he did more of his recruiting in person, while traveling, which must have been one of the things which led to the International Writing Program, which Paul founded after he'd turned over the workshop directorship to George Starbuck, another man of vision in his faculty and student recruiting.

This ramble could go on and on, but I mustn't let it. Let me close with this: my *Discovery* old boy–old girl network was soon replaced by a workshop web. There had followed, from Paul's example, over one hundred graduate writing programs in universities all over the country, and they were overwhelmingly staffed by Iowa workshop graduates, as we'd learn when we went out to give readings and so on.

For example, when I left Iowa at last for Arizona, I found that the seven-person faculty of that large writing program included five I'd known at Iowa — Jon Anderson, Steve Orlen, Bob Houston, Buzz Poverman, and Jonathan Penner. Maura Stanton (I think) joined us later, as did Mary Carter.

The Iowa predominance at various times and places continues. A different sort of example: at the last Miami Book Fair I went to, on hand to sign books and give talks or readings were Jane Smiley, Tracy Kidder, Bharati Mukherjee, Clark Blaise, Stu Dybek, and Alan Gurganus. And in another part of the forest, you and Paul. It was our last meeting. You were there to accept the American Book Award (which Iowa's Ben Santos had won a year or so earlier, as perhaps in another year, had John Edgar Weidman). You accepted, as always, graciously. Paul and I drank free rum. Graciously. As with so many other things associated with Paul Engle, the Iowa Writers' Workshop, and the International Writing Program, it was a stimulating time, a learning time, and a good time.

"I'll Make Your Career"

Paul Engle's name caught my attention for the first time in, if my memory is correct, 1955, in a feature article in *Life* on Iowa's poetry workshop and Paul Engle. I was a graduate student at San Jose State College (now University), majoring in poetry. I had changed my major three times since I had come to the States, and poetry was the latest one, hardly a year old. The previous ones were sociology and American history, both of which I took in hopes of studying something uniquely American, something I could bring home to Japan to make use of for the defeated and devastated nation, but after having made futile efforts for three years to reconcile myself to the highly statistical and prosaic studies, I gave up my pretensions and settled down to a very basic ambition, a truly American one, "Do what you like to do." I used to write poetry in Japan, in the style of the French symbolists, a style very popular among the Japanese in the prewar period, but, giving priority to the national cause and believing that I would have no chance of speaking and writing Japanese in the States, I threw all my poetry into the fire and gave all my poetry books to friends when I left Japan.

When I read the article about Paul and his workshop, I was attracted to a line, which was, as I remember, something like "He looks after his students, even their pots and pans." It sounded pretty Oriental. We have a similar expression in our language. It conveys the image of a man, old-fashioned, but warm and helpful.

I wrote a letter to Paul, asking him for admission to his poetry workshop, and enclosed in it a twenty-page typewritten poem of mine entitled "A Portrait of a Lady," which I had just finished. A daring product in the style of *The Waste Land.*

Paul wrote me back, admitting me to the program. He also told me to get in touch with Mr. Maner, the adviser to foreign students, about a tuition scholarship, which, he said, he had already arranged for me. He said nothing about my twenty-page-long poem. It was also amazing, as I sometimes reflected upon it later, that a professor's permission to attend his class was tantamount to an admission to his school. No Japanese college professor had that kind of power. I mention this because I fail to remember if I was officially admitted to U.I. or not. It may sound silly, but when I returned in 1991 as an Ida Beam Scholar to teach Japanese and Japanese literature, I was told by a faculty member in Oriental Studies that he could find no record of me in the school register. Was I just a private student of Paul Engle?

It took me another year before I finally left for Iowa because I couldn't meet the financial requirements of the university. The foreign student adviser kept saying no to my insistence on working my way through school. I thought Iowa City was something like San Francisco, full of job opportunities. So I worked again for a fruit cannery in California that summer, saved about a hundred dollars and, toward the end of August 1957, set out on a four-day journey by Greyhound bus from San Jose.

From the beginning Paul was very kind to me. I still wonder why he was so kind to a poor foreign student who couldn't even write a poem without making a mistake in English; a poetry student who arrived on campus with a tennis racket in one hand and a T. S. Eliot anthology in the other, which was practically all the English poetry he had read in his life. Maybe my ignorance attracted him.

He would sometimes invite me to his home when he had poets or writers from the other parts of the States or from abroad. A name that still remains in my memory is C. P. Snow; I remember him particularly because I challenged him in a discussion about Shakespeare, saying that Shakespeare was too bloody for the Japanese. I don't remember what he answered, but he was polite enough not to dispute the sensibility of the Japanese people.

This way I also met Nobuo Kojima, a Japanese writer now well-established, whose novel *Huyukazoku* (*The Embracing Family*) became a landmark in postwar Japanese literature, and who has become, since our meeting in Iowa, my lifelong mentor and friend. Paul's invitation, I'd say, really provided me with a fated encounter. He was at Iowa on the Fulbright Exchange Program after he won the Akutagawa Literary Prize, a prestigious award for rising young Japanese writers.

It was a big shock to me when I found that my workshop friends were hostile to my visits to the Engle's, and some of them were even hostile to Paul himself. At a gathering of the students, when I said that I had been invited to his home the day before, someone immediately asked me who else was there, and I sensed the sudden tensing of the atmosphere. I divulged the names of the two other guests who fortunately happened to be from outside Iowa. "Anyone else from the workshop?" the inquirer asked again. "No." Then, the tension relieved, they all started to talk randomly. Someone mentioned an incident that had occurred at the workshop before my arrival; a student was bitterly criticized for his work by Paul, to the extent that it was made obvious to everyone that there was no use in his continuing at the workshop. The other students were shocked. Some of them resented the fact that Paul had done this publicly.

Then someone else started talking about Paul's campaign for raising funds for the workshop. He was critical of Paul's making use of his students, taking them with him to the firms he targeted and having them recite their poems in front of the company executives. "We aren't in a show business," a girl in the group said. She mentioned one of the students in the group had refused to play the role of bard. Paul had, nevertheless, recommended his work to a literary journal.

One day I was called by Paul to his office at the workshop. He showed me a small book and asked me if I knew its author. It was the translation of one hundred classical Japanese poems by Kenneth Rexroth. I told Paul I knew the poems but not the translator.

"Good. You know the poems," Paul said, and explained who the author was. This was the first time I heard the word "beatniks." According to Paul, they drank a lot and drugged themselves to write wild poetry and laughed at our poetry workshop. A teaching assistant, then present, added, "They are calling us 'The Cornfield Poets.'" Paul nodded and asked me if I could write a critical essay on the book. A severe one.

"If you don't feel like doing it, it's O.K.," Paul said.

"I'll do it, Mr. Engle," I said. (My Japanese background prevented me from calling him by his first name; also I found it too formal to call him Professor Engle.)

I took the book back in my room at the Quadrangle and read it. Most of the original poems were familiar to me; so, I could easily see the difference between them and Rexroth's translation, which was more simplified in technique and in emotional expression so that it sometimes verged on vulgarity.

I wrote as I felt, being a bit sorry for the man trying to introduce for the first time to Western readers the little-known classic poems of my country. I brought my finished essay to Paul. A few days later I was again called to the office. I understood that I had been often too lenient toward the translator. Paul said that I should forget my Oriental politeness when writing literary criticism. "Make it tough," he said. "That's our way."

When the second semester began, Paul told me that he had arranged to give me an assistantship for the semester, which, with the stipend of $400, he explained, would require no more work than typing. He went on to say that he was sorry that I had to wait for a semester to get it. I hadn't even applied for a scholarship. I was very grateful.

Donald Justice, who happened to direct the class for Paul for that semester, suggested to me one day after the class that I send my poems to literary magazines. "It's nice to get a few bucks," he said. I remember his words particularly because until then I had never had the idea that my poems would be capable of earning a penny.

But I was then more concerned about my Japanese poems than about their English brothers. I had resumed writing poetry in Japanese sometime earlier. I showed some of my work to Nobuo Ko-jima, who had now taken to visiting me in my room at the Quad-rangle almost every day. He said that my use of the Japanese lan-guage was not up to date. He likened it to the situation into which the Japanese Issei (first generation Japanese immigrants) were drawn, where they retained their old use of the language. His com-ments woke me up, and I began to think seriously of the possibil-ity of returning to Japan.

Toward the end of that semester, on a warm May day, Paul called me into his office after the class and said that he could double the scholarship money for the next year if I wanted to stay in Iowa. I don't remember how I answered, but, as if to make sure that the message of his willingness to help me was heard, Paul added, "I'll make your career."

I remember his words distinctly, because I have often recalled them especially when I felt I was at a turn in my life. My response to it at that time was, however, a vague one, as I did not realize then the full impact of his words, and I was experiencing anxiety over my deteriorating Japanese.

I went back to Paul after the next class and told him that I had decided to leave Iowa the next semester because I wished to go back to Japan to refresh my own language and write poetry in Japanese.

Paul was silent. So, I went on, "I have to make money for my trip back to Japan. I have a friend who has gotten me a job at a Chinese restaurant in Ocean City, New Jersey. I am going to work there this summer."

"I think you'd do better here than in a Chinese restaurant," Paul remarked, giving a wry smile.

I left Iowa in the summer of 1958, and worked at the Bob Chin restaurant on the Ocean City beach. Later I went to New York City and found a job at a travel agency owned by a Japanese American. There I worked for a year and a half to raise the additional money necessary for my travel expenses to Japan.

Paul's influence continued even after I had returned to Japan. When I applied for a teaching position at Meiji University, Tokyo, where I am still on the faculty, Paul's recommendation was my strongest support. I have neither an M.A. nor an M.F.A. Even at a time when the postwar Japanese college system was not yet tightly organized, and education at an American college was valued much more than now, to get hired as a faculty member at a college was difficult. I was told later by Nobuo Kojima, who was a member of the committee that evaluated my application, that Paul Engle's letter said, "Although Mr. Miura apparently does not have a degree from a Japanese College, the work he has done in this country is the equivalent of that done by our own young instructors. I had the pleasure of knowing him not only in the classroom and in my office, but in my own home with my family, and always found him reliable and congenial, with a capacity for joining in conversation with my colleagues, my friends and my children."

So, in the end, Paul did "make" my career.

Engle's Workshop

On Friday, the 23rd of May, 1986, my wife, Jean, and I drove from Oswego, New York, to Hancock Airport in Syracuse, forty miles away, in time for me to catch my flight to Chicago at about a quarter past eleven in the morning. I was on my way back to Iowa City for the first time in twenty-six years to attend the Golden Jubilee celebration of the Writers' Workshop, the world's oldest and most famous graduate program in writing arts. I pondered the unsettling thought that when I'd left Iowa in 1960 the workshop had been about to celebrate its silver anniversary with publication of a volume edited by its early director, Paul Engle. Now, returning, I was more than half as old as the program I had attended. As I flew west it seemed to me that I was in some true sense returning in time as well.

In 1959 I had transferred to the Iowa workshop from the University of Connecticut graduate school. During the fall of 1958, while I was an undergraduate at UConn, I had applied to the workshop, and on January 21st of the following year Paul Engle had written asking to see the letters about me from my teachers John Malcolm Brinnin and Kenneth Spaulding, and from Tom Ahern, manager of the student union, for whom I had run the fine arts festival magazine and the literary reading series. He'd also wanted copies of my published poems. At the end of March, W. F. Loehwing, dean of the graduate college at Iowa, had written to tell me that I had been awarded a graduate fellowship for the academic year 1959–60 in the amount of $530. On the 4th of April Paul wrote to offer me a teaching assistantship of $1,300 instead of the fellowship. He also wanted me to submit poems to be considered for publication in the workshop's silver anniversary anthology, which was to be titled *Midland: Twenty-Five Years of Fiction and Poetry from the Iowa Writers' Workshop.*

I'd written back to say I'd rather not teach as I wanted to get my degree as quickly as possible. Paul replied, telling me about the differences between the English M.A. and the M.F.A., which took longer. I decided to go for the M.A., as I still had a year left on the Korean GI Bill and could transfer my six UConn graduate credits to Iowa, thus in effect finishing my classwork at Iowa in a year.

In the fall I transferred to the workshop. The graduate fellowship was an honor, but the stipend was quite small. Jean and I were pretty strapped, so Paul, even though it was against the rules to give me both a fellowship and an assistantship, arranged for me to become editorial assistant to the workshop in order to bring me back up to the financial level of the teaching assistantship I had foregone. I was to help Paul with correspondence and with the permissions work for both the Random House *Midland* and the Hallmark *Poetry for Pleasure,* to be published by Doubleday. Jean found a full-time job in the Bureau of Labor and Management.

By the 24th of August, 1959, Jean and I were settling into our new apartment on the second floor of Mrs. Keith's farmhouse outside of town. I was to dump the garbage into a ravine, blow snow out of the driveway, and so forth, as part of our rent. Our landlady kept a few sheep, one of which was a ram who inhabited the field I had to cross to the ravine. I was always careful to keep an eye on him and one of the garbage cans between us in case he decided to attack, but he never did. By October Jean was pregnant; her morning sickness was lasting all day, every day, and she was pretty unhappy. This was the first time she had been away from her family for any extended period of time.

Curtis Harnack was on campus with his wife, my fiction professor Hortense Calisher; and Verlin Cassill labored away in the Quonset hut where the poetry workshop was held. Hortense liked to take baths in the tub there because there were only showers available in the apartments where she and Curt lived. Paul Engle and Donald Justice shared the duties of the workshop. At that time Don, a

Floridian who had recently taken his Ph.D. from Iowa, had not published his first book.

Paul, a native Iowan, had been born in Cedar Rapids in 1908. He had studied for the Methodist ministry and preached at Stumptown church at the edge of town, but he'd heard no call and had instead taken an M.A. from Iowa in 1932. In that same year he'd published what may have been the first creative thesis ever submitted anywhere for a graduate degree, *Worn Earth*, which appeared as a volume in the prestigious Yale Series of Younger Poets. Subsequently, he had studied at Columbia and then traveled to Oxford on a Rhodes Scholarship, taking another set of degrees there.

In 1937 Engle had returned to the University of Iowa as a faculty member and had eventually become director of the workshop. Under his leadership the workshop, by the time I'd joined it, had become world-famous as a training ground for young writers. On that first day of class in 1959, Paul asked us how many were from the state of Iowa. Not a single person raised a hand. Paul said, "I'm embarrassed. This is the first time such a thing has happened." I looked around and saw what seemed to me to be a familiar face, and indeed it was — it turned out to be Ed Skellings, with whom I had gone to prep school at Suffield Academy in Connecticut from 1947–1949. Some of my other fellow workshop students were George Keithley, Robert Mezey, Vern Rutsala, Morton Marcus, Raeburn Miller, and Kim Merker. Walter Tevis, John Gardner, and Jerry Bumpus were members of the fiction workshop.

Paul's and Don's styles were completely different. Paul was the feisty, funny, slippery-tongued pepperpot, and Don the practical critic who knew just how to approach each particular poem. Paul never got angry, but Don could sometimes be peevish, especially when he thought he was wasting his time on a poem that had not been carefully worked over before it was submitted for the worksheets.

When I had arrived in Iowa City, I'd been surprised to learn how literally the poets rubbed elbows in all kinds of competitions, including most particularly physical competitions. From this distance in time, it seems as though nearly every day of the semester some of us spent a couple of hours at least in the Ping-Pong room at the Iowa Memorial Union viciously pasting a bouncing ball over a net. It was almost as though some kind of literary superiority depended upon our whipping Don Justice. Many of us tried, but most of us failed. In fact, I can't recall Don's ever losing a game, though I suppose he must have. I'm sure I never beat him.

His technique was maddening. No matter how hard you hit the ball, Don would stand way back and let the ball drop over the edge of the table, out of sight. There, underneath, he would give the ball some kind of gentle, satanic slice, and back it would come, floating over the net. It would kiss the table, but where it would go from there was anybody's guess.

Seeing Don's prowess on the Ping-Pong table, I never dared sit in on the weekly poker games some of the poets — Bob Mezey, Kim Merker, and others — engaged in, but I hear they were marathons. In the spring Ping-Pong would give way to softball, but poker went on forever.

I was the only member of the workshop turning in syllabic poems, some of them written at Yaddo the previous summer. At one point Don said to me, "Lew, you're cheating. Your poems don't rhyme." Dylan Thomas and Marianne Moore had been writing rhymed syllabics, but no one other than haikuists had been writing just plain syllabics. I considered that Don's remark in this case was ignorable, and I went on writing my rhymeless syllabics, as I've done ever since. A few years later I couldn't help noticing that Don's second full poetry collection, *Night Light*, consisted of unrhymed syllabic poems.

Robert Mezey was one of the students I had looked forward to meeting ever since I had learned I would be going to Iowa. He and I had published in many of the same magazines and anthologies, including *Riverside Poetry 3* and *New Campus Writing 3*, which appeared that fall. Mezey was anticipating the coming year when he was to attend Stanford as a Fellow under the latter-day messiah of the neoclassical poets, Yvor Winters, of whom Bob was a professed admirer.

Like Mezey, I had always been interested in the traditional forms of poetry — I was born a formalist, and I wanted a reference book that contained the whole range of them, but I'd never been able to find such a book other than those that contained merely the standard sorts of things: the sonnet, the villanelle, the haiku and tanka, the sestina — mainly the medieval Italian and Provençal forms plus a few others.

What else was there? Perhaps there weren't enough forms to fill a short book. Then, one day while I was browsing through the bargain bin of Iowa Book and Supply on Clinton Street, I ran across a book of poems by Rolfe Humphries titled *Green Armor on Green Ground*. Humphries had laid out "the twenty-four official meters" of the Welsh bards, and he had written a poem in each of these complicated syllabic forms. I bought the volume, of course — I think I paid a quarter for it, or maybe a dollar — and I took it home. After I'd looked it over a while I got to wondering whether, with such forms as these, I might not be able to gather enough material for a book, particularly if I filled it out with examples of poems written in the forms and with schematic diagrams of the forms, which I had never seen in any other book. I discovered, incredibly, that no one in the history of English literature had ever put together a compendium of all the traditional forms, and I asked Don Justice whether he thought such a volume would be useful. He encouraged me, and I began working on the project.

That period of time when I began putting together what would eventually become, first, *The Book of Forms: A Handbook of Poetics*, and much later *The New Book of Forms*, was not auspicious for such projects. The so-called Beat Generation was in the process of consolidating its antiintellectual stranglehold on a generation, and the self-righteous, self-indulgent decade of the 1960s loomed ahead. Christopher Wiseman, a workshop poet from England, one day submitted to the worksheets a parody of the work of the Beat poet Allen Ginsberg. Mezey, however, did not see the humor in it, only the threat, and he reacted by writing, and the next week submitting to the workshop, his response, "A Coffee-House Lecture."

Interesting things were happening off campus as well as on. The Paper Place, one of the first paperback bookstores in the country and certainly the first in Iowa, was being tacked together by graduate students. Upstairs the Renaissance II Coffee House was also taking form, and it was over coffee that Steve Tudor and his friends were starting the antiestablishment student newspaper, the *Iowa Defender*, which was to stand against the philistinism of the *Daily Iowan*. Across the street Kenney's Fine Beers was another hangout for the writers; in all three places we got together for talk and socializing, but at Kenney's, things were generally more boisterous.

One evening, after a group of us had left Kenney's, we walked across the street to see in the window of the bookshop a display of the manuscript drafts of Walter Tevis's novel *The Hustler* and the contract that Tevis had signed, for which he had received a $10,000 advance. One of us asked him, "What the hell are you doing at Iowa?" "Learning how to write," he replied.

It was at the Renaissance II that the first student readings ever organized at Iowa took place. John Gilgun was the entrepreneur. Vern Rutsala and I and one or two others had the honor of inaugurating the series. Others who read that year were, as I recall, Kim Merker, Peter Everwine, Jim Crenner, Morton Marcus, and Bob Mezey, who read his reply to Wiseman. He later included the piece in his first book, *The Lovemaker*, which won the Lamont Award of the Academy of American Poets in 1960 — Paul was one of the three judges. That same year two other books would come out of the workshop, Don Justice's *The Summer Anniversaries*, which had won the Lamont Award for the previous year, and my own *First Poems*, which was published as a selection of the Book Club for Poetry during the summer.

I met Jerry Bumpus at Kenney's early in the autumn. Whether it was on that occasion or another soon after, for some reason we got into a discussion about words that described places where particular kinds of creatures were kept. I said that a herpetarium held snakes, an aquarium held fish, and an aviary was for the birds. Jerry nodded his head amiably and drank his 3.2 beer. "And an apiary is a place where apes are kept."

"Right," Jerry said.

"Wrong," I said. "An apiary is a place for bees."

"Bull," he said, or words to that effect.

"How much do you want to bet?"

He checked his pockets and found that he had three dollars. So did I, so that was the wager. I went to the bar and asked for Irene Kenney's tattered dictionary, brought it back to the table, showed Jerry the entry, and asked him to pay up. "You set me up," he said and wouldn't come through with the three bucks.

What happened next is probably apocryphal; I don't recollect it. In 1976 Steve Wilbers, who was researching his history of the workshop, wrote me a letter and asked in a postscript, "By the way, is it true that when you met Jerry Bumpus you poured a glass of beer over his head while talking backwards? He claims you're the only person he ever knew who could do that."

Whether Wilbers meant pour a glass of beer on Bumpus, talk backwards, or do both simultaneously, I'm not sure. In any case, I wrote back to say I had no specific remembrance of the beer-pouring, but not only can I talk backwards (for some reason), but I can write backwards as well — when I was at sea aboard the USS *Hornet* in the early 1950s, my battle station was behind a Plexiglas plotting board on which I had to write so that the officers on the other side could read it, thus the incident may have occurred as Jerry remembers it. If so, I was getting even for his welshing on our bet, and what I said to him amphisbaenically was without doubt insulting.

The *Esquire* symposium was held at Iowa that year, and a lot of famous writers and editors were present, including, as I recall, Dwight Macdonald and Norman Mailer. I remember a cocktail party — was it at the Engles' or the Justices'? — where I saw Mailer pinned in a corner by Ed Skellings who was gesticulating earnestly and jabbering at him at a great rate.

For me, in the final analysis, the Iowa experience in terms of the poetry workshop was largely Don. One of my books, *Awaken, Bells Falling: Poems 1958–1967*, is dedicated to two great teachers; John Brinnin at Connecticut, and Don Justice at Iowa. In many ways, Don is a diffident and self-effacing man. I sometimes don't think he realizes what effect he had on the minds of many of his students. One of his phrases could set you off. I could give many examples of the kind in which a word from Justice went a long way toward getting one of his students into a project, or simply to raising our self-esteem.

But Paul Engle had his effect, too, and it was at least as large. It was Paul, too, who stood in the line of fire to take the hits, for the Iowa workshop has always elicited a fair amount of criticism, a good deal of it of the sour grapes variety. Readers of the country's literary periodicals are used to these sorts of remarks concerning the Writers' Workshop at the University of Iowa. In my view, the hostility displayed by various writers who have never been to Iowa, and by some few, such as Robert Lowell, who have resided there, is remarkable and largely unwarranted.

First, in defense of Iowa, I would like to point out the simple truth that Paul Engle did not "turn out" poets. Rather, what he did was encourage them to go to Iowa. In this encouragement he was successful, because Iowa has earned a reputation as a gathering place for young writers, and for would-be writers who might never make it — but how can one tell until they are given their chance?

It seems to me that very few young people go to Iowa expecting to be "turned out" as accomplished writers. Rather, they go there in order to be with other young people who are also interested in writing — to talk with them, to fight with them, to be excited by the atmosphere generated in one of the very few communities of the United States where the art of writing is treated as a serious subject.

That any number of mediocre talents seem to come out of Iowa can be explained simply: any number of mediocre talents are attracted to Iowa. In any given year it would be remarkable if the law of averages permitted more than two or three potentially excellent writers to be enrolled in the workshop. The rest, as in any other kind of specialized gathering, must range from good through average to poor. Thus, the appearance every now and then of a Snodgrass, or a Legler, or a Justice, or a Mezey, or a Rutsala, is to be expected and applauded.

In fact, Iowa's workshop does its work quite well. It encourages an interest in writing; it provides an atmosphere in which various levels of talent may develop; it provides competition for the ambitious and talented, and it provides a certain level of excellence which the less talented writer can try to attain. Iowa is an exciting place for the young writer; at times, indeed, it may be a bit too exciting and hothouse, but these are conditions which any intense place must hazard from time to time if it is to accomplish its goals. Stereotypes to the contrary not withstanding, Iowa is an essentially unacademic place. Most of the learning process takes place not in the classroom but in the private bull session at the Union or at the local bars; in the library and bookstores where students introduce themselves and each other to all kinds of writing, from the avant-garde to the conservative.

The measure of Iowa should not be taken by the unreasonable yardstick that it does not "produce" uniformly excellent writers, but by the fact that it encourages the young to write seriously, to develop, to learn something about the art and the craft of writing. And to fight like hell for one's own point of view and kind of expression.

He Made It Possible

In 1960, the word "Iowa" signaled a place beyond my imagining. Having grown up in a small town, in an area of eastern Long Island which few citizens left unless it was to retire to Florida, I felt venturesome just to have made it as far west as Chicago. University of Chicago professor Napier Wilt sometimes digressed during his seminar on the works of Henry James to speak of his own childhood in Iowa City. He reveled in describing the mud and pigs at the front porch. His memories convinced me that I should perhaps never try to drive to such a cultural netherworld. Therefore, when it fell to me to travel to Iowa City for an interview, I rode the Greyhound.

I took no chances, but followed the other passengers through the rear door of the nearest building and asked the man at the desk if he could please tell me how to find the Burkley Hotel, where I had been told I might find a room. "This is it," he said. In the morning, I asked the same man to help me find the University of Iowa. He pointed past the front window across Washington Street. "There it is," he said.

I knew little more of Paul Engle and the Writers' Workshop. I held a commission in the army. To delay having to go on active duty, so as to have time to explore my involvement with poetry, I needed to become, somewhere, a Ph.D. candidate. I knew that the workshop was home to young writers, but it was dumb luck rather than research that sent me to Iowa City.

The poet John Logan first told me of the Iowa workshop. The notion that out there in the wilds of Iowa there existed a group of young writers was right up my alley since, my lieutenancy not-withstanding, I fancied myself avant-garde. Something more or less unknown, original, and vaguely disreputable in the eyes of the general public suited me. The writing of poetry was still then a gratuitous art form by any ordinary standard, and that's the way I preferred it. The Beats were still current. Also, I was a rebel jour-nalist, and my idea of the serious writer was more Hemingway and Ginsberg than Stevens and Pound.

At that time, few writers who found their circuitous ways to Iowa City knew much about the workshop beforehand, or about Engle. I was aware of the time he, his wife, and one daughter had been taken hostage by escaped convicts from the state prison in Anamosa while vacationing in a second home the family owned in Stone City, Iowa. That had made the national news, complete with the quirky information that Paul had convinced his captors to let him go to his study to complete a book review due shortly at a Chicago newspaper. After the convicts left (and were quickly recaptured), Paul went on television. He told a story of family preparedness: how one of the Engles had secreted a weapon (was it a pair of scissors?) in a sock, while another boiled water on the stove, and how he himself talked sense to the escaped prisoners. Only many years later, while writing about it in his memoirs, did Paul confide to me his fear at what he supposed the men might do and his shame at not jumping one when he thought he had the chance.

Such confidences stand in contrast to Paul's image around the workshop. Paul was, rather, bigger than life. He spotted tal-ent quickly and talked about it. He raised money for writers and talked about it. He spoke of the great poets he knew. He went to battle during those times when university miserliness or disregard threatened the workshop, and he thanked the uni-versity publicly whenever it came through. He did not often speak of his own writing, though he continued to add to his bib-liography. Having been welcomed to the literary world with considerable fanfare — his first collection of poetry, *Worn Earth*, won the Yale Younger Poets Prize for 1932, and his second book,

American Song, was greeted by a front-page review in the Sunday *New York Times* book section, written by the estimable J. Donald Adams — he nonetheless soon turned to carving out a wider place for writers within academia. Thereafter, his writing may have been taken somewhat for granted — by himself and by others. The dynamic of the literary world, which today devours and moves on, even then tended to set aside the writing of those who labor publicly.

To me, Paul was the boss man in the World War II barracks building which housed both the workshop office and its classes. Donald Justice was on the job as poet-teacher, while Paul raced to and fro, within and without the university, playing scout, host, diplomat, adviser, and fund-raiser, as well as, when he had a chance to sit down, teacher and writer. He seemed indefatigable.

And always a quick study. Our poetry class was taught in tandem by Don and Paul, with Paul frequently excusing himself to answer the phone in the back room, sometimes returning to announce a new donor to the program. (I believe I remember his bringing back from a phone call the announcement of the "Iowa Natural Gas Fellowship," which made us laugh.) Hurrying back to class, he would take a quick look at the poem under discussion and, without knowing what had been said so far, nonetheless wade in with remarks useful and to the point. And then, like as not, the telephone would ring again.

At the time, I was photographing, as well as potting and still playing a little trumpet — what an easy time it was for poor students. Paul gave me funds with which to attend the first meeting, in Bloomington, Indiana, of what would come to be known as the Society for Photographic Education. And he paid my tuition when my budget needed it. He did that and more for all of us on the spot.

To us, the money, but more so the community and the focus on writing, made all the difference. Paul kept his focus, and ours, on the individual writer and his or her place in the community of writers. Today's writing programs sometimes resemble stressed-out writers' conferences compared to Paul's version, but of course it was a calmer time. Make no mistake: Paul delighted in our public successes and used them to win funds.

But Paul's effect went way beyond the writers he knew personally and aided directly — even though there were hundreds of us. It was Paul's energy, his robust language, his demand that you listen and see, his unflagging stamina, his inescapable force, that opened a door in American colleges and universities through which hundreds of teaching writers and thousands of writing students would pass.

There had long been some teaching positions for teachers who also wrote. If they wrote seriously or wrote much, that was acceptable, but only if they held the Ph.D. and walked the walk of scholars. Because of Paul, however, writing programs sprang up all over the country — most of them following the unacademic, energetic model of Iowa's — and university administrators came to see the vitality such programs afford an institution as a whole. The master of fine arts was increasingly accepted as a sufficient teaching credential for a writer, and the wisest administrators came to understand, as Engle's Iowa had all along, that a truly gifted writer needed no degree at all.

Those of us who found a salary, a niche, a project, a task, a duty, or a calling within the university expressly because we were writers owe to Paul Engle the core of our lives. He did it. He made it possible. In the beginning, no one gave him permission. The university sometimes supported him, but sometimes, especially at the beginning, merely tolerated him.

Paul could throw a mean party. He could tap dance and he could steamroll. He could go your way or he could go his own way. At any moment, you could not tell for sure if he had you in mind or a wider vision of an active literary community in which you held a small role. His public image was defined to the point of shielding his private life from exposure. He had, in any case, an absolute vision of literature in culture — first in these States and later throughout the world, and once he was in position to act upon it, he did so steadfastly until his death.

Iowa born and raised, Paul was both knowing and in-the-know: given his effectiveness with all sorts of people, he might well have been called a "country slicker." Let me offer an example.

I stayed in Iowa City as what I like to call "a graduate student bum" for three years, writing poetry while teaching speech and composition for the university, but in January of 1963, I finally had to go on active duty. As an army officer, I held many jobs, but the one that eventually took all my time, Foreign Military Training Officer, was distinctive in that it had political origins and consequences. Robert Kennedy was reported to have conceived of the program, and in the course of my duties I worked with embassies, the State Department, and the Pentagon. I was allocated funds and given unusual freedom in running my program precisely because military brass fears the Congress, which not only votes on budgets but also hands out general's stars one-by-one.

Then it was 1965 and the Vietnam War was accelerating. My job protected me while my colleagues were being shipped over on three days' notice. That's when a call came from Iowa City offering a faculty position in the workshop. To arrive in Iowa City in time, I would have to arrange a three-month "early out" for "seasonal employment." This was going to be iffy because the word was out that, once Secretary of Defense Robert McNamara returned from an upcoming visit to Saigon, junior officers like myself would be "frozen" for the duration. Thus, within a few days I would have to gather signatures that usually took weeks, and then drive to Fifth Army Headquarters in Chicago for final approval — before McNamara's return. Was there even much of a chance? First, I needed a letter from my prospective employer.

Paul's letter was thrilling, not to say brilliantly calculated. First, he explained the job, pointing out that my work with foreign soldiers was appropriate since the workshop was welcoming more and more foreign writers. And then . . . then he recounted his recent dinner with President Lyndon Johnson at the White House. (Paul was a member of the original National Council on the Arts.) It seemed he had been seated next to Attorney General Kennedy and across from Defense Secretary McNamara, both of whom, it appeared, expressed pointed interest in the workshop, its foreign students, etc. I "hand-carried," like they say, Paul's inspired letter from office to office, and my application for an early out sailed through.

Perhaps it is in the nature of sons to feel that they have not thanked their fathers enough. I content myself with the memory of Paul's enthusiasm for young writers, his joyous storytelling, his affirming presence — memories which remind me that he damn well knew what he had wrought and, I believe and hope, knew too what it would mean to the rest of us long after he took his leave.

Every Shut-Eye Ain't Asleep

I graduated from L.A. State College in winter 1961 and applied for a passport with intentions to visit Paris; I got a draft call to take my physical instead and had to get into graduate school immediately. Henri Coulette and Wirt Williams were teachers of mine at L.A. State, and both were Iowa alumni, with creative dissertations for their Ph.D.'s. I asked Christopher Isherwood to write for me also; Isherwood was the only writer I knew who did not believe in school of any kind for writers; he would bring his friends to class, Auden, Spender, Heard, Huxley, his next-door neighbor Charles Laughton, and Laughton's wife Elsa Lancaster; with this sort of assemblage you were less inclined to miss classes, and since I was working graveyard in the post office at terminal annex, attending a 9:30 to 11 A.M. Tuesday/Thursday class on English writers between World War I and II was a hazard.

Since I was admitted to Iowa with no fanfare, and no financial aid, in mid-winter, I decided to drive from Los Angeles, in a '54 Chevy, loaded with jazz records and books, and got as far as Needles, California, before I broke down; I spent an entire afternoon getting a wayward mechanic to look at my engine, and when he could find nothing wrong other than five quarts of oil missing, I decided to return to L.A. and do without wheels. I flew to Chicago and then boarded Ozark Airlines to Iowa City, the mail run; in less than an hour I was chatting with Paul Engle and his daughter, Sarah, in his office in the temporary buildings near the river.

I had left my bags in storage at the Greyhound station. I was early for apartment hunting, having arrived between semesters, and when I brought up the subject of housing, Paul said,

"Mrs. Lemme." Mrs. Lemme was a fixture in the Iowa City community; her husband owned a shoeshine parlor on the main drag, and they entertained the great musicians of the era, black men and women who needed a place to stay on a tour through the Midwest. Had I been more experienced, a little less green, I would have visited Mrs. Lemme's house, checked out her accommodations, and decided on home cooked meals and conversation that might translate into subject matter. I never explored Paul's option, and visited the bulletin board in the housing wing of one of the main buildings. I was assured every entry had to sign an antidiscrimination pledge.

It was twenty below, and I wore a tweed car coat that was not insulated, and not long enough. I had pretty much decided to move on to Chicago and New York when I stopped into a local beer joint named Kenney's, with a jukebox and many 3.2 beer drinkers in attendance. I remember looking for anything to play on the jukebox, and found only two tunes worth mentioning, "Moaning" by Art Blakey and the Jazz Messengers, and "Softly As in a Morning Sunrise" by the Modern Jazz Quartet. I was not going to miss this town, and after a draft was about to retrieve my bags and head east. Vern Rutsala and Lawson Inada were at a table with a few poets, and Rutsala approached me as if in waiting: was I Mike Harper from Los Angeles? I was amazed at his ease of approach, and soon I was seated at a table in front of a pitcher and popcorn. Inada was from Fresno and a student of Philip Levine, and, I was soon to find out, a jazz collector. I quickly recounted my efforts at apartment hunting and Rutsala mentioned that Alan Pike, a musician on leave from the faculty of Tennessee A&I, had just left town; perhaps his roommate was looking for someone to replace him. Inada invited me home to eat, and we stopped at 419 E. Washington St., where I met Donald Marsh, a medical student from Fort Madison. In a few minutes I was gathering my bags from the baggage claim at Greyhound, many changes in a very long day making sense of what was called "The Athens of the Midwest," Iowa City.

Rutsala and his wife, Joan, were expecting a baby, and Matthew was born soon afterward; and I spent many an evening learning what I could about the pecking order of the workshop, how to get poems on the worksheet, whom to assuage, what posture to take on rhyme and meter; there were no open forms to negotiate. I had more to worry about because I was in a fiction workshop with Philip Roth, and also his Contemporary Seminar; nine units of Roth, and six in poetry workshop. Fifteen units was a normal load for an M.A. student; thirty units to complete the degree, take an examination, and write a thesis. In my case I was to submit a collection of poems, *Blues and Laughter.* As a midyear student I was out of sequence with almost everything, and insecure.

Inada, who had two roommates and was looking for more space and privacy, soon moved into the same building I was in, with no furnishings. The landlady was a "liberal" Jewish woman who lived in Des Moines, and when a small apartment on the same floor became vacant, I told Lawson about it. From his arrival on I could hear his music collection through the walls of his apartment, and I could count on sophisticated and *lowdown* programming from early morning to very late at night. Lawson also received care packages from Fresno, full of exotic delicacies from his parents; and he sometimes shared them.

Immediately I was in the university library perusing the theses of previous graduates from the workshop, on an upper, isolated floor; there I looked over the competition. It took me a few weeks to get through all the binders. I had heard a few stories from Coulette and Williams about their fellow students, and who were worthwhile teachers. Justice had already won the Lamont Award for *The Summer Anniversaries,* and Snodgrass the Pulitzer in poetry for *Heart's Needle.*

Philip Roth's Contemporary Seminar was small; each student was expected to present a critical reading of one book on the syllabus; I volunteered for the first book which was William Golding's *Lord of the Flies.* I thought I was out of my depth to begin with and turned in my report of about twenty pages after reading the paper aloud to the class. I did not get my paper back from Roth, and after a few weeks I made an appointment to ask about it. It was marked with a "B−" and no comments anywhere, so I asked how

I could improve it; Roth's answer was "don't plagiarize." I was also in a fiction workshop with Roth and had turned in a novella of eighty pages I was waiting to discuss. I asked him what he meant by plagiarize, and he asked who'd written the paper. I said "I wrote it." Roth said I'd made reference to several of Golding's subsequent novels, published only in England. By this time I was standing up in his small office.

Roth had a habit of asking me about James Baldwin, whom I'd never met, but whose essays and novel *Go Tell It on the Mountain* I had read earlier. I knew Baldwin's "Sonny's Blues," also. The *Partisan Review* had published "Sonny's Blues" in an issue of 1957, and in the same magazine was the only criticism published on Golding in America; that issue was missing in the Iowa library. Isherwood had loaned me three books by Golding published in England, but not in America, when I was doing my own independent project on fables and connecting them with the prefaces of Conrad and the notion of narrators that were not authors but vehicles to a layered shale of voices (Marlow).

Roth and I were at war from that meeting on, and I held my tongue in class, but not in Kenney's where I saw him occasionally. Finally, I told him all black people didn't know each other, that Baldwin was born in Harlem in 1924; I was born in Brooklyn in 1938; did he know all Jewish writers?

At the end of the spring semester, I turned in my last paper to Roth without discussion. I was returning to L.A. to take the lifeguard exam which was a *live* swim on a specific date. The night before I left, Philip Levine got his jaw broken above Irene Kenney's bar in an after-hours fight. I also met W. D. Snodgrass briefly that same evening, and heard Philip Levine insult his old student Lawson Inada at Don Justice's house. Poetry then hit the news, and Paul Engle threatened to sue the athletic department because a wrestler had manhandled Levine and Bob Mezey at the party I had briefly visited and left.

So Iowa was an immersion in another kind of segregation, not only in housing but with regard to the company and behavior of writers, in and out of class. I spent most of my downtime with black athletes. I lived in an apartment building which housed the black quarterback Wilburn Hollis, and a defensive back from Chicago, Bob Tucker, who lived behind me on the same floor.

One day I was playing a record by Miles Davis, *Kind of Blue*, and Inada knocked on my door to find out what I was playing. I showed him the album. So much did Lawson love the first side of *Kind of Blue*, he was afraid to turn it over and be disappointed; what he'd heard was side *two* of *Kind of Blue*. Hence the title of my thesis, *Blues and Laughter*. These pieces were improvised monologues, and they were terrible, but the best I could do at the time. I had begun as a playwright, mostly one-act plays which I had turned in to Isherwood as a student. They were efforts at discourse and chatter, inside commentary, among musicians, in the idioms of speech of musicians, with no attempt at buffering the cursing, the banter, the obscenity of wordplay. Isherwood would say "send this to *Encounter* magazine," edited by his friend, Stephen Spender, and I would quickly have them returned, often with no comment. But I was interested in the speech patterns of innovators who were telegraphing a special vernacular, a melding of speech and decorum I felt precious and unique to the American tongue. Roth did not encourage these explorations, and my efforts at poetry were conventional, though not in rhyme and meter. I could not talk to Paul Engle at all about these matters; and Justice was too formal for me, and too southern, though always helpful, even generous. I was not in anybody's circle of friends.

My second semester put me in a small hotel behind a candy factory on the main drag, a room with no windows, until I could arrange to move into a garage behind a black homeowner on E. Prentiss Street, out near the A&P. I froze in that garage, but I offered space to one of Lawson's old roommates, Johnny Hodgkins, who was also working on a master's but with no thesis in writing. Johnny was from Mineola, New York, and later was to visit from the language school in Monterey, California, while doing his stint in the army. I was further deferred in a miracle, even though I passed my physical administered in Des Moines. I was examined by a young Iowan intern, female, from Council Bluffs who told me where the blacks lived in Omaha. I had already visited Des Moines for the Drake Relays where Wilma Rudolph and John Thomas, both Olympians, performed in exhibition. Without a car you had to hitch with friends; trips to Fort Madison, the Quad Cities, Chicago, Detroit, St. Louis were chores on the bus or train. I was always aware my experience would have been different if I'd gotten my '54 Chevy to Iowa intact.

During football season at Iowa, Tod Berry integrated the concession monopoly controlled by a southerner who did not like blacks. Tod's wife had just delivered; Annette was a poet in the workshop, and we visited mother and child in the infirmary. Tod shared his anxiety over having no assistantship for that semester, and how was he to feed a wife and newborn? He offered me a pennant concession on Saturdays for home games, and I took it, because this meant beer, popcorn, and movie money if the Hawkeyes won. My spot was the train station where the railcars brought alumni from elsewhere in the Midwest. I knew the names of football players Hollis and Joe Williams, Larry Ferguson, Cloyd Webb, Dayton Perry, Al Hinton in particular, a painter. And I knew the basketball player Connie Hawkins, who attended Boys' High in Brooklyn and was ineligible to play his freshman year at Iowa; also Don Nelson and Andy Hankins.

The stories of black athletes at Iowa during that era can be summed up in "20 W. Harrison," the rented house the athletic department leased for the black active players, and which was used as a recruitment perk for "recruits" in fully subscribed "black and white/salt and pepper" parties. Frank Davis, who had been the Iowa Golden Gloves heavyweight champion and had wrestled professionally, and played an extra year for Forrest Evashevski, was in training to pass the physical therapy course of study; unfortunately he took classes with medical students, who raised the curve, and Frank was always studying for exams while parties went on constantly at 20 W. Harrison. One evening they sent for "The Padre" to calm Frank down. When I got to his apartment on the second floor, Frank was buck naked with a .45 caliber pistol in his hand, muttering, to himself, "I'm in a world of trouble." He had begged his housemates to quiet the record player so he could study, had cajoled and begged, then shot through his floor to a hushed ground floor audience. I took Frank out for a walk, then a drive in his old battered Ford, and when we returned the house was dark. He could study. And passed, despite the curve. Frank's father was an economist at Fairleigh Dickinson University and had served as a Fulbright Professor in West Africa; Frank accidentally shot a youngster when he himself was but fifteen and avoided scandal, in part, because of diplomatic immunity. He was also a brainy guy who felt a compulsion to entertain his classmates and fellow teammates with minstrel antics of the worst kind, and I reminded him I would not go out in public with him if he didn't change his demeanor. And Frank from New Jersey, shaming his ancestors.

I left Iowa City by train in freezing rain with a paid ticket to fly to L.A. unused in my pocket. I left as soon as I could gather my effects, give away blankets to Oliver Jackson, send home my records and books. I was sick with the flu but I had learned legions of what the anthropologists called the Useless Curiosity, the gathering of meaningless facts for future application. What were these?

I knew I had missed much by not investigating Mrs. Lemme's. I knew I had learned very little in L.A. during the early 1950s. In civics class, in 1954, at Dorsey High, I remember no discussion of the Supreme Court decision of Earl Warren; in Latin, the teacher forbade me reading aloud. At L.A. City College, a Dr. Bell had whispered to me I should not try to master the microscope — we were studying nematodes — I was not going to be admitted to medical school, this by a Ph.D. from Berkeley. When you are surrounded by Ph.D.'s in airmail in the post office, unable to find jobs except working for the government, you alter your expectation, or you bide your time.

I saw the best football game of my youth on television, with Calvin Jones from Iowa beating Jim Parker from Ohio State. I was a senior in high school and this was the first football game which focused my attention exclusively on line play. Jones was a three-time All American at Iowa, a legend among the black recruits in the 1950s as Emlen Tunnell had been a legend in the 1940s. This tradition was important to me, workshop or no workshop. Jones was later killed in a plane crash en route to an all-star game in Canada, and the black players took his loss personally, particularly

Al Hinton, who later went on welfare in Iowa before graduating. Hinton hosted my return to complete my master's while living in Black's Paradise, a set of rooms owned by the largest landlord in Iowa City. Welfare, Iowa-style, was one hundred pounds of sugar, one hundred pounds of flour. Hinton was also a painter. Hinton would whisper to me, at 20 W. Harrison, that he needed someone to teach him to draw, that no one took him seriously as an artist, that he wanted to go to graduate school in painting. So I spoke to Oliver Jackson, from St. Louis, whom I'd met late in August 1961. I was returning from my lifeguard duty in L.A. and was strolling down Iowa Avenue trying to find an apartment when a figure came into view on the opposite side of the street; the figure crossed to my side in midblock, and before I could ignore him he chanted, "Don't ignore me; I've been waiting for you all summer; where you from?" Two grown black men, on the streets of Iowa City, both graduate students — Jackson was in the M.F.A. painting program — was a public event at the time. Jackson and I became fast friends. Jackson was a draftsman who painted on a huge scale; I helped carry his canvases to student exhibitions. We were almost stopped once in broad daylight for stealing. We went to free movies on Sunday night on the campus, and the best movie I saw in that year was *A Raisin in the Sun*, which catapulted our spirits beyond the possible. Jackson's expertise ran the gamut from Beethoven to Charlie Parker, and he would drag me along to the art library where he would peruse the oversized art books of the masters, turning the pages so quickly they were a blur. He had total photographic recall of these plates, from Dürer to Rembrandt, Goya to Michelangelo, and back again. He was an inspiration because he validated what I knew about black men and ambition, and we discussed what never got touched in seminars, our sense of aesthetics.

My first publication while at Iowa was in *December* magazine, a small lyric named "Discovery." My first impression of the magazine involved an interview with Ralph Ellison by Richard Stern, "That Same Pain, That Same Pleasure," in which Ellison spoke movingly about elegance, a sense of style, his Oklahoma boyhood, and creating a standard of rhetoric and democratic values that have kept me in stead to this day; for him, Ellison, "literature was a study in comparative humanity." His sense of the possible was the only place I could locate myself. Later, I was to meet Ellison and his wife, Fanny; Fanny Ellison had been a graduate student in drama at Iowa, but she was not allowed to act in plays, though she learned much about stagecraft, putting on several of Langston Hughes's plays in Chicago. It was Fanny who would not allow Ellison to teach at Iowa in the workshop, so bitter were her memories of discrimination. It was Fanny who told me about the benefits of Mrs. Lemme, how much she learned about life, the arts, and how to place people in the social hierarchy which is race and class in this country.

I learned a respect for psychic window peeping in Iowa City (not only at 20 W. Harrison, which was an underground station for many of the fantasies of the locals, farmers from out of town, a cadre of screamers from moving cars) and the voyeurism nascent in the "criticism" of contemporary writers. I also learned the maneuvers behind opinion expressed in the college/university dossiers, and why certain people, particularly people of color, did not get jobs despite good academic records. This was why when I could not get a job in California, I had to ask Henri Coulette to check my dossier and give me his sense of my file. He told me to expunge it, all of it, though he would not rock the boat by specifying his reason. At that time it was illegal for recommenders to mention race in dossiers under California law, and all of my recommenders, two from Iowa, had broken the law. It took L.A. State six weeks to find a place for me to student teach at Pasadena City College (where Jackie Robinson had starred as an athlete before transferring to UCLA). This was 1963 and Birmingham was calling. Freedom Riders had traveled the Midwest raising consciousness, and funds, and I remember refusing to hold hands with Iowa students while they sang "We Shall Overcome." I thought this was hypocrisy, their political action clubs, their zeal for social change, with no large black population, and a covenant of gerrymandering, and worse, tormentors in cars, yelling obscenities as black students walked up the hill from the library, or downtown to window shop.

I did not get to Waterloo, Iowa, where the strikebreakers came from elsewhere in the 1930s; this was a black community I would have learned from. I knew Black Hawk Indian legend; I knew the Iowa Indians met regularly at the confluence of three rivers in Des Moines; I knew the T. S. Eliot of the "objective correlative" was not his exegesis of O'Neill's *All God's Chillun Got Wings.* I had quarreled with Dr. Swerdlow in his O'Neill seminar while I was writing plays at L.A. State; it was Swerdlow who'd loaned me his copy of *Invisible Man* by Ellison. Swerdlow had taught me Zola, Flaubert, and Balzac, and a seminar, "The Epic of Search," where I postulated a different sense of history and race than my classmates, writing papers on Ellison, Baldwin, and Faulkner, not to mention Twain's view of black men in "Huck and Jim." I remember one conversation with Vance Bourjaily in Kenney's about whether I could create white or black characters, and whether one could write out of one's experience and truly depict what one did not know. I reminded Vance that evaluation was always a two-way street, and that idioms were shared whether one was aware of the inheritance or not. This was a matter of form as well as vision, and I was too attuned to my own ancestry to evacuate in a world that had been a true test to them, hence my quarrels with observation and talent.

"Every Shut-Eye Ain't Asleep," one offered on the lonesome road, rural or urban, to the fellow traveler; "every good-bye ain't gone" comes the answer.

My mentors were not my teachers mostly because I was incorrigible, would not listen, and blundered in my own way. Iowa gave me that opportunity. Paul Engle bought Charles Davis's house in Iowa City, and Davis invited me to Yale to teach in 1976. When I read Paul's letter in my dossier he mentioned a certain "flair" and sympathy for letters; I wrote a monologue for Elvin Jones, the jazz drummer with Coltrane, with a coded "flare" in the schizophrenic line between artistry and entertainment. On the football field Tunnell was an artist; Hinton told me that Calvin Jones saw to it that Alex Karras would be toughened up for the pros; Calvin had promised Karras's older brothers. Big Jim Parker was the fixture that made John Unitas a great quarterback. Willie Fleming and Bobby Jeter took Iowa to the Rose Bowl when Evashevski let Fleming play, as a sophomore, against Michigan; from that game onward Fleming scored two touchdowns a game. Hollis and Sandy Stephens were two black quarterbacks at Iowa and Minnesota during the season I sold pennants at Hawkeye home games. Byron Burford apologized for his Mississippi background by teaching all he knew to Oliver Jackson as a painter; Jackson even learned from Lasansky, and sold paintings to his faculty sponsors; he was not about to give "Night, Death and the Devil" away. And Hinton is teaching painting at Michigan. Keep your eyes open! The past is not even over; "who knows but on the lower frequencies I speak for you."

A Tale of Two Fathers

This is a love letter to Iowa, and to Iowa's favorite son, Paul Engle, who, in the spring and summer of 1961 (when I was a very proper young woman in Calcutta, writing escapist short stories in lined notebooks while a suitable bridegroom was being handpicked by my father), came to represent for me that seductive combination of "go-for-it!" brashness and "You-never-know!" optimism that is the spirit of America.

That spring I was waiting to hear from the admissions offices of Bryn Mawr, Mount Holyoke, and the Sorbonne. I couldn't have located Pennsylvania, Massachusetts, or Paris on a blank map of the world, but I etched these sites with romantic intensity and flamboyant abandon in the imagined map of my future. I hadn't applied to the University of Iowa, because no one in my family had yet heard of the state of Iowa. Nor for that matter, had any of us heard tell of Nebraska, Nevada, Idaho, Ohio, Oklahoma, Montana, Arizona. . . . My father, always the patriarch, had selected the schools and programs, and even written the rough drafts of my college applications. He had short-listed Mount Holyoke and Bryn Mawr because, at that time, they were exclusively women's schools and offered "womanly" enough disciplines, such as education and English literature. I have no idea why I was allowed to apply for a program in public administration at the Sorbonne other than that I had just won a prize in an international French-language contest by writing an essay on *Les Miserables*. My father didn't seem to mind what my sisters and I studied as long as we avoided coeducational classrooms and professional careers. Modern young women in modern young India, my father explained, had the luxury of learning what they wanted to learn — by which he meant the liberal arts — while sons, poor fellows, were forced by tradition to slog through medical school or engineering school so that they could get the respect and the financial security they needed to fulfill their roles as generous providers.

Going to school, my two sisters and I accepted, was about acquiring skills that would make us interesting but financially dependent companions of Calcutta's future patriarchs. In 1961 we could already recite enough Racine, Shakespeare, and Matthew Arnold to initiate bright conversations over tea and samosa; we could hum enough lines from Rabindranath Tagore or Gilbert and Sullivan for after-dinner entertainment; we could construct floral arrangements of passable beauty and balance from whatever sprigs and sprays the gardener scrounged together. And I could write stories of tortured souls that neither my family nor I, thank goodness, recognized as autobiographical.

I can't remember back to any time in my childhood when I didn't think of myself as a writer. By age three, living in a raucous and fecund Calcutta household that included Mukherjees of four generations, I had made myself a proficient reader, a devourer of whatever tabloids, movie posters, romance novels, detective stories, ghost stories, Russian tearjerkers in Bengali translation, came into the house courtesy of the many uncles, aunts, cousins, and neighbors. But that compulsive reading was just a preparation for writing. Even at three, I was making up wild, weird, introspective stories in my head. Outwardly I passed as a normal kid, which in my neighborhood meant an obedient, social miniadult with decent manners. My secret, writerly self, however, inhabited rough landscapes and rude emotions. I lived *for* and *through* these stories. They shocked me; they thrilled me. They convinced me that my persona was the authentic me and I the imposter.

I might have escaped the obsessive life of a serious writer if that spring of 1961 an African American theater instructor from Los Angeles hadn't come to our house for dinner, and my father hadn't introduced me to him as "the daughter with the gift for the pen."

"The daughter with the gift of the pen," the theater instructor had repeated. "I like it, man!"

"I'm sending my daughters to your country," my father boasted, "all three of them. Take your dowry money and invest it in yourselves, I've advised them. Oldest one I'm packing off to Day-tree-oyt, youngest one to Vassar College. Only question now is where best to send the middle one given her gift of the pen?"

The theater instructor hadn't missed a beat. "Paul Engle. To Paul Engle in Ames."

"Paulengle," my father repeated. "I like it, I like it very much, man! I send her to a person, not to an institution. Hello, Paulengleinames!"

That very night he dictated a father-to-father kind of letter to a man he knew nothing about but seemed, uncharacteristically, willing to trust with the informal guardianship of my oversheltered sensibilities and moral conduct. To my father's I added a more standard letter of application, a list of honors and prizes, and six short stories beautifully penned on letterpad paper. Very early the next morning, with my mother chanting good luck prayers for me in the backseat of our ancient Vauxhall, the chauffeur rushed the fat envelope to the main post office in town. The envelope was addressed to MR. PAUL ENGLE, AMES, USA.

Right name but wrong city, we discovered much later. But no error so slight could keep apart lives destined for intersection. The application reached Paul Engle; he was that well known an American figure. Get on a plane, be in Iowa City in time for the fall semester, Paul Engle responded. He even offered a tuition scholarship. For my father, Paul Engle included a special letter. He had daughters of his own, my father was not to worry, Paul'd personally help me through any adjustment problems that cropped up.

And he did. When I tried to negotiate my first Iowa winter in pretty but frail Indian summertime sandals, he took me to his house, rummaged through the basement, and found me his equestrian daughter's riding boots and thick wool socks. When I was hungry for American literature (which had been carefully withheld from me as "too unseemly for our little ladies" by the teaching nuns in my Calcutta school), Paul introduced me to novelists like Ken Kesey in person so I would know that serious fiction subverts both head and heart. And best of all, long before my discover-the-person-you-were-really-meant-to-be time ran out in America's heartland, he invited me home to have tea with a young writer who, he explained, had just hitchhiked in from Cambridge where the young writer'd been Bernard Malamud's star student; then, right there in the middle of his drawing room, he transformed himself into a fatherly Cupid and let fly his arrows. The arrow-struck married in Iowa City during a lunch break between classes, have stayed married, making Iowa their inspiration for fiction as well as their home base.

So Jasmine and I, two honorary Iowans, thank you Paulengleinames for opening up closed worlds.

The Fellowship

About to enter the celebrated Clinton Street group therapy center, Kenney's, I met Rod Terry, on his way out. After we'd spilled ideas on some weighty matters — night, the stars, Thelonius Monk, tyranny — he dipped to the mundane and asked if I planned to apply for a writing fellowship.

Rod was in at least his second year in the poetry workshop, I nearing the end of my first in fiction. A recent foolishness had left me desperate for money. "How do I apply?"

"See Paul at the Quonsets on Thursday."

"What time?"

"Any time after lunch. He stays 'til everyone's gone."

The Quonsets were down and away from the main campus, along a bank of the Iowa River. At least two had classrooms used by the Writers' Workshop. At least one had offices. I supposed that one of the offices was Paul Engle's. "What about an appointment?"

"Don't need one."

"Application form?"

"Just be there."

On my way from San Francisco the summer before I'd stopped at Lake Tahoe to visit my sister and, in the plunging, uninformed way of a greenhorn, managed in a few hours to turn $45 into nearly $5,000 playing blackjack. After I arrived in Iowa City I upgraded my quarters, taking luxurious rooms over the common garage at the Blue Top Motel in Coralville, then began searching for a clean, well-lighted place where now and then I might flee from the rigors of writing to enjoy a few sips of local beer and the music of conversation.

During the search, I began talking compulsively about my Tahoe adventure, not as much to brag as to explore an experience that had been like falling from a tall building into a passing truckbed full of marshmallows. "I was lucky," I confessed, "but I doubt I could have won that much on luck alone. Don't you?" One listener agreed and suggested I test myself at a country tavern I'll call Second Chance. "I hear said they do some after-hours shuffling."

The next night I drove to West Freedom, where, in a shack with two rickety looking tables and a badly chipped mahogany bar, I found several men in overalls discussing corn futures. When they paused after a dispute over December prices, I introduced myself, announced that I was looking for a clean, well-lighted place, then spoke the line that in other spas had been turning eyes on me like fleets of searchlights: "Playing blackjack for a few hours at Lake Tahoe recently, I won several thousand dollars." Six-foot-five-inch proprietor/bartender, Ham Hammerbrock, had given me only a couple of blinks but now closed on me like an eclipse. "Fill us in, young man." There were only three fingers on one hand and a scar that semicircled from his temple over his forehead to his nose. He listened to my story with eyes as well as ears, now and then nodding as if to authenticate details. When I started my by-now-well-polished ending, he bent so close his garlic-on-burgundy breath rushed my nostrils in full assault, forcing me to take a couple of leans back. I sucked in air offended only by smoke, then put the finish on my story:

> Slightly inebriated, courtesy of the casino, I reached for my cigarette lighter and felt pocket after pocket bulging with chips. I'd just split aces with the dealer showing bust, normally a safe thing to do. But, when he arrived at 21 on a five-card hit, I felt my face tighten. A moment later I watched him scrape away ten raspberry-colored fifty-dollar chips, leaving me to gaze at my instantly hopeless 20 and suddenly pathetic 19. I knew then, the way you know your own shoes, that my luck had gone AWOL. "Mister," I told myself, "it's time for you to go home."

Ham slapped the working side of his good hand on the bar and bellowed, "Did what you had to do!" I felt pats on the back from the others and heard Ham say, "I think you found that place with the clean lights you was looking for, Mr. Phil. You be sure and stick around 'til after I bolt the door." About three beers later the bolt went on and Ham prepared the bar as a priest would his altar, his last step being to place within reach of the four of us who'd stayed, two fifths of a bourbon called Pleasant Surprise — "Whiskey is Whiskey," said the label — and a card that read:

LOSERS CAN BE WINNERS!
THERE DRINKS ARE ON THE HOUSE!!!

Ham did the dealing, those three fingers moving like sheet lightning. After about forty games of blackjack, I'd won only gas money. A bad night, I told myself, and certainly one was due.

During the frigid months that followed, I drove to Second Chance often, as often as four times a week. I'd get ahead, sometimes by $50 or $60, but always fall back, usually going home with a little more or (more frequently) a little less than I'd brought in. It wasn't only the possibility of turning my luck that drew me but, increasingly, the game itself, its flow, the very feel of the cards and of course that hard-nosed country camaraderie.

I kept waiting for a bank-buster, a Tahoe night.

It didn't come.

I'm not sure when the nightmarish recognitions began. I don't think I was having even previews before Second Chance's doors went shut. I recall speaking aloud to myself many times as I made my way home, not spouting Dostoevskian recognitions, rather sputtering dry, pointless admonitions — "You should have taken a hit on that damned thirteen!" — inevitably concluding with one or another of the gambling fool's delusions: "The cards just didn't fall." "You didn't bet right." "You'll win a bundle next time."

By the time snow had surrendered to sleet and the apple trees were popping buds, Ham had let us regulars know that Second Chance would close for a while, long enough for him to have the bar resurfaced. "I'd like to attract a finer clientele," he confided to me. "More folks like yourself, Mr. Phil." During the card games, he'd let out a roar of support when I'd draw a twenty-one and a groan of pain when I busted. On my very last day there, as I sipped my final beer, I for the first time noticed above the cash register the weathered print of two elephants and a giraffe standing before a Barnum and Bailey circus tent, all watching me with eyes as sympathetic as Ham's.

Monsters with faces like gargoyles were soon nudging me out of sleep and whispering my disasters:

1.) I'd written only one short story I could stand (preserved to become, much later, the first chapter of my novel, *Defending Civilization*).
2.) I was drinking constantly.
3.) I was gutter-broke.

Partly blinded by the afternoon sun, I zigzagged to the back stool in Kenney's, squirmed onto it, found the silhouette of Irene's round face, and ordered a draft.

"I detect a troubled gait," she remarked.

"The darkness disjoints me."

"Only the darkness?"

Irene was a hands-on Rogerian and like all great Rogerians could read your feelings in a gesture. If necessary, she'd transform herself into a mother, a sister, a friend, or an adviser, whatever it took to help you get back on your road, or, if necessary, find another.

Today I was indulging in solitary suffering and didn't want any of the above. I presented her with the lesser but related problem: "Know anything about the fellowships Paul gives out in the spring?"

"A little," she said, drawing me a foamer. "I think they're mainly for the writers who've put in at least a year."

"Rod said you don't have to apply. Isn't that strange?"

She blew off some foam and slid the beer my way. "Paul isn't big on paperwork."

"I was in the army and nearly court-martialed after forgetting to sign for a Jeep. I've figured ever since that something will go wrong if I don't sign something. I worry about signing papers and after that I worry about them being lost."

"One of my more troubled patrons."

"The army does that. I applied to the Iowa workshop twice, for fear the first application would get lost. Lucky I did."

"The first one got lost?"

"No. I received one letter saying, 'You're not accepted,' then another saying, 'You're in.' I threw the first one away."

"A lie."

"Is it a good story?"

"No." She was wiping a glass with the towel that lay over her shoulder. "And it's not true." She stopped wiping and was eyeing me. "Is it?"

"I'm not saying. I learned in Verlin Cassill's Craft of Fiction that you have to leave the reader with uncertainty."

She snapped the towel at me.

Since my Iowa days I've heard that Kenney's has appeared more in American novels than any other bar. Writers drank at other Iowa City bars and taverns but didn't write them into their works. There are no doubt many reasons, like the beer at Kenney's being tastier because Irene didn't put too much of a freeze on it and Miles Davis coming off the Wurlitzer and stories so enviable you knew you were in a nest of imaginations. But the main reason was Irene.

A gentle eastern European writer I'll call Fred, then in his mid-thirties, began threatening to destroy a beautiful novel manuscript he'd been working on for more than a decade. Like most of us, he had no copies of his work because in those days copy machines just weren't available and few writers bothered to use carbon paper and onion skin. This would be Fred's second novel-assassination, same novel. Kara, his wife, had met him when, seven years earlier, she'd seen a wild-haired man tossing sheets of paper into the Chicago River. (No one who knew Fred had to ask why he didn't choose fire. He enjoyed suffering and preferred his suffering to be extended and romantic. Even page-by-page burning would be too quick. How many more self-lacerating thoughts he could have walking along a river bank at dusk, watching page follow page to oblivion!) He'd started again after he and Kara were married and now had a couple of hundred pages completed. Within a few hours after she sounded the assassination alert, several of us took Fred to Kenney's.

We'd warned Irene of his intention, and she was soon wringing out of him a full confession: he was indeed, once again, perhaps tonight, going to do away with his creation. She surprised him, all of us, when she said, "I'll go down to the river and help you throw the pages in."

"You will?" His head had been listing. It came upright. "Why?"

"You might change your mind and try to save it." She wasn't all worked up. In fact, she was stacking glasses, not even looking at him.

"You wouldn't want me to do that?"

"No."

He'd been holding onto the stalk of celery she'd for some reason stuck into his Bloody Mary. I heard it crack. "But . . . you must say why."

"Because it's clear you have to stop being a writer is why." Her tone was cool. "A banker who doesn't like money should get out of banking. You don't like words. You've made the right choice."

"But . . . but you don't understand, Irene." He pressed his palms to his chest. "I love words! That's *exactly* why I must destroy this novel!"

"Nonsense. If you're going to do it, at least be honest with yourself. You don't love words. You're like a parent with an ill child who can't cure the child and therefore must kill it. You do not deserve to be a writer any more than that parent deserves to be a parent. Give me the novel. I'll throw it in for you."

Fred stared at his Bloody Mary and seemed to shrink.

We talked around him, not about his novel.

In a few minutes he stood, bowed to Irene, shook each of our hands and left.

Would he or wouldn't he?

In the days that followed we inquired of Kara, not of him. "How's the novel going?"

"Still growing, little by little, day by day."

We inquired on and off for a year.

Then Kara said. "The river-watch is over. A publisher has accepted the novel."

We took him out again. To celebrate. This time Kara came.

When the novel finally appeared, the reviewer for the *New York Times Book Review* called it "a rare work of art."

"You're wonderful, Irene!" I now blurted. "It will never matter that you don't have the small answers."

"What's that supposed to mean?"

"It means I love and admire you even though, in that great lexicon, your memory, there's nothing more about the fellowships. Is there?"

She shook her head, and I knew I'd read her mind, whose thought was, "What problems are going to come through that doorway next?"

The afternoon beer had turned me into Holden Caulfield. How many would apply? And how, if Paul didn't have written applications, could he determine fairly who got money? Would he confer with Don Justice, the executive director of the workshop? With other writers who taught us? Would he base the decision on a review of manuscripts? On classroom performance? Both? On what basis would he, say, compare Vance Bourjaily's students with those of Philip Roth or Verlin Cassill? Could you get a fellowship if you also had a teaching assistantship? If so, could you . . . ?

Ack!

These days departments and programs distribute booklets with detailed information and instructions, even forms, but academic life in the early sixties was much less formal. At the Iowa Writers' Workshop informality reigned. At the beginning of a semester you showed up at whoever's workshop class you'd chosen, and the instructor accepted you because you were there. Teachers in 1961–62 were (in poetry) Paul, Don, and Mark, and (in fiction) Vance, Verlin, or Phil, not Dr. or Mr. Engle, Justice, Strand, Bourjaily, Cassill, or Roth. The only roll call I can remember was at Don's house before a Friday night poker game when he said, "Does anyone know if Marvin's coming?"

Part of the informality were the Quonsets, former military shacks made of corrugated steel that looked like half-buried oil cylinders. When you went to class in one of them, you wore anything from shorts to an overcoat, depending on the weather outside, which was going to be the same inside. Each class was scheduled for three hours one day a week. Students brought snacks, soda pop, coffee, rarely wine or beer, now and then a friend, sometimes a pet. Dogs slept; cats went from lap to lap. I heard that when someone brought a parrot to a class Paul was teaching he said it could remain if it didn't dominate the discussion. When you arrived in a classroom, the desks usually stood in neat rows facing front, but, even before class started, the desks were turned to as many points on the compass as there were egos in the room. A disputatious young man in Verlin's Craft of Fiction course lost an argument over a detail in Hemingway's *Soldier's Home* and turned his desk to the back wall for the rest of the afternoon. Now and then someone would slide three desks together and take a nap.

The writer of the work being discussed in workshop listened and usually swallowed without comment both positive or negative responses, interrupting only to request clarification or correct a misreading. When the general discussion ended, the writer had a chance to explain his or her intention, to ask for further clarification, to request ideas as to how to revise, to complain about the discussion, or even to make a speech. Workshop was the place where a writer learned how his or her work was experienced by others, and that was surely its greatest value. Hearing a discussion of your poem or story, though mostly rewarding, could also be intimidating. Yes, you tried to detach yourself from your manuscript but you couldn't always because, whatever a teaching writer might say about the artifact not being its creator, you felt both possessive and protective, maybe even had playground reactions as I did after Harry Williamson dampened a favorable response to my one good story by saying he thought he should "warn" its writer (we were always the anonymous "writer" though everyone usually knew who'd written what) about a tendency to descend to the farcical. I wanted to raise my finger like a protagonist in a Bernard Shaw play and proclaim my loyalty to the farcical, asserting that my vision of existence was of an endless farce, that it had been such from not long after my birth when I was informed that I would someday die ("No, we can't tell you when!"), that I giggled at the most serious parts of serious movies and that I unproudly gushed with laughter at funerals, that I found most human endeavors farcical, including farts which, I would say, is why everyone laughs at them, and that I would in all my writing depend on, if not, like the captain on a crumbling ship, go down with the farcical. Everyone (including me) was saved by my respect for Unwritten Workshop Rule Number One: *Never praise or defend your own work.* A week later, after my stew had cooled, I began to find some value in Harry's comment.

In those days there were too few women in graduate programs, too few African Americans, too few Hispanics, too few Asians, too few anything but white men. Paul must have begun to correct such imbalances early however, because, judging by the noncreative writing courses I'd taken and by other classes I'd visited at Iowa, there were more of the "too few" in workshop than in other graduate programs. And there were many more than there had been at the other two universities I'd attended.

I carried my fellowship questions to the Black and White Coffee Shop, where writers sometimes stopped before class, and there found first-year fiction writers Freeman Solberg and Red Clark in a back booth collaborating in a penetrating exploration of why certain writers' despicable characters are likable and other writers are just despicable. When the explorers pulled in their sails, I said, "Do either of you know anything about the writers' fellowships Paul gives out every spring?"

"I don't," said Red.

"What's a fellowship?" said Freeman.

Some help.

"Like an assistantship but with no teaching," Red explained.

"What's an assistantship?" Freeman, I later learned, was in the navy and until recently had been coming from the Rock Island Naval Station to classes. He was as yet unfamiliar with academic ropes.

Katy Dohr from poetry, second year, joined us. I was sure she'd shine light into our booth because she seemed to know how all things, from cars to governments, worked.

"What do you know about the writing fellowships?"

"All I know is that I and almost everyone who got money last year is happy with what he or she got, even the ones who got less than they asked for."

"You can ask for an amount?"

"Yes. Whatever you think you need."

"And then?"

"Paul asks you why you need it. You tell him. He might urge you to raise the amount. Sometimes he urges a writer to lower it. It's sort of negotiated."

How irregular! Imagine! Granting someone an amount he or she actually needed! What could be more offbeat? Why wasn't that most trustworthy of university bodies, a committee, involved? And what was the chance to negotiate all about?

"Just show up," Katy said. "You'll understand."

A weekend passed during which I stopped drinking and suffered through no more than half-a-dozen postgambling nightmares, most of them the sleeping kind. I sold some books, picked out smaller living quarters for the fall semester, was introduced to a beautiful woman named Sorrow, and by Wednesday finished a short story that I disliked but promised myself I wouldn't deliver to river or creek.

I arrived at the Quonsets before noon on Thursday. A line had formed. I inquired and was told that this was indeed the line for Paul Engle. I didn't join it until Katy came down the hill because I felt like a mouse and wanted a good mousetender beside me. Just after we got into line, Rod arrived and took the place behind me.

"Why are you shaking?" he asked.

"Guilt, I think."

"I don't get it."

"It's a short story too long to tell."

"Listen in," said Katy.

"Huh?"

"It's hot and he's keeping the door open. I can almost hear the conversation in there now. Get close to the door. Listen to me, then let Rod go ahead of you and listen to him. You'll see, I mean hear. It's not so bad."

"You don't mind?"

"You think we've got secrets?"

"What about Paul?"

"He probably wouldn't care. In any case, he won't know."

"Okay. I'll . . . try it."

I'd spoken to Paul a couple of times but only now realized that he had one of the most evocative human voices ever to swim in air. I heard it dog-paddle to determine why Katy, though she was able to graduate in June, wished to stay through the summer; freestyled through questions aimed at finding out how she felt about her writing; nicely sidestroked through a few gentle inquiries about her housing needs. Katy was a guiding dolphin, providing direction without slowing between rocks and cliffs. She'd requested $400 for the summer. Paul said he would approve $600.

As Katy had glided in, Rod splashed, was soon a long-distance swimmer doing the Australian crawl, quickly leading Paul into turbulent waters. He requested support for another year, giving as his main reason his pregnant wife, Diane, whom, I'd been told, was also a poet. "I have family needs now, Paul." Paul calmly did a crawl beside him, gently splashing questions. Did Diane have time for her own writing? What was Rod doing to carry his part of the family load? When did he plan to begin looking for a teaching or other job? Did he have any very recent works Paul might see? As the two swimmers maneuvered through these reefs, Rod's strokes became uneven, were soon reduced to thrashing and water-treading. "Haven't been able to produce as much as I'd like to have . . . because of the family situation." Eventually Paul led him into a quiet lagoon, not, I think, the haven Rod had expected. He'd help Rod find a job that would leave him plenty of writing time and time off for classes. He said he'd invite Diane to apply for a fellowship that would help her finish her degree. Meanwhile he'd recommend support for Rod in an amount equal to any pay he would make at his local job. When Diane had her degree the two writers could leave on equal footing. Meanwhile Paul could try to help them both line up permanent post-M.F.A. employment.

Rod's swim had exhausted and unnerved me, and, I went in like someone doing the breaststroke with broken collarbones. "Hep . . . hup . . . hellope . . . all."

Paul, who must have seen many looney-tooners come through his doorway, looked up at me stoically from a wooden swivel chair in front of a desk that faced the wall. The desk was bare except for a business-sized envelope with a flap whose edge was jagged. He was slender and mobile-looking (a swimmer perhaps) and had piercing eyes that worked themselves into a smile as he pointed to the chair between us.

Wanting to make up for my babbling entrance, I mumbled the words I'd been rehearsing as I'd eavesdropped. "I want you to know how grateful I am that you invited me . . . to your house last fall when . . . that time you . . . were having . . . a few students — over . . . to meet . . . ahm, Philip Roth."

His puzzled, penetrating look was saying, "What do your remarks have to do with anything we're sitting here for?" and slowed me to a dog-paddle, about to become a dead man's float. "Sorry." My hands did a tandem shrug. "I was going to ask for money. Actually I'm broke. But . . . the point is, you shouldn't give me any."

Each statement sent his head back as though he were avoiding jellyfish. "Then why have you come?"

"Well . . ." My eyes searched the room. A preferred answer might be posted on one of its bulletin boards. I found nothing and had to give the one I had. ". . . desperation."

"Go on."

"On?"

"Why the desperation?"

"Ahm . . ." Dizziness struck. I become dizzy under stress. Tears were also rising. And disconnected thoughts flooding in, crazy thoughts that more than once have sent me scudding to a psycho-therapist. Like: *Nothing is easy, even rare moments of success.* And: *My brain never works when it should.* Such thoughts! Nuthouse-quality. Oh, the dizziness! Suddenly I was back at St. Anselm's Church, San Anselmo, California, twenty years earlier, kneeling in a confessional, but this time the priest behind the screen was at the same time both our pastor, Father McGarr, and Paul Engle. Thoughts whirlpooled: *Two persons in one being, like partway imitation of The Trinity. No! I'm there too. Three persons! All in one being, that being my waking dream.*

"Are you going to answer?"

"Sorry, Father. When I arrived here, I had a lot of money . . ."

"Father?"

Shit! "Paul. I'm sorry. I had money but I . . . I frittered it away." I told him the Tahoe story. A good thing. It got me outside of myself. I told it in the only way I knew how, with awestruck wonderment and a few embellishments. I reminded him (though that might not have been necessary) that I'd given up part of my teaching assistantship after arriving in Iowa.

We were in a deep channel. He was circling me protectively. "Go on."

I for the very first time told the Second Chance story. I started in an odd crumbling tone, a ship collapsing in a typhoon, but by the end it sounded, to me at least, relatively calm and flowing. I didn't leave out a thing, including my skimpy output of two stories, total, one for each of the two semesters I'd been enrolled. Finally I felt it necessary to confess that I might be an alcoholic, wondering aloud whether it was an accident that one of my two favorite short stories was Frank O'Connor's "The Drunkard." I remember ending with the statement, "I fear I may be a broken man at an early age."

He was now treading water the way a dolphin, going almost vertical, seems to tread while observing something strange like a floppy walrus chasing its tail in circles. "Here's what," he said at last. "I'll provide you with enough money to get you through until June."

For a flickering second grateful, I then groaned against the dreadful anticipation that there might be a terrible condition: that I then leave. Forever! Total banishment! Why not? I was a drunk and a gambler, all in one! And there had been very little creative output! Avast! Maybe the first expulsion in Iowa workshop history!

"I appreciate you having seen me through this year," I mumbled.

He ignored me. "If between now and June you present a story in writing that's as good as that Tahoe one and the Second Chance story are orally, I'll recommend you for a fellowship for next year."

"Really?"

"In a place like this, being a storyteller is a good thing. But you don't have to let yourself be a fool to come up with a story. Where do you think Ham got the money to build that bar in the first place?"

Ham? He knew Ham? Probably did. He knew many people. I guessed: "Suckers like me?"

"No more need be said." He turned his swivel chair, picked up the envelope with the torn flap, peeled off a tiny piece of the flap, a piece half the size of the nail on his little finger, then removed a stub of pencil from his shirt pocket and somehow managed to write something on the fleck. He turned the chair back and handed it to me. "Take that across the street to the Iowa Foundation and give it to one of the ladies at the counter. She'll present you with a check."

I stood, closing my fist around my fellowship, and went out tail first and smiling.

Thank You, Paul

Paul played a pivotal role in shaping the course of my literary career. I would like to pay my tribute as a testimony to his boundless magnanimity and love for thousands of aspiring writers like me.

It was in 1962. I had my master's degree in English from Taiwan, having just completed a thesis on Eliot and published a translation of "The Waste Land," and had begun to teach in a high school in Hong Kong. But under the British colonial education system, all non-British degree holders were treated as cheap labor; I was asked to teach an overload of basic English with minimum pay. I was totally tired out every day; there was no room to develop my budding creative impulse. In the midst of this frustration which weighed down on me like a heavy lid, Paul came to my rescue. I had sent him a few English poems I had written and a chapter from my Eliot thesis, both of which were, in retrospect, far from in publishable form. To my surprise and delight, I received an immediate response from Paul. He showered me with praises I didn't deserve and offered me a scholarship which eventually brought me to Iowa City. At Iowa, I had the opportunity to work with Paul, Donald Justice, Mark Strand, and Edmund Keeley, and was able to embark on the translation of twenty modernist poets from Taiwan which Paul saw through to its publication by the University of Iowa Press in 1970. To ensure that I would work worry free, Paul went out of his way to bring my wife and daughter to Iowa. This was a difficult period in Taiwan in which wives were not allowed to join their student-husbands immediately; they had to wait at least two years, if not more. Paul went to Taipei to negotiate for my family's exit permit and U.S. visa. Paul was always concerned about a writer's well-being and would make any effort to create an ambiance in which a writer could work at his or her maximum. Many writers, both from within the U.S. and from countries around the world, will testify to this.

Paul's totally selfless offer of assistance to young writers came, no doubt, from his conviction that a better, borderless world can be achieved with totally open and unimpeded dialogues between and among writers from all nations. To provide for such a common-wealth of writers, Paul, later joined by Hualing, had gone to great lengths to create channels for writers to break through local restrictions, quite often political in nature, and to come to Iowa to participate in these unimpeded dialogues. Take the case of Y. C. Chen, who was unjustly put into prison for ideological dissent in Taipei. Paul went so far as to get an American attorney in Taiwan to defend him. Paul and Hualing continued to defend cases of ideological oppression of writers in the People's Republic of China as well as in East European countries. The magnanimity with which Paul did these things had its origin in the triple dimension of his love: (1) in the deep reaches of his heart, his measureless love for poetry and literary creations, (2) in his conviction that humanity, in its untarnished splendor, will shine and speak across national borders and ideological boundaries, and (3) in his commitment to achieve a world community of writers whose unimpeded dialogues will eventually lead to the emergence of a true-to-type United Nations.

For myself, and for many writers who have come from other parts of the world, I would like to say, "Thank you, Paul." If, as the myth goes, Orpheus after his death was metamorphosed into various forms of nature singing his lyrics, we are then your trees, rivers, and mountains forever singing your songs, here and everywhere.

"Next Year You Can See for Yourself"

Paul Engle changed my life.

I'd begun reading American poetry in the early sixties, first in Helsinki, at the U.S.I.S. Library, and then back in England after my year in Finland. In the poems of James Wright, Theodore Roethke, Anne Sexton, William Stafford, W. S. Merwin, and James Dickey, I found language and images that suggested all kinds of new possibilities to my own restless imagination.

In Helsinki, I'd met Chester Anderson, a Joyce expert and Fulbright Scholar at the University of Helsinki. We began a lifelong friendship in the fall of 1963 and it was Chet (best man, "best Chet," at my wedding many years later) who gave me a list of American creative writing programs, with the name "Iowa" at the top. (Funny-looking word, I thought. Is that where the Mormons are?)

Back in England in the summer of 1964, I spent some time at the American Embassy in London, looking at information about creative writing programs, and made the decision to try to go to Iowa. I applied to enter the program and to support myself for two years with a teaching assistantship in French.

Late in October of 1964, I received a blue airmail letter from Paul Engle in Iowa City. The information in the letter was definitely of interest—Paul assured me of acceptance into the program and of receiving the assistantship—but the large and very scarlet maple leaf Paul had enclosed in the letter especially thrilled me— a living piece of the landscape I aspired to enter. What also thrilled me were Paul's words: "Next year you can see for yourself." And so I did, as he promised. And I have an American life, thanks to him.

Over many years, Paul Engle helped thousands of people, and it's possible he sent out thousands of Iowa leaves inside blue airmail letters, but I took the gesture entirely personally — it was magic to me and has always stayed with me. It was a poet's gesture, all right.

I found in Paul's own poems, which I sought out, the kind of vigor I later encountered in the man. Having been raised on the sonnet, I responded to the music and firmness of form of *American Child* while finding in its images intimations of a country very different from the one I began in, vivid details of the new world that was to become my own:

Now she is all the seasons in one child:
Her eyes are summer and the summer sun
Full with a great earth warmth, open and mild,
Her hands are autumn when the crop is done,
Her rapid fingers harvesting ripe touch,
Her hair is winter drifted with blonde snow,
Her mouth is spring and overfilled with such
Cry as you hear when the webbed ducks northward go.

Minnesota has been my home for twenty-five years, and so I know about harvest and snow and children and ducks and the north — and the large maple leaves (the kind that are whirling in late October as I write this).

I have two main memories of Paul. One is of his voice, his utterly distinctive voice, some witty confluence of Iowa and Oxford, clipped, firm (like the poems), a gleam to the phrasing, a natural cadence, a warm tone. It was a welcomer's voice: it invited.

At the same time, there was something of the fencer's manner about his voice and speech — he seemed always to enjoy encountering a lithe or outspoken conversationalist, one with whom he could thrust and parry, one whom he could *engage* in conversation; there was an obvious relish to the way he delivered well-turned phrases and frequent *bons mots*. There was also a decidedly mischievous and funloving, ever-young quality to the voice (he must have been quite a boy).

That tone and manner are well preserved in a paragraph such as this (from the introduction to *Seems Like Old Times*):

Of course there are risks. The mild frost of a university air can kill the tender plant. Excess of self-consciousness can slow down a talent which has little momentum. An English novelist, V. S. Pritchett, laments that the American university may induce "an unnatural hostility to vulgarity" in the writer. Have no fear. They will not lose their vulgarity.

I read that and I hear Paul's voice. I hear, if you'll allow the synesthesia, the gleam.

My other main memory is of Paul the Great Convenor. Lord, that man loved to get people *together*— he must have had a convening gene in him somewhere. The workshop, and the International Writing Program were, of course, a massive convening of many years' duration.

For myself, I remember a number of communal excursions — a football game that first fall (the enemy being icy invaders from the north, the currently reeling Golden Gophers of Minnesota)— followed by a party at the house, where I discovered bourbon; an excursion to Chicago and the Playboy Club (What were we doing there? Did we go anywhere else in Chicago?); a visit to Des Moines one time where we were entertained royally in the penthouse suite of one of the patrons of the program, of the kind Paul was so skilled at courting.

Even after I'd left Iowa, Paul's kindness reached me; thanks to him, I was invited to a conference at the Library of Congress in the early seventies and had the incomparable pleasure of sharing a platform with N. Scott Momaday (among others) and hearing Momaday recite:

Remember my horse running.
Remember my horse.
Remember my horse running.
Remember my horse.

Unforgettable.

And when I came to Iowa City in the mid-eighties to give a reading and a talk to members of the International Writing Program, a favorite memory is of a lively, loquacious dinner in a Chinese restaurant on the outskirts of town to which Paul and Hualing had invited, oh, a few people. . . .

I didn't know Paul that well, probably, finally, though I always liked him. (I was also very full of myself at the time and may have been hard to know.) My first year at Iowa was the program's last year in the huts by the river and his last as director, and I never actually took a course from him. But he made a huge impression on me, that father to so many writers, and I'll always be grateful to him.

In the week Paul died, I was visiting the James Wright Festival in Martin's Ferry, Ohio; there I had the opportunity to pay my homage to the poet who has meant so much to me. And when I heard that Paul had died at O'Hare, between planes, on his way somewhere, as I said my prayer for him it seemed to me that it was somehow appropriate for death to come to him this way — while he was still in the saddle, or had his boots on (or whichever expression might fit).

He who had told me I could see for myself is gone, but his example lives on in me and in the many other writers whom he honored, at the times in their lives when they were most in need, with his tireless generosity and support. God rest him.

New World Symphony

I want to scold the state of Iowa at least a little bit.

You did not accord Paul Engle a minor fraction of the honors he deserved.

But you were simply being human. Saint Matthew said: "A prophet is not without honor, save in his own country." Matthew was speaking of every locality on Earth. How can anyone seem remarkable who was born where we were born, grew up as we grew up, who looks like us, who talks like us, who jokes likes us, who eats like us, who makes the same dumb mistakes that we do?

Why should you have paid homage to Paul Engle, when you could see him every day, if you wanted, and he was no dumber or smarter, or a better or worse dresser, than your brother Frank or your cousin Ed?

So it takes an outsider like me to give his word of honor that Paul Engle, in addition to being one of you, was a glamorous planetary citizen on the order of Duke Ellington or Charlie Chaplin, say. Or Martha Graham, the great dancer and choreographer, who died ten days after Paul died. Or Antonín Dvořák, another great artist, who wowed your great-grandparents when he lived and worked in Iowa precisely because he was so much unlike them.

Very well.

Let the climax of this memorial service be the performance, or the reading, or the viewing, or whatever, of a work of art by Paul Engle which is obviously as majestic as Dvořák's *New World Symphony*.

Silence.

Nothing.

What remains are the Writers' Workshops. And those have always been here, haven't they? Like the river and the old State Capitol?

Before I came to Iowa City to teach in 1965 and '66, I could name only three things I knew for sure about your state: Corn, pigs, and the Writers' Workshop. There was only one such world-famous workshop then. Now there are two, the newer one for authors from other nations, the International Writing Program. There wouldn't be a Writers' Workshop worth a nickel here if Paul Engle hadn't committed his whole body and soul to their creation. So are the desks and file cabinets and duplicating machines of those on-going institutions — the New World Symphony, so to speak, that he left us? You think I'm nuts?

His New World Symphony, which is an Old World Symphony, too, or simply a World Symphony, is the enormous body of litera-ture created, and which is still being created, by men and women who gained or regained self-confidence as artists right here in River City. Excuse me, I meant to say, "right here in Iowa City." The line "right here in River City," of course, comes from Mere-dith Willson's *The Music Man.* That's a natural slip of the tongue to make, since Paul Engle, a real human being who was among you until very recently, was as virile and exciting, and hilarious, and rascally, and playful, and encouraging, and inspiring, as Meredith Willson's wholly fictitious Music Man.

"Seventy-six trombones led the big parade."

The current mayor of Prague, Czechoslovakia, in case you don't know it, who is also a novelist and my translator, studied writ-ing here. So did Flannery O'Connor and John Irving and Gail God-win, and John Casey, who won last year's National Book Award for fiction.

Pigs and corn?

Somebody started to assemble a history of Paul Engle's Writers' Workshop, I'm told. The person, while riffling through musty files, came across the name of a former student who became world fa-mous, although nobody recalled that he had studied there. He had changed his name after he left. That was the problem. He was just

Tom Williams at the University of Iowa. But then he changed his first name to "Tennessee."

I was rescued by Paul Engle's Writers' Workshop in the mid-1960s, and he didn't know me, and I don't think he had ever heard of me. He didn't read that kind of crap. But somebody else out here did, and assured him that I was indeed a writer, but dead broke with a lot of kids, and completely out of print and scared to death. So he threw me a life preserver, which is to say a teaching job. That same autumn he threw another to the world-class writer Nelson Algren, and yet another to the Chilean novelist Jose Donoso. All three of us were headed for Davy Jones's locker for sure.

Paul Engle should get a posthumous medal from the Coast Guard for all the lives he saved.

No writer in all of history did as much to help other writers as Paul Engle.

I miss him because I loved him.

One last thought: To hundreds of writers all over the world now, Paul Engle wasn't merely an Iowan. He was Iowa!

Mentors, Fomenters, & Tormentors

Mentors, Fomenters, and Tormentors

I. BACK TO SCHOOL

Most everyone agrees that the period just after World War II, when the colleges were full of GI Bill veterans, was the Golden Age — or Golden Moment — of American education. Still, there were times when with its overcrowded classes, long lines registering in field houses, married students living in barracks and Quonset areas, it seemed much like being back in the service. And it, too, could lead you into dangers.

Once out of the navy, I decided I'd have to get out of music; I simply hadn't done the groundwork necessary by the time you're twenty. I felt, though, that I belonged somewhere in the arts and decided — on the absurd grounds that I had the basics: the English language — to try playwriting. I had seen somewhere — *Life* magazine? — an article about Paul Engle's writing workshops at the University of Iowa. My mother pulled some strings among old school friends in that area and got me admitted. I soon found, though, that I couldn't study playwriting in the workshops and must persuade someone from the theater to take me into one of their courses; sadly, I succeeded. The theater was in the hands of an aged tyrant named Edward Mabee, a crude and bullying businessman type who had championed a costly new theater building with advanced stage machinery and elaborate equipment. This "ideal" physical plant, with its demands for popular and financial success, had quickly driven artistic life out of a once vital program.

My playwriting class was taught by a woman who'd been a classmate there of Tennessee Williams — a first version of whose *The*

Glass Menagerie had been rejected as a master's thesis. Already stung by its success on Broadway, she called him a one-shot writer; then, months before my class with her, *A Streetcar Named Desire* had opened. Known generally as "The Bitch"— such language was not then used on campuses — she was rumored to be the model for Blanche DuBois.

From the first, she and I were at war. The first law of her formula for plays was that the leading character must be likable. I raised the specters of *Macbeth* and *Medea*; she retorted that you had to learn the rules before you could break them. She paraded my first scenario—based on Trevor-Roper's *The Last Days of Hitler*— through the classroom between pinched fingers as if it were a dead rat's tail, meantime holding her nose with the other hand.

She proposed that, as a class, we jointly compose a scenario according to her formula. She picked the central character and situation: a young girl in an orphanage who dreams of becoming a concert pianist. Her mentor, the kindly headmistress, knows that she cannot succeed in this aim and wants to teach her a digitally related but humbler skill, typing. The required obstacle is that the girl has reached the age of graduation and the antagonist, head of the board of directors, is determined she must be ejected on schedule into a hostile world. Need I dredge up any more?

A first draft completed, she asked each of us, in turn, for criticism. Each found it good — some remarked on the economy of cast and setting; one thought it might do a year in New York, then have a profitable run in little theaters. When she got to me — having sedulously avoided my help in the "communal" composition of this document — I collected my nerve and said I thought it was gawdawful. I no doubt played some variations on this theme. After class, one of the others — all theater majors — pulled me aside: "You idiot!— don't you know that play is in her doctoral dissertation?" I was the only one who hadn't known!

Still, my plays were terrible; only my teacher's doctrines could have made them worse. I wandered back into the creative writing department and soon was sitting with, though not signed up for, the poetry workshop. I had no intention of writing poetry but there, at least, I felt I might learn something about one of the arts. The students were extraordinarily gifted, some doing exciting work. Better, I could admire my teachers: they cared about their subject; they *knew* something about it.

I was terrified and exhilarated at once. I had never even heard of New Criticism or of T. S. Eliot. I suddenly realized that, through my two years at a small college, I had taken A's in every course without understanding a word. I hadn't even known there was something you *could* understand. For two years, I read as if possessed; I was too scared to say Word One.

Among the workshop students was a gruff, bearlike veteran named Hood Gardner, several years older, silent, glowering, obviously respected by the others. Earlier, in the art department under Mauricio Lasansky, he'd made some beautiful copper engravings; before that, he'd designed a striking lamp for an industrial design class, then a new typeface for a typography class. All he did bristled with invention; now he was in the fiction workshop writing a muscular novella. Almost at once, I attached myself to him.

One noon, I followed him to the barracks apartment where he lived with his wife and baby son; I couldn't have been more awestruck by a shah's palace. On the wall was one of his copper engravings; near it, his own map of the tiny Pacific island where he'd been stationed — a map accepted by the National Geographic Society; opposite, a rack of primitive spears and arrows his native workers had given him. The phonograph was playing a violin concerto by Delius, of whom I'd never heard. Hood sat, solid as a magistrate, in a gnarled diamond willow chair or held his naked baby son by both hands, dunking him in the kitchen sink, while we talked about Sartre — just then appearing in English and a heavy influence on Hood's novella. Hearing that the brightest of the student writers and intellectuals met there almost every night, I vowed to beat down the door if necessary.

Again, I was both terrified and exhilarated; my wife was only terrified. Most veteran's wives worked: Hood's wife, Betty, was a clerk at the psychiatric hospital; mine taught primary grades in a small town nearby. Leaving the Gardners' after our first evening there, she started to weep hysterically: "We must never, never go back there. Never. I feel so stupid, so ignorant. I know they're all making fun of me." In the small church-related college we'd both attended, she'd been bored half frantic by her education classes; now she wanted to flee anything livelier. I felt equally ignorant — but how else to correct that? Persuaded, finally, to return, she grew at ease, was liked and accepted. After several semesters as a listener, I was admitted to the poetry workshop. I'd found something I might be able to do.

Both fiction and poetry workshops were directed by Paul Engle — who had not founded them but was largely responsible for their success. It had once been expected he'd become a fine, perhaps a great poet; this had not occurred. As a fellow student once said, if Paul had a choice between two ways to do a thing — a simple, straightforward way, and a complicated, difficult, underhanded way that was nearly as effective — he would always take the latter. A related predilection I think ruined his writing — again and again, a poem would broach a real and moving subject only to collapse into sentimentality or hot air. That same predilection, however, made him a superb administrator. And it may be that any such large and expensive program needs a person similarly gifted at its head.

Engle could be — and on occasion was — a brilliant teacher. He led us into the French Symbolists, Baudelaire and Verlaine, then did close analyses of Rimbaud's "Le Bateau Ivre" and the magnificent "Memoire." Multiple corridors, landscapes of expression opened, ways of meaning I had never imagined. Later, knowing Engle had lived in Germany, I brought him the Rueckert texts set by Gustav Mahler as "Die Kindertotenlieder" and which I wanted to translate. Sensitively and precisely, he pinpointed the strengths and subtleties of those poems. Yet, as I've noted elsewhere, if I'd presented those as my own poems, he'd have thought them sentimental or overemotional.

The problem lay, I think, in his own writing's history. Coming from a small town in Iowa, he'd been celebrated, when young, for long lined, loose poems of a sort called (wrongly) Whitmanesque. Later, these had been attacked by the New Critics and writers influenced by the Symbolists, Pound, and Eliot. Now he was championing those very writers who had savaged his early work.

This might bespeak a willingness to see that one's opponent was right — perhaps, though, only that they were stronger. In any case, converts are liable to be stringent and dogmatic. Ignoring the real causes of his early work's artistic failure (an emotional and intellectual dishonesty which had also insured its popular success), he was obsessed with symptoms.

There were other problems — not least, that he was seldom present. He traveled about the country, later the world, spotting with great accuracy promising young poets and luring them to Iowa City. With missionary zeal he badgered administrators, legislators, businessmen for the funds to support those students, their courses, the writers who taught them. Even when in Iowa City, his mind was usually taken up with such problems; criticism of student work reverted to a sort of knee-jerk New Criticism. It is the classical dilemma of American education: those of highest ability don't want to administer; those of lesser ability are bound to administer for lesser purpose.

And deeper problems. Engle enlisted many students with more promise, on the verge of more achievement, than his own. That must have been hard to live with. He was. Subtle and energetic, he held the purse strings for graduate students — often specially vulnerable because their wives were supporting them. There were ready ways to destabilize their psyches. It was normal to be invited to his country house, a rundown estate in Stone City, for a party — then be asked to cut down some small trees on the grounds, to mow the lawn, to do other menial tasks. Much too often, people came to Iowa City on the promise of grants which never materialized. Supposedly ongoing fellowships might suddenly be canceled. He turned his back while one student became embroiled with his attractive but fiercely neurotic wife, then walked in on a scene not quite actionable, but embarrassing. I suppose all creative programs may have some students whose work is blocked; we had far too many exceptionally gifted students unable, for long periods, to produce anything. True, such students often contributed greatly to others' work through generous criticism, but their own work and careers faltered. Surely part of the cause lay in their relations with the director.

Even this might have served as a preparation for what one would soon meet in the academic and literary worlds outside. Once, at a party given for Robert Penn Warren, Paul shocked everyone by telling his recurrent nightmare. He was a prisoner, he said, in a concentration camp where he'd been singled out for a specially degrading punishment. Along the camp's outer rock wall, about six feet off the ground, was a series of holes or depressions. Brought out naked before the massed prisoners, he had to bend over and grasp his ankles, then hoisted by the guards, put his feet in two of those depressions. The guards and prisoners jeering at him, he must then draw out one foot at a time, moving it on to the next hole and so proceeding around the wall like a fly. But, he said, after a while he found he could do this surprisingly well — better, in fact, than anyone had ever done it. In time, he was simply whizzing around the wall while guards and prisoners, no longer jeering, looked on with amazement and admiration.

We were astonished not only by the horrors of this dream but also that he would recount it at a party where many (Warren not least) would understand. If only his poems had offered such revelations! At parties, though, horrors were not scarce: one evening I was met at the door by Engle's wife who, though approaching derangement, still seemed appealing. "Well, Mary, how's it going?" I asked. "Oh, I don't know," she said in the hearing of everyone; "I love him but it's so awful!" A few moments later she went on, "I went over and had most of my plumbing out last week. He might as well have that; he's had all the rest." Such scenes moved us sometimes to sympathy for Engle, sometimes for her, but we all knew either sympathy could be dangerous.

For years, Engle was very generous toward me, then without informing me suddenly cut off my fellowship. I had recently been divorced and had support payments to meet; this could have put me in serious trouble. Fortunately, another teacher, Rhodes Dunlap, warned me, then added me to *his* list. When I had so many to feel grateful toward — such scholars as Victor Harris, Rhodes Dunlap, and John McGalliard, not to mention, for the moment, my writing teachers — it was sad to leave with bitter feelings toward the very person who had, chiefly, made this possible. I think it fair to note, though, that my feelings were reciprocated. When I attended a reunion some years later, Paul, as master of ceremonies over a vast luncheon, was able to recognize and introduce to the group every person in the room — industrialists, legislators, teachers, former students. There was a gratifying wave of laughter when he had to ask who I was.

II. THE BIG BOYS

Engle's absence had one splendid side effect: substitutes. Ruthven Todd, the Scottish poet, came during my first year, though I only got to know him later — relieved to escape his rocky upland farm in Scotland, he seldom left his stool in a local bar. Later, there were Reed Whittemore, Karl Shapiro, Robert Lowell, John Berryman — besides those who came for shorter periods: Warren, Brooks, Tate, Ransom, Ciardi, Dylan Thomas, Jarrell.

When I first heard Lowell was coming, I scarcely dared believe it. Soon after I'd started in Iowa, I fell in love with the poetry of William Empson, author of *Seven Types of Ambiguity* and of our most intensely ambiguous, highly intellectual poems. Having written several villanelles in imitation of Empson's, I then moved on to Lowell. Lowell's early poems — *Lord Weary's Castle* had recently won the Pulitzer Prize — had overwhelmed young readers, much as Swinburne's had an earlier generation in England. I cannot say we understood them. I cannot say I understand them now — or even that Lowell understood them. But, after the dry, etiolated language and attitudes of Eliot, we were ravenous for their vigor. A Lowell poem seemed like some massive generator, steel jacketed in formal metrics against its throb of rhetoric and imagery. Even before we'd heard he was coming, I'd been writing like him.

Until his arrival, he was the one topic of conversation: the time he had done as a conscientious objector, his periods of madness, his past violence. We were surprised to find that, though tall and powerfully built, he seemed the gentlest of mortals, clumsily anxious to please. Talking to you, he'd lean one cheek on his fist, or rest his chin on the back of one straightened hand; the elbow that supported that hand and head, though, often rested on empty air. Meantime, his free hand, its wrist cramped at a sharp angle, the first two fingers pointing, made jabs and clashes in the air. This broken wrist — often associated with weakness or effeminacy — seemed in him to betoken almost an excess of force, leashed but undiminished.

Lowell's massive, unwieldy appearance seemed an objective correlative to his mind and personality. Almost devoid of graceful expression, he often broached an opinion or subject in the most jolting and awkward manner — sometimes he seemed simply off the track. Soon, though, the mass and power of that mind overbore doubts or objections.

You could never predict his opinion, what associations he might draw toward any subject. That, of course, may be almost a definition of brilliance — that it throws out unexpectable ideas. Yet this was so marked in Lowell that I sometimes wondered if he did not, like certain British writers I've known, deliberately seek outlandish responses either to spark conversation or to appear clever. Surely a sort of aggression was embodied here — on a level, though, that provoked thought, not mere controversy.

However high the expectations, almost no one was disappointed by Lowell's teaching. He came, one semester each, for several years and usually taught at least one course in masterpieces of English poetry. For each session he picked a poet or even a single poem, then for several hours would free associate to that work. Wyatt, Raleigh, Milton's "Lycidas," Landor, Tennyson's "Tithonus" — week after week we came away staggered under a bombardment of ideas, ideas, ideas. None of those works would ever look the same again; neither would our estimation of an adequate response to the work of art.

His workshops were, if anything, more powerful. When Lowell "did" your poem, said one student, it was as if a muscle-bound octopus came and sat down on it. Then, deliberately, it would stretch out one tentacle and haul in mythology, a second for sociology, a third for classical literature, others for religion, history, psychology. Meantime, you sat there thinking, "This man *is* as mad as they said; none of this has anything to do with my poor, little poem!" Then he began tying these disciplines, one by one, into your text;

you saw that it *did* have to do, had almost everything to do, with your poem.

My friend neglected to say that two days later you would run into Lowell on the street and he'd say, hunching over you with a concerned smile, "I've been thinking about that poem of yours — you know, the one with the rather grand language — and I was all wrong about it. Now, what it's really about is . . ." and he was off again, hauling you with him through new galaxies of idea and association. Who could feel less than grateful for a mind so massive, so unpredictable, so concerned?

No less exciting was the Greek poetry workshop—taught jointly by Lowell and Gerald Else, then the leading American classicist. The students were poets from the workshop; none of the others had taken any Greek. (I had taken beginning Greek twice and Homer once, but none of it had taken.) We moved through the *Iliad* at exactly six lines per meeting, taking apart every sentence, each and every word, to identify its root, the nature of any suffixes and prefixes, additions, eccentricities of Attic or Ionic speech, departures from normal syntax or usage. This two-hour class followed an unvarying format: for the first hour, Lowell went through our six lines throwing out incredibly provocative, far-reaching theories about their meaning and implications; for the second hour, Else went through the same lines telling what they *really* meant. The class seemed almost a liberal education in itself; even Else said that doing the *Iliad* so slowly taught him things he'd never noticed.

This incredible force and extension of Lowell's mind seemed to me frighteningly involved with his extreme personality changes, his manic-depressive episodes. Little by little, month by month, the reach and power diminished, area after area of that mind were sealed off. Finally only a weary, gray shadow remained. Then, as that dammed-up force began to reassert itself, he might grow fiercely destructive to himself and others.

In his writings, Lowell intimates that if his wives were hectoring or slighting to him, that recalled his earlier situation with his mother; he felt that the nature of affection. Once, in some conversation, I started, "Oh, marriage is always . . ." He, no doubt dreading my probable truism, concluded, ". . . a rat-fight." When he could endure his situation and its concomitant depression no longer, he usually got a new girlfriend and broke into manic violence. I knew he could not have been easy to live with, that he had chosen and contributed to his situation, yet that made it no less painful to observe. I still felt something close to awe for him and found it hard to be friendly to anyone who was less than deferential to him.

Fortunately, he had no violent episodes at Iowa; I was never present when he did. There, I met his wife only briefly — if I recall, five times, of which she was in bed, three. She was apparently ill quite often; sometimes, after he had talked with some of us downstairs, or brought us home from some party, we might be received in her bedroom. Usually languid and exhausted, she once or twice became so excited at the mention of an absent acquaintance that she would get out of bed to "do" them. These imitations were exquisite, crackling with energy, but you never wanted to leave the room for long.

In time, I came to be one of the senior workshop members; my work was liked by Lowell and others — not merely, I think, because it resembled his. I did not care to recognize how exact, how exacting, that resemblance was, apparently content just to win a place among writers and teachers whom I revered.

The person who most jolted me into other directions was Randall Jarrell. I was able to study with him through the generosity of Catherine Drinker Bowen, the biographer, who'd given a lecture at Iowa City, then returned her fee to be given to younger writers. This, plus a fellowship from the Rocky Mountain Writers' Conference, took me to Boulder, Colorado, the next summer. Since this conference was to last only three weeks — most are even shorter — I expected little more than a respite from academia and a decaying marriage.

I thought I had some notion what to expect of Jarrell. Knowing he and Lowell were close, I assumed he would, in some way, resemble his ponderous friend. I knew Jarrell's poems, especially those about World War II, and thought him the only American poet serious enough to deal with the cataclysm. Expecting him to concur with other poets and critics who'd seen my work, I selected a sample, including pieces admired by Robert Penn Warren, Ransom, Brooks, and Tate. (It *did* seem odd that no two had liked the same poem!)

We met; I was flabbergasted. Slender and graceful, with a pencil-line mustache, his manners and vocabulary were those of a spoiled but lively little girl. "Gee," his voice skated to a high note as he lounged almost seductively against a stone wall, "don't you just love Colorado? I think Colorado's simply *dovey*!" If Lowell had come down on me like an avalanche, Jarrell came like an alpine skier schussing across that broken surface and piping (as Lowell recounts in an actual memory of him), "I feel just like an *angel*!"

His classes were as startling. Instead of discussing our poems in class, he read and analyzed other poems, beginning with an hour-long exegesis of "Frankie and Johnny." This ballad, in Brooks and Warren's version, he thought one of the half-dozen best poems composed in America; after his explication, I could scarcely dissent. The next class session, we tackled "Prufrock." He demonstrated, again, that we had read and/or heard even this standard text but had understood nothing. Neither had the critics and teachers we'd consulted. Hankering after big ideas and impressive terms, we'd thought the poem somehow depicted Eliot's movement toward religious belief; we had no suspicion that the poem contains a lady or that Prufrock feels an urge to "go through certain half deserted streets" to her apartment where, despite the women who "come and go" there, he will ask an "overwhelming question." His intent throughout the poem is, of course, to dissuade himself from any such venture.

Most of the students were distressed that he discussed their work only in private. If I was, I knew I'd been so enlightened that I could scarcely complain. Lowell's analyses had tended to the highly intellectual; Jarrell's, the emotional and personal. To my surprise, he actually *cared* about the exact dramatic scene and situation, about who was speaking and for what purpose. Could that be as important as grand ideas and terminology? Having nailed down these matters, Jarrell sensed impeccably what specific choices of language revealed about the speaker's character and emotions.

In "Frankie and Johnny" — which most teachers would have dismissed — we hadn't even realized that everyone except the judge is black, that Frankie is a prostitute and Johnny her pimp (not pander), or that she finds him in bed with Alice Fry — wearing a Stetson she must have bought him. "Did you ever meet a man," he asked, "so happy-go-lucky that he might come to the dinner table with his hat on? Could you tell more about a man's character if you wrote a whole book?"

Again discussing the details of clothing, Jarrell revealed more of Prufrock's character than most critics do in *many* volumes:

My morning coat, my collar mounting firmly to the chin;
My necktie rich and modest but asserted by a simple pin

It's as if, said Jarrell, the man had been born in a morning coat which he'd shed and grown anew every six months; as if a tortoise came up to you and said, "I know I'm old and my neck is all wrinkled, but just look at my shell . . . my beautiful shell . . . my beautiful *tortoiseshell* shell!" Absurdly, it is Prufrock's collar (surely an old-fashioned, high, starched one) which he imagines "mounting firmly" — language suitable to Roland or Galahad before a bastion. Prufrock will mount firmly neither bastion, stairs, nor lady.

Against the women he fears might mock his thin arms and legs, his thinning hair, he can marshal only the richness of his necktie, then having done so, must correct himself with the thoughts that "we rich people must be modest." Yet that must be balanced with, "but that's my problem: I'm too modest; I must be more assertive." Then, countering that, "But I simply can't stand assertive people!" So he must insert the "simple" pin — an adjective defining precisely what he is not!

Jarrell must have spent five minutes on those lines — every second of it revealing. He moved on to the climactic scene where the imagined lady will finally turn to Prufrock, throwing off her shawl to leave her arms open, her throat and shoulders bare, then — in the very epitome of cruelty — turn toward the window to dismiss him: "That is not what I meant. That is not it at all." We hadn't even known the poem had such a scene!

In private conference, Jarrell was remarkably kind, I think, to most students' poems. He may have thought many lacking in talent, so not worth troubling. He regarded highly the work of one man among the younger students and of one little old lady. Having lost her husband, this lady had taken a job as a government stenographer. Sent to Guam in the Marianas, she'd been assigned to record court-martials. What she'd seen there had been so cruelly unjust, so unjustifiable, that most of her beliefs had collapsed. Now she was writing poems about those cases. Meantime, the older participants (whose presence paid for the fellowships of younger students like myself) tried to coax her back into their more comfortable acceptances. Jarrell said that one of her poems had moved him to tears; he always encouraged her work but knew, I think, that her age might make the loneliness of such knowledge unendurable.

His attitude toward my work was harsher and more public: "You're *some* good." He thought me nearly obliterated, though, by the influence of Tate, of other New Critics, most especially of Lowell. "Do you know, Snodgrass," he crowed, "you're writing the very best second-rate Lowell in the whole country? The only trouble is there's only one person writing any first-rate Lowell: Lowell." Sitting on the patio, surrounded by tables of students with their cokes and sandwiches, he'd pick up one of my poems, loudly declare a line or two, then slap his thigh, howling, "Snodgrass, you *wrote* that! You really *did*! *That*!" Or he would whoop, "What are you trying to do? Turn yourself into a fireworks factory?"

If Lowell had seemed like an octopus, Jarrell was like a dolphin, swiftly slicing curvets through the sea, uttering outrageous messages in almost supersonic squeaks, bumping sharks to death with his nose and, in a closed tank, liable to kill every other creature just for fun. I often thought that if the wit of his everyday conversation hadn't kept me weak with laughter, I might have hit him.

In the sheaf I'd given him, he had liked only two poems — both translations. One was that passage where Ovid tells of Jupiter as a white bull carrying off Europa; the other, one of Rilke's "Sonnets to Orpheus." I'd done both pretty much as exercises — the Rilke because I'd seen a printed version so poor I thought I couldn't do worse. These made sense to him, he said; they embodied an emotion he could experience. I think it hadn't occurred to me that counted. He thought my own poems academic exercises: they didn't, on the one hand, make much sense, or on the other, have such magical language that you could get along without it.

Because of my Rilke translation and my poem called "Orpheus" (which was, he must have guessed, about my failing marriage), he sent me to look up Rilke's "Orpheus, Eurydice, Hermes." Unquestionably a masterpiece, it depicts, in nearly surreal images, Orpheus' fearful journey into the underworld, where he will sing to regain his wife. Utterly changed by death, she must be led along by Hermes, the messenger god, following Orpheus' voice back to the upper world. As always, Orpheus must not look back until they reach that realm but is wracked by fears she may not be following. As always, just at the threshold, he turns. The god is horrified: "O but he is looking at us!" She, in response, speaks one syllable: "Wo?" — "Who?" It isn't that she hates you, Jarrell said; not that she is wicked; not that you are worthless. It is simply that she has no idea who you are. Is there anything you can do with fancy language, he asked, to match the sheer invention of that? — the utter bleakness? I began to see what he was getting at.

In a strange way, I, too, may have affected Jarrell's life during that conference: I may have brought him together with his second wife. During registration, she had asked who this Jarrell was; having signed up for fiction workshop and children's writing, she wondered if she should take him also. I told her to drop everything else. She took him so completely that both soon became scarce at the conference. If you saw them at all, they were holding hands, cooing and ogling each other like adolescents as they sauntered away — evenings, to dance; daytimes, to his match with the local tennis pro. Someone who'd known him earlier at Greensboro told me he'd seen Jarrell and his first wife skipping across campus together, then cuddling in the back row of the movie, the day before their divorce proceedings began.

Despite all his brilliance, despite all I was learning, I could not always be sorry to lack Jarrell's company. On the opening day, I had noticed Jarrell's racket and asked if he'd like to play; he replied that he was very good and didn't like to play anyone who wasn't. I backed off, but later had a minor revenge at Ping-Pong. No, I didn't beat him, but I did scare him — I think I was the better player, but simply couldn't want to win any game that badly. Again, at the end of the conference, the students did skits and songs and I got to "do" Jarrell. In time, I grew grateful to him: he'd been right; my poems improved.

Not, though, at once. Over several years, other pressures grew. My marriage fell apart and I had to take outside jobs to meet support payments. I was desperate at not being allowed to see my baby daughter. Partly because of the marital failure, partly because my writing was blocked, I went into therapy. There, I noticed that of the two of us, the doctor and myself, one sounded like a textbook; it wasn't him. Similarly, my poems weren't finding my own voice or any subject I really cared about. All this, together with musical influences I've described elsewhere — and Jarrell's influence — led me to write markedly different poems, in particular a cycle of poems about my daughter which first brought me general notice.

At the time, strange to say, Engle and others in the workshop were more sympathetic to my new poems than was Lowell. He, genuinely worried for me, said, "Look; you've got a mind. You mustn't write this kind of tear-jerking stuff!" Some years later, he made a similar shift and found pretty much the same resistance from *his* mentor, Allen Tate.

John Berryman, who came one semester, was more sympathetic. Reading these poems about my daughter, he seemed, if not wildly enthusiastic, encouraging. Several lines, there, still contain revisions he suggested.

By that time, however, my life was in such turmoil that I saw rather little of Berryman. I was working, first, in a grubby small hotel, then at the Veterans' Hospital. My impression is that his classes were no less stimulating than either Lowell's or Jarrell's. He is harder, though, to sum up: not quite so ponderously intellectual as Lowell, nor emotionally brilliant as Jarrell. Full, though, of startling insights. He took us through the ending of *A Winter's Tale* and selected passages of "Song of Myself." Reading the miraculous last section of the Whitman, he looked up and said, "You know what that proves? That proves most people can't write poetry."

His writing classes were specially valuable, partly because he made specific assignments to a roomful of already highly accomplished students. When they handed in their assignments one day, he sat a moment leafing through the papers, paused to look at one, then glared at the class. "It just is not right," he said, "to get a sonnet like *that* as a classroom assignment." He was looking at Donald Justice's poem about how the angels, driving Adam and Eve from Paradise, raise above the closed gates their dazzling and fearful wings. Later, he assigned us to write a poem in stanzas about a death; I wrote about a patient I had looked after at the Veterans' Hospital, "A Flat One." I later had to comb Lowell's language out of this piece, as well as its symbolist stasis, but felt grateful to Berryman for a poem it wouldn't have occurred to me to write.

He once said that the poet's career should consist of, first, finding who they were, finding their own voice. Then, though, they would have to set about finding their opposite — the thing and voice that they were not. Finally, they would have to make a synthesis of these oppositions. This has a relation — never an easy one — to his own career and his effect on students. He tended to jolt you out of any easy definition of yourself or your limits. The poem was for him, more than either Lowell or Jarrell, a leap into the unknown.

Meantime, his own career seemed stalled. Some time before, he had published *Homage to Mistress Bradstreet* which won multiple awards and which many had said was the great American long poem. By this time, no one was saying that. No one was reading his little pamphlet *His Thought Made Pockets and the Plane Buckt*, which contained a number of concentration camp poems and several sketches toward the loopy brilliance of the *Dream Songs*— his finest achievement. All the cockeyed fancydance and fireworks of those poems was now going into talk at cocktail parties, bars, all-night drinking sessions. If he didn't seem to be involved with any women just then, made passes at none of his students, he made up for that. Once he'd had a few drinks, you could not get away; if his monologues couldn't stop you, he would grab your arm or would sing — surely the worst I ever heard. Unlike the quiet little man who walked about campus wearing a pork pie hat, this Berryman was frightening; I started avoiding him. He got into a fight with his landlord, thence into jail, and finally out of town with the semester unfinished. He was already well into the drunken wallow of his later years.

Others I recall in scantier detail, some because my personal affairs became so demanding, some because they came for shorter periods, some because they were simply less noteworthy. Karl Shapiro took the workshop for a semester, but commuted from Chicago only one day a week. Considering his position as editor of *Poetry* and the rambunctious heresy of his recent critical *dicta*, we were astonished at how vague he seemed about student poems. He often brought along the magazine's coming issue and discussed its poems instead. Even here he was oddly noncommittal, almost evasive. Asked why he had picked this or that poem (the undertone of which always meant, "Why *that* instead of my poems which you praised but rejected last month?"), his answer usually ran more or less that, well, it's not very good but the writer did some fine poems fifteen years ago and people would want to know what he's up to lately. We couldn't figure out just what he liked or wanted; we wondered if *he* could.

Of those who came just for an evening's reading or lecture, then a workshop meeting, easily the most notable was Dylan Thomas who came, I think, twice. We had the usual longed-for scandals: the stevedore's language, the crush on a dumpy local waitress, the Tournament of Insults at the chairman's party. One year, having fallen in with truck drivers, he rolled off the train dead drunk and announced, "This is the night I don't go on!" He was rushed to the writers' Quonset office where the bathroom had an actual tub, dunked in icy water, shucked back into clothes and brought to the Old Capitol's senate chamber where he proceeded to give one of his most beautiful readings. Before and between poems, his speech was slurred, shambling, obscene; suddenly, for the poem, he would shift into that sonorous, nearly Shakespearean voice still so familiar on recordings. The effect was so electrifying that one couldn't help wonder how much it might be calculated. The audience — many of whom had admired Eliot's dry and weary renderings — was forced into difficult reappraisals.

His meetings with the workshop, like Shapiro's, passed over the students' poems; he read, marvelously, his favorites — Hardy's

"Ah, Are You Digging on My Grave," Hodgson's "Eve," suggestive limericks, Ransom's "Captain Carpenter." At less disastrous parties he retold the myths of his own malfeasances — e.g., about the well-meaning London landlady who, not realizing he could only stomach a glass of milk and one of beer in the morning, brought him breakfasts of eggs and sausage, bacon, lox, ham. When every drawer in his rented room was filled with decaying delicacies, he'd had to move out. Alas, my only direct contact was to point him once toward the men's room.

The others who came for such periods were frequently New Critics — Brooks, Tate, Warren, Ransom. As they were also southern agrarians, dialect problems sometimes developed. Warren, moreover, paced and mumbled. Tirelessly, he would stalk back and forth across the platform muttering enigmatically, then turn suddenly to declare "AND!" Then he'd turn his back again, pace off several more stage lengths, whirling again to exclaim, "Theahfoah," or "Lak a ploohm!"

Ransom, the sweetest and courtliest of southern gentlemen, perhaps of mortals, once announced that he did not like the essay he'd prepared and would, instead, tell us about the "dipodics" which his friend, Harold Whitehall, had just declared to be the basis of much poetry. All the learned scholars of the university sat transfixed, watching in awe and perplexity, their heads pivoting in unison from left to right to left to right again as if at some very slow Ping-Pong match. Before them, Ransom, with a conductor's follow-the-bouncing-ball gestures, recited:

> The NOATH wind doth BLOW
> and WE shall have SNOW
> And WHAT will the ROBin
> do THEN . . .

"Now you see," he explained, "theah's somethin' missin' theah; it wasn't enough. So they had to add somethin' ":

> pooah THING!

On the stairway, leaving another occasion when he *had* read his prepared lecture, I heard a senior professor ask a colleague, "What's this new critical term he's invented? Metapause — what does that mean? Metapause!"

All eccentricities and even extremities of opinion aside, these critics and writers all brought an air of intelligence, seriousness, commitment to and concern for literature. One never doubted — as so often since — that one belonged to a genuine university community, a body of scholars, critics, and writers who, even when dead wrong, truly cared about their subject.

Only one visitor brought a sense of intellectual posturing and emptiness — John Ciardi. His own poems, when he read them, seemed null or pretentious. Yet, because of his translation of Dante — surprisingly tone-deaf but still daring to use the appropriate lowdown language in the *Inferno*— one still had hopes for this workshop. He began by remarking that as poetry editor of the *Saturday Review of Literature* he received hundreds, even thousands of poems weekly; as soon as a poem lost his interest, he stopped reading. When he taught, he drew, instead, a blue line across the page at the point he would have stopped if not paid to continue. This already seemed questionable practice on several scores, but we held our peace. He turned to one of the student poems — a piece by Bill Stafford about how cedar trees manage to cling even in the rockiest, steepest cliffs in spite of high winds and pounding salt spray. "On this one," he said, "I'd have stopped right there where it says that whenever you come to such and such type of ocean cliff, as like as not, you'll find a cedar." What was wrong with that, we asked. "What that says 'as like as not'— that means 50 percent of the time. I've been on lots of beaches and cliff sides; you don't find cedars anything like 50 percent of the time." We protested that the phrase surely meant "often," but with a hint of admiration for the tree's toughness and tenacity. He replied, "But that's the point; you've got to say what you mean.

"I met a case like this the other day. One of my students was writing a story — he'd been a marine in the war — about a troopship he'd been on. He had a phrase, 'When we arrived in midocean . . .' I tried to explain that you just couldn't say that." By now we had broken into a clamor. He went on, "You can't 'arrive' in midocean. 'Arrive' comes from the Latin, 'ripa' or 'bank'; 'Ad ripum'—'to the bank or shore.' There's no bank or shore in mid-ocean! But you couldn't explain that to him — he was a marine!"

I'd never before wanted to defend an American marine. But none of us did — we had sunk into disbelief that we'd heard correctly. He continued, "Now look at this poem by Robert Frost — 'Mending Wall.' It starts, 'Something there is that doesn't love a wall . . .'" The example proved *our* point, not his, but no one wanted to talk about it. Better just get away as quickly and politely as possible.

III. CONTINUING EDUCATION

Of course, I encountered most of my teachers again. I cannot say many of us came to good ends. My best friend at Iowa, Hood Gardner, who'd taught me at least as much as any faculty member, lost his first teaching job, came back to the university, changed fields several more times, and ended up making detailed medical drawings for the university hospitals. His son, a paratrooper, was killed in Vietnam. Hood and Betty broke up; he remarried. When I revisited Iowa City to give a reading, he seemed downcast and bitter. Even so, when he died unexpectedly, he remained a demigod for his second wife and step-daughter. My own daughter, who was raised there, said they often picnicked beside his grave where they had installed a tube in the ground and dropped sandwiches down for him.

I ran into Ciardi in Detroit at parties given by Charles Feinberg, a wealthy oil executive who collected manuscripts. I was not surprised to hear Feinberg relate that Ciardi had decided to become the first rich American poet. Not only was his deep voice to be heard over National Public Radio, but on the side he was selling real estate. I doubt that he reached his goal; too many had a head start on him.

I reencountered Shapiro when I read at Nebraska where he taught. I was much concerned at that time with the problems of raising children and we shortly got into a heated argument on the subject. Shapiro declared that one should raise a child "like a sexual weed," giving them all freedoms they demanded so that they might grow up fully vital and sexually fulfilled. I suspected this would have precisely the opposite effect, abandoning them to the scant mercy of terrifying energies and drives. At the dinner table, a sullen and flirtatious teenaged daughter kept throwing bits of meat from her plate at me.

As we started to leave for my reading, Shapiro appeared wearing a flamboyant shirt which provoked an outburst of scolding from his wife. Smiling—apparently having provoked the desired reaction—he slunk off to change. After the reading, we had just arrived at the chairman's party when he and his wife said they'd have to rush me away—their daughter had been at a dance and she might bring the boys home with her. In part, I was relieved to find how little his passionately argued convictions affected his conduct. That also made it clearer how he'd passed through so many allegiances: dedicated Jew, converted Catholic, Communist, academic beatnik, conventional prosodist, etc.

For a long time I avoided Lowell—partly to keep my language and poetic practice free of his. But also, conversely, because he had written me that he was taking my poems about my daughter—which might never have been published without his support—as a model for his own. I found this, in one I had nearly worshiped and whose style had so dominated me, hard to live with. I even became afraid—perhaps mistakenly, though not without evidence—that he might be influenced by some of the destructive elements of my own life and behavior. When I did visit, his wife and I became steadily less friendly. If I did not see him during any actual attack, I did just before and shortly after; the changes were appalling.

Once, I visited his class at Boston University. It seemed this couldn't be the same man; I have seldom encountered anyone duller. I struggled to inject some life into the class, but my deference to him, my unfamiliarity with the students' work, my shock at his state—all conspired against that. As we left the building, he hovered over me much as before, saying, "I always feel you should be as numb as possible in class—not say too much that's interesting. You ought to give the students a chance—not just obliterate them."

During that same weekend, though, we had one splendid evening: in his study we stayed up working on his translation of Rilke's

"Orpheus, Eurydice, Hermes" — the same poem Jarrell had shown me years before. At the time Lowell was influenced by the late poems of Ford Madox Ford — which he'd read me at length during the day — and was moving on from the *Life Studies* poems toward an even prosier style. I was astonished both at the liberties he took with the original and at the flatness and slanginess of his renderings. I have never held a brief for literal translation, but it hadn't occurred to me that one might take the original simply as a springboard into a related, but different, poem. Jarrell had once said, about his own splendid translations, "I would never try to second-guess Rilke!" I had agreed. Now I had to rethink my position: after all, what was good enough for Wyatt in his version of Petrarch just might be good enough for us.

If my poems had once pushed Lowell toward a simpler surface, he had now moved into areas of language I wouldn't have dared. For instance, in that poem's ending:

> Far there, dark against the clear entrance,
> stood some one, or rather no one
> you'd ever know. He stood and stared
> at the one level, inevitable road,
> as the reproachful god of messengers
> looking round, pushed off again.
> His caduceus was like a shotgun on his shoulder.

I recall that I had qualms about "no one you'd ever know" which now seems, however un-Rilkean, brilliant. I still don't know what to think of that shotgun in the last line. In any case, though I'm glad there are more literal versions, I still see no reason to regret the existence of Lowell's.

We must have worked for three or four hours, until around two A.M., when Stanley Kunitz came in. Kunitz, who was usually unfriendly to me and many of whose opinions I had thought foolish, now worked over the same poem with Lowell while I took a lesser role. I remember being surprised by the quality and cogency of Kunitz's practical criticism. I came away drained but exhilarated; if someone had had a tape recorder, they could have produced a marvelous document on the poetic process.

And old magics could be reborn. Once, at the New York City Ballet (an evening when Villella had been especially breathtaking), I ran into Paul Engle during intermission. Much of my rancor had abated; he seemed changed. His wife had been committed, then died; he had remarried a Chinese lady whom everyone adored and who adored him. He had lost the workshops at Iowa; taking his funds with him, he had initiated, instead, an International Translations Center, something quite unique in the academic world. Yet that serious defeat, and surely the change in his affectional life, had made him humbler, more humane. We agreed to meet later for a drink.

Coming out of Lincoln Center together, we ran into Lowell on the street. Their enmity, too, seemed to have faded. On my book jacket Lowell had described Iowa — in a sharp slash at Engle — as the "most sterile of sterile places." I later discovered that, several years before, Engle had been suddenly hospitalized while in New York. Lowell had visited him there and they had grown friendly again. Each now seemed thoughtful of the other's feelings: Engle carefully stepping around difficult subjects; Lowell, in his heavy-handed way, blundering into painful areas but turning quickly to put an apologetic hand on Engle's sleeve or make a counterbalancing compliment. Lowell suggested we go to his place at the Dakota for a drink; when I said that my wife, Camille, was coming in on a plane around midnight, he suggested that I pick her up and bring her there.

When we arrived, they were busily conjuring up the greats of the past generation — Engle recalling that after Robert Frost's son had killed himself, Engle walked the beaches of Cuba with Frost, talking him out of suicide. "How little good," Frost had said, "my health has ever done for anyone dear to me."

Lowell told of being with Pound when he first heard of Eliot's death. Pound responded in three statements, each delivered, after a pause, in a different voice: first, the official pronouncement, "my old comrade in the arts is dead." Then, the voice of personal loss and half-humorous complaint, "Now, who will understand my jokes?" And finally, a rush to generous acknowledgment and praise, but in the voice an Idahoan would use speaking of a horse trainer or auto mechanic: "Well, you've got to admit he was one *hell* of a poet!"

It was one of the evenings of a lifetime. It was punctuated, however, at roughly forty-five-minute intervals by the appearance of Lowell's wife, Elizabeth Hardwick, on the balcony above their two-story living room. Once again, she was in nightgown and socks and would peer over the railing like a figure on some medieval clock tower, calling, "Cal! Cal! Don't you know the time? You'll be an absolute wreck!" Camille, Engle, and I would get up, embarrassed, and tiptoe for the door. But as soon as she was out of sight, Lowell would wink and whisper us back for just one more drink. Even knowing how difficult Lowell could be to himself and, surely, to his wife, who could resist such talk and such company? There we would be for the next incarnation forty-five minutes later.

That was not the last time I saw Lowell, but things were never so rich again. Gradually, I thought, his work was losing force and direction. Above all, he seemed unable to find the feel of his own passions, became as gray and indecisive as that father he describes in his poems. With the passions went the voice — he showed me poems which tried to recapture the wildness of the earliest poems, the clarities of *Life Studies*, or just any defined voice. Meantime, he became the center of an industry, surrounded by sycophants or those who founded careers on his. Acclaim grew as the poems diminished and he declined, I thought, into a public figure.

After our last meeting, there were a few letters — chiefly about his divorce and remarriage to Caroline Blackwood in England, a life which he detailed rapturously. It seemed improbable this could last. Back in New York again, he died shortly before his taxi reached Hardwick's apartment. In the meantime, he had used her private letters in his poems — an act which many, I among them, thought execrable. It is no doubt a failing that I have never ended a marriage amicably — love converts too easily into hatred — but I, too, would have died before going back into the apartment of someone I had once loved, then had so profoundly injured.

As for Jarrell, he remained as outrageous in manner, as brilliant in perception. When I was teaching in Detroit, he came for a visit; he read, among other things, his translation of Goethe's *Faust*. He was the best Gretchen I ever heard; there wasn't a dry eye in the house. Later that day, I took the Jarrells to the Detroit Institute of Art where he soon discovered a wild and mangy cat by Kokoschka; guards stared, appalled, as he called the length of the gallery to his wife, "Pussycat! Come see the kitty!"

Although, in general we became friendlier, I tended to keep my distance, knowing how cutting he could be at anything less than total acquiescence. Several times, he had sliced me to ribbons: once, earlier, in my barracks apartment at a party I had given for him; once at the opening of a Lowell play in New York. I had come in to review *The Old Glory* for the *New York Review of Books*. At the party onstage after the opening, Jarrell collared me: "That's one of the half-dozen best plays ever written in America. Isn't it?" I answered that I liked it very much; not that much. For weeks, I licked my wounds.

Jealousy, I think, was a crucial problem for Jarrell; he could scarcely have felt anything less for the power of the play, for Lowell's public position, his power in New York's intellectual and artistic circles. Jarrell lived in Greensboro, N.C., and his poems, finally better than Lowell's, I think, were ignored. But jealousy was a quality he could not forgive himself and it played a factor, I think, in his final breakdown. It must have been difficult to accept the two daughters of his second wife, Mary; once he had accepted them, even harder to accept their maturity and loss. Even more significant, of course, must have been the death of his mother.

In any case, he, the one poet of that generation I'd thought might escape madness, was hospitalized too. His cleverness was surely a hindrance: I am told he could usually talk his way around his doctors. I think this same quality contributed to a falling away in the later poems — it took something as fearsome as the war to shock him into seriousness, out of the displays of wit and elegance that could provide a way out. Back home, on leave from the hospital, he was struck by a sports car. He had driven an Austin-Healy himself, and whether he picked it or not, would have thought that a worthy destroyer. His wife, who had not been present, long insisted his death an accident; no one else thought so. Lowell, Jarrell, Schwartz, Roethke, Berryman — a whole generation of gifted but dangerously driven poets — had each in turn passed into fearful neuroses, usually involving bad behavior, drunkenness, new girlfriends, deaths which suggested no great drive toward a longer life. Jarrell's loss was particularly tragic; a rich career might still have lain ahead. We were deprived not only of a superbly gifted and moving poet, but an original, daring mind and probably our best critic.

As for John Berryman, I not merely avoided, I practically fled him — he was too dangerous. After pawing the wife of a well-known younger poet and former student all one evening, he had struck the man over the head with a full whiskey bottle (which could easily have killed him), then jumped on him, breaking a rib. Once, visiting Detroit, he managed to get my lady friend in the backseat of a car, my wife and myself in the front. Instantly alert to the hazards, he began pursuing the lady around the backseat. Hearing her protests, I stopped the car and said, "John, this is a proper lady who does not like to be mauled." "What?" he said, "You mean you don't fuck?" Everyone gasped. "Oh! It's that word. That's what bothers you: the word: P-H-U-Q-Q. I promise never to use that word again." We all dissolved into giggling. Such little-boy naughtiness may be amusing to recount afterward; it might have seriously damaged a number of people, some of them innocent.

I did hazard his company once more; this time, I almost injured him. Arriving in Los Angeles for a reading, I was met at the plane by my old friend, Henri Coulette. He grabbed me by the arm, glared in my eye and snarled, "Listen, you son of a bitch, try anything and I'll kill you." "Hank, what did I do?" I gasped. "Nothing," he said. "We've had Berryman here for a week and I just can't stand any more trouble." All week, Berryman had refused to sleep or eat, stayed up all night monologuing, collapsed during readings, went to the hospital, propositioned the nurses, roamed the corridors, went back out against doctors' orders, collapsed again. Everyone was frantic. Now he was at the Green Hotel in Pasadena, watched over by students till sufficiently recovered to be shipped home to his wife.

At the door of his room I was greeted by a young woman built roughly like a hydrant, with a great shock of black hair and arms thick as my waist. "Hi," she said in a gravelly baritone, holding out her hand. "My name is Vivian Cienfuegos. I'm lookin' afta John. If he gets outa bed, I belt 'im in the chops!" She knew how funny that was. Tough and savvy, a sociology student who hadn't the reverence for him that literary students felt, she put up with no nonsense. Every time he reared off the bed with some obscene proposal, she laid a massive forearm upon him, delivering him safely to the mat. When he awoke and spoke to me, I, wanting to demonstrate friendship and not realizing how frail he was, thumped him on the chest. He fell back, choking and coughing uncontrollably. She and I looked at each other, terrified. He did recover though and she, in large part, was responsible. He mentions her, gratefully, in a poem but neither he nor the literary world gave her half the thanks she deserved.

In any case, I kept away after that. His case was the most frightening of all. I knew that a great many brilliant men's achievements and problems centered around their attachments to difficult and powerful mothers. Only after I'd read John Haffenden's and Eileen Simpson's books on him did I realize this was even truer for Berryman than for the others. I did know I didn't want to see this splendid man either throwing away his life and energies in childish nastiness or in being rescued and nursed back to life by versions, comic or tragic, of his mother. The only literary lessons left there lay in the print of his poems; the extraliterary lessons were too fierce to learn close by. It is only surprising he lasted so long before stepping off that bridge in Minneapolis.

I finally met William Empson in the seventies, when I had long imagined him to be dead. He had been living in England but an economic crisis had forced him out of retirement. At the University of Delaware where I taught and where he came as a visiting distinguished professor, I met him at a party given by Kay and Gibbons Ruark. He no longer wore the great spade-shaped beard I had seen in photos; he no longer smoked a pipe and a cigarette at the same time. When I told him how much his poems had meant to me, he seemed not quite sure what I meant.

A bit later I met his wife, a large woman, somewhat younger. When I told her how long I had admired and wanted to meet

Empson, she replied, "Well, you *may* have been in time." All evening, she spoke with maximum disrespect for him and maximum aggression against everyone there — especially if they showed an interest in him. The insult aside, her remark was true enough; I may have exaggerated in saying I met William Empson. He came to life only for a moment at the mention of Marlow's *Faustus* and talked shrewdly about its probable political censorship. Then he fell back into fog, maundered on aimlessly or stood silent on the borders of conversation.

As I was going home, he happened also to leave the house, following his wife and another man. There were rumors that in England her lover lived with them and that Empson usually got up to make their breakfast. It was drizzling; as he hurried across the lawn to catch up, she shouted, "Bill! Bill! Get out of that grass. You'll catch a dreadful cold! Have you no sense at all?"

The New York Times
Book Review

Section 5

Copyright, 1934, by
The New York Times Company.

SUNDAY, JULY 29, 1934.

TWENTY PAGES

A NEW VOICE IN AMERICAN POETRY

Paul Engle's "American Song" May Prove a Literary Landmark

AMERICAN SONG. A Book of Poems. By Paul Engle. 102 pp. Garden City, N. Y.: Doubleday, Doran & Co., Inc. $1.75.

By J. DONALD ADAMS

THIS is a heartening book, and a portent of what the Thirties seem sure to bring to creative literature in the United States. Rarely is a first book of poetry reviewed on the front page of this section, or for that matter, any book of contemporary poetry, but Paul Engle's "American Song" has a natural title to that place. Both on the ground of its own distinguished quality and for its significance as an indicator of changing mood and temper among creative writers of the youngest generation, it merits the widest possible attention. Mr. Engle may not fulfill the high expectations which are aroused by a reading of his book, though it is hard to believe that he will not, but if "American Song" does not prove in the long run to become something of a literary landmark, this review may be set down as an unfortunate venture in prophecy.

My conviction regarding its significance is strengthened by a recent reading of the other first books of poetry—both, like Mr. Engle's, products of the Middle West. They are scheduled for publication later in the year, and mention of them must be reserved for their appearance; it will be said here only that one cannot dismiss as fortuitous the sudden emergence of three young poets so far above the average level and so evidently united in their attitude toward the world we live in. It is not a poetic renaissance, however, that is in my mind, so much as it is a conviction that these young men are bidding a determined farewell to futility, that they either have a faith or are working toward one. They have id enough of negation in life and literature; their heads are lifted and they do not fear to look ahead. That change in temper is not discernible in poetry alone, though it is only natural for its manifestations to be first appreciable in that field.

Paul Engle, though he is not a truer poet than Elder Olson, whose first book we are soon to have, is more definitely a voice, articulate with the aspirations and convictions which are forming in his generation. He is a native of Iowa, and at present a Rhodes scholar at Oxford. In this book of his there is the voice of a confident young America, strong in its love of place, proud of its heritage, sure of its destiny. His ears are not insensitive to the older melodies of Europe, nor are his eyes shut to the beauties of her scene and the pageant of her history; but he knows his native wealth and demands that it be held not cheaply, and with feeling for its true values.

"The American dream," for Paul Engle, is not dead, but the most young thing in the world. The quotations with which he introduces his book sound the keynote of his faith. This, from Sir Thomas [...] the [...]men are already past [...] and [...] are already past

Paul Engle.

their first sleep in Persia." And this, from William Blake: ". . . and all the thirteen Angels Rent off their robes to the hungry wind, and threw their golden sceptres Down on the land of America . . ." One of the most heartening things about Paul Engle's poetry is that his love of America is not a blind

love; its flame is not dampened by sentimentality, but is blown hard and fierce by resolution, courage and pride. Harshly and with frequent injustice, we have done great things, but they are not enough:

. . . (You gave us shoes
For our feet, shirts for our backs,
will you not give us
Power and peace for our hearts?)

It is in the poem with which he concludes his book—"American Remembers"—which was awarded Poetry's prize for the best poem about the Century of Progress Exposition, that Mr. Engle gives

fullest expression to his Americanism. Here in the space of eleven pages he has written our history to date—the facts of it that truly matter, which are the spiritual facts, with the compact quality of poetry and the fervor of a prophet. For my own part, it is difficult to recall another piece of writing of equal compass in which there is so

strong a distillation of all that has gone into the making of the American land and the American people. It is a poem strongly felt, strongly forged, and native to its core. Its compact quality has already been mentioned, and here it should be added that a part of the distinction of Paul Engle's poetry lies in its achievement of density and depth without the sacrifice of clarity. Here again his work is marked off from that of the poets of the Twenties, and here lies what seems to me to be his superiority to such a poet, for example, as Hart Crane.

By grace of it, he is likely to win a wider audience and to be better understood. Yet his lines are not infrequently closely packed, and his phrasing and his figures are often as arresting and sharply cut as Crane's. It is verse, too, that has the beat of life in it, that has thrust and movement, the vigor that springs from the understanding use

of verbs and the knowledge of how to give motive power to descriptive words, as when he writes,

the thin
Roots of wheat grip the soil with
fibrous
Fingers that clutch the rain to the
stalk's heart,

or

Churning a wake of pale foam in
the torn
And tideless estuaries of my mind
Where the shy fish of memory leap
and shatter
The quiet water, their dark scales
gleaming

Among the longer poems, "The Troubadour of Eze" is remarkably effective in its handling of an excellently conceived theme. Meditating in a village of the Alpes Maritimes that is redolent with history, Engle contrasts its past with that of his own land, and comes, through many fine and quickening lines, to this intensely felt and powerfully written summation:

Here to my town has the world's
great power come over
The torn, dream-furrowed ocean,
and now waits
A stronger form that the New
World alone
Can give to its old and proud
nobility.
But if my town, like Eze, should
fail, and leave
No nobler symbol than a fallen
stone
The world fails with it, and it will
be beat
To swing the huge, gnarled war
club that is doom
And crush again the patient walls
of Eze,
Hurl into its centuries-quiet mouth
The half-remembered chant of
misery,
Forget that New World image, and
beat back
The towers of all our towns into
the earth.

"Complaint to Sad Poets" is Mr. Engle's challenge to the school of writers sick with self-pity both for themselves and their times:

The terrier bitch that whelped its
litter today
Under the bars where the dirt is
moist and dark
Shames and defies you with the
quiet logic
Of life that works its ancient way
out, knowing
No fullness but to live, strongly to
live.

Like Stephen Vincent Benét, Paul Engle is alive to the beauty of American place names, and the homely names of American things, and he drinks deep from that well from which every creative artist must—love of place, the sense of being somewhere rooted:

O wood thrush crying in Kentucky
hills,
O gray gull poising over Puget
Sound,
Sing down our hands from cursing
at the sky,
Give them again the feel of friendly
ground.

Under the Chippewayan woods, the
wide
Iowa prairie, Illinois loam sheet—
O meadowlark in blue stem—we will
watch
The birds of Francis gather at our
feet.

It will be interesting, incidentally, to observe what effect this young poet's residence in the ancient mellowness of Oxford will have upon his work and his temper; one inclines to believe that it will serve chiefly to sharpen his already vivid sense of contrast and to deepen his national consciousness. Whatever the outcome, Paul Engle is a poet to be watched, a writer who will play his part in the resurgence of creative force that will mark this decade in our literary history.

The July 29, 1934, essay by J. Donald Adams in the New York Times Book Review.

A gathering of students and their spouses at the summer house of Paul and Mary Engle, Stone City, Iowa, ca. 1951. Among the notables are (back row, left to right) Sarah Engle (in the arms of Barney Weinberg) next to Andrew Lytle (later editor of the Sewanee Review*); (row two, sitting) Mary Engle and young Mary Engle with Paul Engle; (row three) short story writer James B. Hall sitting on the floor next to Paul; (row four, second from left with pipe) poet and later director of the writing program at the University of Massachusetts Joseph Langland; (front row, last on the right) novelist Warren Miller.*

The barracks, ca. 1954, home of the workshop until 1966.

BE IT EVER SO HUMBLE. *The home of the Program in Creative Writing has for many years been these "temporary" barracks on the bank of the Iowa River. The architecture will be recognized by veterans and married students as "World War II Ghastly." We feel toward them the sort of tender affection which the pioneer had for his disintegrating but loved log cabin— his kids were born there. We lived cheerfully in them; the writer needs nothing fancy, just a piece of paper. He is the cheapest artist!*

More barracks, ca. 1955.

In 1957, Paul Engle presented the French consul with a copy of Homage to Baudelaire *at the University of Iowa's centennial celebration of the publication of* Les Fleurs du Mal. *The book, which contained translations from Baudelaire and original poems by workshop poets, was handset and printed at the Typographic Laboratory and issued by the Cummington Press.*

The workshop fiction staff during a criticism session held as part of Creative Arts Week, May 1961. Left to right: Philip Roth, Vance Bourjaily, and George P. Elliott.

Midland *was published in May 1961; this photo dates from that period. Left to right: Donald Justice, Christopher Wiseman, Henri Coulette, Paul Engle, Michael Harper, unknown, Robert Mezey, and Nicholas Crome.*

Left to right: Edmund Keeley, Mark Strand, Vance Bourjaily, Paul Engle, and R. V. Cassill, ca. 1964.

The workshop staff, 1964–1965. Left to right: visiting British fiction writer David Pryce-Jones, R. V. Cassill, Robert Williams, Richard Yates, Paul Engle, Mark Strand, Eugene Garber, George Starbuck, and Fred Will.

The door to John Berryman's barracks classroom, 1954.

Far from the Ocean

Robert Lowell at Iowa, 1953

O to break free, like the chinook
salmon jumping and falling back, . . .

I last spoke with my old mentor, Robert Lowell, in the spring
of 1974. He was to give a reading that evening in a plain, some-
what dingy little room above the bar at the Queen's Elm Pub in
South Kensington, a working-class section of London. The event
took place under the auspices of the Writers Action Group. But
who the sponsoring writers were and why the reading was to take
place in this rather unlikely venue I don't now recall, if, indeed,
I ever knew.

I had neither seen nor talked to Lowell in twenty years. Not that
that's so remarkable. Because when I was a student of his in 1953
at the now much praised and often maligned writing program at
the University of Iowa, I was just that — a student in his poetry
workshop. The writing program at Iowa was, at that time, the only
one of its kind anywhere in the world, small, and not yet a point
of focus for much of anyone except Paul Engle and a handful of
graduate students. Lowell's class numbered about twenty-five.
John Berryman, Lowell's successor, cut the class to a core of thir-
teen. The survivors included W. D. Snodgrass, Donald Justice,
Donald Petersen, Jane Cooper, Shirley Eliason, Philip Levine, Paul
Petrie, Melvin Walker LaFollette, William Dickey, Henri Cou-
lette, and me. We certainly had, at the time, no sense of ourselves
as anything special.

Our aims as fledgling poets were modest: to learn to write poetry
well, and later to find a job somewhere, probably teaching litera-

ture. We were savvy. No poet we knew of, not Frost, not Auden, not Williams, had made a living from his art. We didn't, like later generations of workshop students, expect to go out and teach courses in creative writing. And we certainly didn't expect to be employed at prestigious and powerful universities. Any kind of college or university teaching job was hard to come by in the 1950s; moreover, our degree field was highly suspect. Donald Justice began his post-Iowa teaching career at the University of Missouri; Henri Coulette, at L.A. State (then a college); Paul Petrie, at the University of Rhode Island. Most of us kept those jobs the rest of our lives, except for occasional sorties as visiting writers to other more glamorous institutions. Children of the Great Depression and survivors of World War II, we knew how to dig in and hold on.

One of my workshop peers Philip Levine claims in his essay in praise of John Berryman that Lowell behaved like a Boston Brahmin, was bored to death with all of us and our poems, and played favorites in the classroom. I must have been even farther from the center of the action than I knew, because I recall neither his boredom nor overt acts of favoritism. If anything, Lowell permitted, whether from generosity or sloth, a wider range of what might be called "amateurism" than Berryman would allow later. In fact, Donald Petersen's description of Lowell's classroom manner seems to me entirely accurate. ". . . he praised what he could in our poems and diffidently suggested that we consult other poets' works, to see how it was done this or that way. He seldom suggested any specific revisions."

I think Lowell saw himself simply as our instructor, and us as his students, certainly not his equals either in knowledge or skill, even our passion for poetry not entirely to be trusted, so he did not encourage familiarity. At thirty-six, he met all strangers, I imagine, with a certain natural reticence anyway. No doubt the notoriety brought him by the Pulitzer Prize for *Lord Weary's Castle* and an appointment as Consultant in Poetry to the Library of Congress, as well as by his personal troubles, contributed to his caution. He may also have been feeling still a bit bruised by the harsh response of the critics (including his longtime friend Randall Jarrell) to his most recent book *The Mills of the Kavanaughs*. In my own case, even if he had encouraged us to a bolder relationship, I certainly would not have been ready.

In fact, I can't claim to have *known* either Robert Lowell or John Berryman except in terms of what used to be called, rather chastely, the student-teacher relationship, a phenomenon which has pretty much been erased from workshop life. I was the poetry workshop's marginal man. I think I still am.

By marginal, I mean I was the greenest person in the room there in that corrugated steel barracks that served the workshop as both classroom and office. The barracks was one of fewer than a dozen remaining on the east side of the Iowa River after World War II had ended. There were one or two encampments of them elsewhere, converted by the university into married student housing. None of the classrooms in these huts had air conditioning, so on a hot day they were like bake ovens, and when the rains drummed down on them, all talk ceased. Paul Engle had managed to commandeer two of these buildings for his fledgling program; the director's office in the main one was the only administrative office on campus that could boast a full-size bathroom with its own shower, and a toilet remarkable for its fiery hot water flush. Nonetheless, the workshop quarters were basically humble, and so was I. What I didn't know about poetry, the enormous amount I hadn't read, were facts borne in on me every day by the presence of my fellow poets whose educations were far superior to mine, as well as by a string of brilliant mentors at Iowa beginning with Karl Shapiro and Wallace Fowlie and ending with Robert Lowell and John Berryman.

Let me stress here that I'm being neither modest about myself nor exaggerating the literary prowess of my fellow poets. The next to youngest member of the workshop, at twenty-two, I had a Yankee backwater high school education — good but thin, and a B.A. from a third-rate midwestern university. Donald Justice, by contrast, had a master's degree from the University of North Carolina; William Dickey had a bachelor's degree from Reed College and a master's in literature from Harvard; Jane Cooper had done summer work at Oxford, attended Vassar, had her degree from Wisconsin, and was on leave from teaching at Sarah Lawrence. They knew their stuff.

I was marginal also because I didn't live in Iowa City. Married student housing was booked up years in advance. I lived in a Czech section of industrial Cedar Rapids and hitchhiked twenty-five miles daily to and from the university, sun, rain, or snow. A situation I didn't find at all unusual. My first wife and I had been married only a year and were on our first car, a used '46 Ford, a wedding gift from her father. We'd been teaching high school in a small town in the far northwest corner of Iowa, hardly a lucrative proposition in the 1950s or anytime for that matter. I had no family, and hers could provide us with only the most meager assistance. So we were living on the frayed shoestring her high school teaching salary provided and paying rent on a tiny two-room apartment in a little frame house. (John Berryman attended a party there once and commented to my wife that the bathroom was so small there wasn't even room enough in it to fall down if you got drunk.) I had no scholarship help from the university (I'd done nothing to deserve one) and was in the workshop more or less on sufferance while I worked on an M.A. in English. In any case, in the 1950s, the writing program played no great role at the university. Kept on a short leash by a skeptical administration, it had at most only two or three assistantships to offer. It was a lean operation in lean times.

The fall Lowell arrived was marked by a sense among us that the ante had definitely been upped, that the workshop was moving onto a higher level. The mood was one of excited uncertainty, a sense that we were about to be seriously challenged. Not that the workshop had not been staffed by accomplished and highly recognized poets before — Karl Shapiro was still editor of *Poetry* magazine, in fact, when he commuted in from Chicago by train for his workshop classes. Perhaps our sharply heightened sense of anticipation was due to the fact that Lowell's fame was still very fresh and because he was known to be a complex and difficult man. He had completed a hospital stay only months before, recovering from one of the psychopathic episodes that continued to plague his life to the end. Of course, he had the added cachet of his Harvard background; of having camped out in a Sears tent, in his student days, on the lawn of Allen Tate's house in Tennessee, until the Tates took him in; and of having studied with John Crowe Ransom at Kenyon College.

In addition, he was a Boston Lowell, related to both James Russell and Amy, a fact that probably played differently with each of the students in the workshop. Some of us — like Paul Petrie, Henri Coulette, myself — were not long out of the military, and had odd, mongrelly backgrounds distinguished more by luck and tenacity than by bloodline or old school ties. Without the GI Bill, we would probably not have come this far, or to this particular place. Our reactions were probably less matter of fact than, say, Donald Petersen's (who'd known Lowell at Indiana), or Donald Justice's or Jane Cooper's — more a mixture of curiosity, amusement, and awe.

I can still see Robert Lowell, sometimes, standing on the walk in front of the barracks — its large front window filled with a many-branched red geranium grown vivid and gangly and monstrous — smoking a cigarette, leaning slightly forward, talking seriously if briefly to one of us. He was a large man, fairly tall, somewhat stoop-shouldered, and wore rather thick glasses. In fact, the brightness of Lowell's eyes and the low, mumbling, almost lisping quality of his voice remain in memory almost as powerfully as the Pindarlike lines of the poems in *Lord Weary's Castle*. ("And blue-lung'd combers lumbered to the kill. / The Lord survives the rainbow of his will.") The eyes, distorted behind the glasses, were thick-lidded, aquatic, or like those of a man looking at you through bull's-eye glass. The voice was surprisingly southern, with a hint of fatigue or wistful amusement or complaisance in it. He was younger-looking than I had expected, and his clothes always looked as though he might have slept in them.

In addition to Lowell's workshop class, there was the more or less impromptu one we ourselves convened around the lunch table once or twice a week in the dingy and steaming cafeteria in the basement of the old student union: a kind of expanding and contracting court of complaint, a floating seminar in practical criticism, a rump parliament in literary theory, where we fed on each other's praise and harkened to each others' criticisms. Poems were handed around, sometimes scribbled on, lamented over. The talk was freewheeling, unfettered, sometimes even preposterous. No telling how many bad lines and bad poems perished in those sessions. Probably not enough. But our little seminar brought us together in knowledge and ignorance and friendship. I learned an immense amount from my friends over those lunch hours.

Lowell's classroom demeanor was thoughtful and scholarly and marked by irony, offhandedness, and occasionally, dogmatism distilled to arrogance. "Looking at things a different way was always difficult for him," Paul Petrie recalls, "though he sometimes made a visibly painful effort to do so." Certainly, there was none of the all-out, energy-charged passion sometimes crossing the border into the histrionic that was later John Berryman's trademark. Lowell was deliberate, almost ponderous on occasion. He would lean forward across the wooden desk, his ever-present cigarette sending up its slender ribbon of smoke, waiting for our comment or reply. Other days he was more relaxed. "At that time," Jane Cooper remembers, "Lowell still hadn't done much teaching, and he seemed like an amateur in the best sense. Studying with him was like listening to inspired gossip, full of brilliant almost casual observations of how a poem could be made. . . . He always stressed what was most human in the work of contemporary and modern poets, most of whom he knew personally." His knowledge of poetry was broad as well as deep and his admiration for certain European poets, Rilke chief among them, was rivaled only by his respect for Virgil and Catullus. It may have been partly Lowell's influence that caused Henri Coulette and others to enroll in courses in the classics department, and which caused me later to undertake a translation of Rilke's *Letters to a Young Poet*. He had a way, however indirectly, of pushing you.

I remember two conferences with Robert Lowell, although there almost certainly were others. The initial one was a kind of get-acquainted session. All of us in the workshop were asked to turn in poems we'd been working on that might make up a set of worksheets for upcoming class meetings. Time has mercifully wiped from my mind any recollection of the poems I handed in, except that they were totally inadequate. Poor, lame, shrill little creatures.

Had I been more mature as a writer and more knowledgeable I would have been embarrassed for them; instead I was hopeful. Lowell was kind; he found an intensity in them worth mention. He talked about Hart Crane's poems and his own, and about how intensity, while of value, sometimes obscured what one was trying to say. "It takes time," he said, speaking of the process by which good poems finally get written, then added laconically, "You can't hurry it." None of my poems made that first worksheet; none of them deserved to.

As a young poet, I idolized the work of Hart Crane; I loved its quirky vocabulary and its powerful compression. And I found similar qualities in *Lord Weary's Castle*. By the time Lowell left Iowa, the cover of my copy was dog-eared and the dustjacket in tatters.

What I thought most affecting in the poems of Crane and Lowell was their powerful emotional drive, their strong, enjambed rhythms. Lowell's poems, in particular, seemed marked by a tone of mourning and yearning older than the poems themselves. I associated this feeling, perhaps willfully, out of my limited background, with jazz—with, in retrospect, the blues, rather than with his recent Catholicism or with classical elegy. I'm sure I didn't articulate this view either very well or very confidently back then. I was keenly aware then, as I am now, that on any immediate level, any such connection must seem wildly fanciful. Very well then, let it.

Perhaps I made of Lowell and of Lowell's poems what I needed to. I was a Boston boy myself, and carrying all the bad psychic baggage of my mother's early death, my father's desertion, and the string of foster homes I ran away from. Like Lowell, I was damaged goods. And still full of confusion, rage, and need, I read his poems as texts of anger and lamentation. I had only recently dumped all the constricting prejudices of my lace-curtain, Irish Catholic upbringing, rejected the church, and was living in freefall; Lowell had desperately embraced the faith I had cut myself loose from and then abandoned it, apparently as disappointed as I had been with its dogmas. Perhaps, in some way, I was the adopted son of his spiritual searching.

We never discussed any of this, of course. At least not beyond the surface details. I think I may have told him about my brief career, after my mother died, as an eight-year-old, would-be hooligan in the care of my aunt and uncle in Charlestown. I was from the wrong side of the river, of course, but he'd been something of a thug himself in grade school. And there is a sense in which evasiveness, rage, and rebellion, those poisons that leak from the wounded soul, are the same no matter what side of the river you're from. Perhaps he saw in the sometimes strained language of my student poems — he was an exceptionally alert reader and, as the result of his own troubles, heavily into Freudian and Jungian psychoanalysis — a tension akin to his own. Perhaps, in these sessions where nothing particularly noteworthy seemed to be going on, I was learning what could be done with the fear and inconsolable grief, the miserable knowledge, that come with too much pain experienced too soon.

So Lowell's poetry and teaching have carried over into my life in a way he could not have guessed and might not even have wanted it to, a way I never realized until I began to write about it here. Wouldn't it be curious, if, of all of his students at Iowa, I was after all the one uniquely equipped by a wretched childhood, to benefit from the full panoply of what he had to offer? It's even possible I was so involved in this silent dialogue of souls that I never noticed what others saw as his faults.

What I learned from him technically now seems to me of another order of importance. For example, after several decades of writing, I ditched uniqueness of idiom as a literary value, much as Lowell himself did in *Life Studies* in response to the urging of William Carlos Williams to use common speech. The early 1950s were a period of intense literary formalism in poetry presided over by Frost, Tate, and Ransom, as it had been earlier, by Yvor Winters. But in truth, during my time in the Writers' Workshop, I never felt entirely comfortable with rigidly defined poetic forms. I appreciated them and practiced them for their beauty and music, but I also felt that I was repeating the past, repeating work already done and done better by the masters of those forms. Whitman and Williams called. And the formal demands of my own spirit.

At Iowa in 1953, I was somewhat aware, as I think most of

us were, that Lowell was struggling with a similar disaffection, that he had begun to find rhyme and scansion a "hurdle," an impediment "to what you want to say most forcibly" as he wrote Williams later. And it would be four more years before he published his first relatively unmeasured verse. It would be even longer before I would make my own small revolution in *Some Versions of Silence*. My work over the last decade, while it shares Lowell's late passion to say clearly "what happened," has also moved yet further away from his in the direction of an often wholly improvisational method.

Certainly, I owe my early belief in revision to Robert Lowell. His reputation as a tireless reviser of his own work preceded him to Iowa City. An obsessive craftsman according to the literary grapevine, he was an aggravation to his publisher, Farrar, Strauss & Giroux, revising lines and phrases in his poems even after a book had gone into page proof. Robert Giroux tolerated this expensive habit, apparently because he felt Lowell was already a major poet.

One day, in a class given over to talking about revision, Lowell surprised us by handing out dittoed sheets of one of his long and as-yet-unpublished narrative poems — "The Banker's Daughter." It was an uncharacteristic act of humility. The poem, as he perfectly well knew, was so unfinished as to have some real clinkers still in it (e.g., "Ring, ring, tired bells, the king of Rance is dead . . ."). Nevertheless, he read it to us and then talked about European history and its possibility as subject matter and what he was trying to accomplish in the poem.

"The Banker's Daughter" in particular, of his recent long narratives, had caused him a lot of trouble and indecision. He had already cut it by a quarter in the 120-odd line version he showed us. When he finished reading it, he said. "It's a bit too long, I think, and slack in places. Do you think it's turgid?" Donald Justice remembers someone said, "Yes."

A year or so later, I saw, in the *Partisan Review*, a very much shorter version — fifty lines or so. And a year later, in another magazine, still another longer version. The version he finally printed in part one of *Life Studies*, six years later, is about a third the length of the draft he presented to us that spring afternoon in 1953, with the result that the poem is more sharply focused and clearer. It was one of the last poems Lowell would write in his grand manner.

My last meeting, as a student, with Robert Lowell, took place at the end of the fall term. Everyone in the class had turned in "finished" work, and he was to offer a final opinion. I'd had a miserable season; my poems were still strained and clumsy and marred by melodrama and a lot of false emotion. I had a pile of ruled pages full of doodles and pencil-smeared failures. Most of one notebook was given over to a poem I was trying to write about my mother's death and the devastation that followed. I told Lowell that all I had to show him was the notebook and that there was nothing in it polished enough to be worth his looking at. He advised me to turn it in anyway.

A week later, when I went in for my conference, I found him, to my surprise, encouraging. I think it was during this meeting that he asked me the details of my growing up in Boston and Charlestown, and my years in foster homes. It was certainly during this meeting that Lowell suggested I try a narrative framework for the poem. Clearly, the lyric forms in which I'd been laboring so unsuccessfully were too narrow to accommodate the material I was trying to cram into them. Later, when I reached the privacy of the student union lounge or my library carrel and opened the notebook to see what comments he'd made, I found a 3 × 5 card tucked between two pages; the grade of B had been written on it in blue ink. Below it, the accompanying note read, "I think your writing is surely getting somewhere. It's hard for me to judge 'My Glass Brother' in its present form, but your language is intense and your stanzas are compact. You should write more, I think." It concluded with a short sentence: "I expect you will be publishing soon." I was stunned.

For a long time, I had trouble imagining what he saw on any of those pages, beyond perhaps an image or a line or two, that might have led him to write such a comment. I told myself that he was just being kind to a struggling young poet. So I thought, until 1955, two years later, when Karl Shapiro at *Poetry* accepted and published "My Glass Brother," a lyric poem laid down on a narrative base, drafts of which I'd been struggling with for three years by then in spiral notebooks. Only a half-dozen lines and phrases from the draft Lowell saw survived, I think, into the final version. But, in Lowell's eyes, they must have been enough.

Robert Lowell may have disliked his days in Iowa City. In fact, he commented openly on the "sterility" of the Midwest on the dust-jacket of De Snodgrass's Pulitzer Prize—winning *Heart's Needle.* But if he found life in Iowa City "a pretty dormant, day to day thing, a rather rustic pastoral after Europe," he also found it remarkable for its "light, space, and cleanness." And in at least one letter to Allen Tate he wrote that his students were pretty good. Whatever else may be true, twenty years later, Lowell remembered this period of his life with pleasure and a certain amount of pride.

That evening in 1974 Lowell entered the Queen's Elm Pub in South Kensington in the company of half a dozen people. One woman, thin, pale skinned, and aristocratically beautiful, stood out. It soon became clear she was Lady Caroline Blackwood, his third wife. In her full-length fur coat she seemed out of place amid the scruffy audience of students and writers crowding into that dim, tiny meeting room above the bar. About thirty folding chairs had been arranged in several rows. And there were one or two other odd pieces of furniture, including a straight-backed chapel pew. The event had been virtually unpublicized, and it was clear the Writers Action Group wasn't expecting a large audience. Lady Caroline paused a moment beside her husband, and then took a seat in the back, at some distance from two silver-haired matrons of the Empire properly gloved and hankied who'd arrived early. Lowell had aged greatly since I'd seen him last. He was partially bald now and wore the remaining hair, now pretty thoroughly silvered, long in the back and on the sides in a kind of lanky tonsure. He seemed overweight and tired, or at least languid.

After a few minutes had elapsed and he was seated, I went over to speak to him. I hadn't expected him to remember me, and at first he didn't. Or if he did, it was only as part of a moment buried deep in the past. But then, his memory seemed to clear, and he began to speak warmly of his days in Iowa City and his class of aspiring poets, asking about Donald Petersen and recalling Phil Levine ("he had a little diary about Spain, didn't he? Rather nicely written, didn't you think?"). As we sat talking, we were interrupted by a young girl from Radcliffe who wanted him to sign a book for her. By way of introducing me, he said, "This man was a student of mine at Iowa almost twenty years ago. That was a great place. Only twenty students — all of them good. Most of my students from there have published books, you know." Then, turning to me, he said, "That was a golden time, wasn't it?" I hesitated a moment in mild shock, because like many others I'd shared for years the general myth of his unhappiness at Iowa. I don't know what I'd expected him to say, but it wasn't that. Then I laughed and said, "Yes, it was."

That night Lowell read only translations — of Villon ("After hearing Villon in the original French, I have a strong desire to revise it."); of Dante ("I'm going to skip the next six lines; it's prophecy and obscure."); of Leopardi ("Someone once said that, in his poems, the splendor of the writing overcomes the misery of the subject."). The group that had accompanied him to the reading were friends who'd assisted him with the translations, and they preceded him, reading the poems in the original languages: ancient Greek, Italian, French, German, and Russian. He himself read well, punctuating and emphasizing his commentary with what my wife later characterized as his "little boy gestures." A young writer friend, an American, who accompanied us to the reading that night said that Lowell's brief introductions to each poem had struck him like "whole semesters of coursework"; and the poet himself, as "a broken man, a felled giant." Lowell's voice was the same low, melancholy voice I'd heard for the first time nearly twenty years earlier, back in those converted steel barracks by the Iowa River, still strong if tired and a little slurred perhaps by drink or medicinal drugs.

At the end of the evening, my wife, my friend, and I said goodbye, and Lowell signed books for us in his almost completely unreadable script. (I've only now figured out why his inscription has remained a puzzle to me all these years. Below the printed "For Robert Dana / With Keen Happy Memories of Iowa / 1952?" he'd scribbled only his *first* name — "Robert.") He rose from his chair then and asked how long I'd be in England, and said rather wistfully, or so it seemed, "Well, it would be nice to get together." But I was leaving in a couple of days for the States and he, for Italy. I shook his hand and thanked him for the fine reading. Then, my wife and friend and I separated ourselves from the crowd, descended the dark stairs, and walked out into the chilly London night. I never saw him again.

Mine Own John Berryman

I can't say if all poets have had actual mentors, actual living, breathing masters who stood or sat before them making the demands that true mentors must make if the fledgling is ever to fly. Some poets seem to have been totally self-starting, like the cars they used to build in Detroit; I'm thinking of such extraordinary examples as Emily Dickinson and Walt Whitman, who over a hundred years ago created not only their own gigantic works but the beginnings of something worthy enough to be American poetry, and they did it out of their imaginations and their private studies and nothing more. But, then, they had the advantage of being geniuses. And neither was from Detroit. I think also of those poets who had to be poets, whom no one or nothing short of death could have derailed from their courses — John Keats, Dylan Thomas, Arthur Rimbaud — and who outstripped their mentors before they even got into second gear. There are those who were lucky enough to find among their peers people of equal talent and insight to help them on their way — poets like Williams and Pound, who for the crucial early years of their writing careers ignited each other. Though, of course, Williams tells us in the "Prologue" to *Kora in Hell* that Ezra benefited also from the scathing criticism of Williams's father, William George. Williams tells us that his father "had been holding forth in downright sentences upon my own 'idle nonsense' when he turned and became equally vehement concerning something Ezra had written: what in heaven's name Ezra meant by 'jewels' in a verse that had come between them. These jewels — rubies, sapphires, amethysts and whatnot, Pound went on to explain with great determination and care, were the backs of books as they stood on a man's shelf. 'But why in heaven's name don't you say so then?' was my father's triumphant and crushing rejoinder." Pound himself showed Ford Madox Ford some early verse, serious stuff, and Fordie laughed so hard upon reading the work he actually fell on the floor and "rolled around on it squealing with hilarity at the poems." Pound said that Ford's laughter saved him two years of work in the wrong direction. Terrible conditions have driven others to take up the pen in an effort to write their way out of the deepest nightmares imaginable — Wilfred Owen in the trenches, Edward Thomas in his melancholia, Hart Crane in the slough of Cleveland. In some cases it worked.

As for those of us here in the United States of America in the second half of the twentieth century, we have developed something called Creative Writing, a discipline that not only flourishes on hundreds of campuses but has even begun to invade the public schools. It has produced most of the poets — for better or worse — now writing in the country. One can only regard it as one of the most amazing growth industries we have. Thus, at the same time we've made our society more racist, more scornful of the rights of the poor, more imperialist, more elitist, more tawdry, money-driven, selfish, and less accepting of minority opinions, we have democratized poetry. Today anyone can become a poet: all he or she need do is travel to the nearest college and enroll in Beginning Poetry Writing and then journey through the dozen stages of purgatory properly titled Intermediate Poetry Writing and Semi-Advanced Poetry Writing, all the way to Masterwork Poetry Writing, in which course one completes her epic on the sacking of Yale or his sonnet cycle on the paintings of Edward Hopper, or their elegies in a city dumpster, and thus earns not only an M.F.A. but a crown of plastic laurel leaves. Do I sound skeptical? Let me sound skeptical.

But I also must in fairness add that it is impossible for me to imagine myself as the particular poet I have become — again for better or for worse — without the influence of a single teacher, my one great personal mentor, and amazingly enough I found him at the head of a graduate class at the most unfashionable of writing industries, the much-maligned Iowa Writers' Workshop. He was, of course, John Berryman, not yet forty years old but soon to be so, with one book of poems to his credit and stuck with the job of teaching poetry writing — for the first time in his life and for the last.

I did not go to the University of Iowa to study with John Berryman; in 1953 his reputation was based on *The Dispossessed*, that first book, and it was no larger than it should have been. The poem "Homage to Mistress Bradstreet" had not yet appeared in the *Partisan Review*, though it soon would and would create shock waves through the then-tiny world of American poetry. The attraction at Iowa was Robert Lowell, whose second book, *Lord Weary's Castle*, had received the Pulitzer Prize, and whose singular voice had excited young poets as far away as Michigan. I among them journeyed to Iowa and enrolled in Lowell's writing workshop and audited his seminar in modern poetry; this was the fall of 1953, America under Eisenhower ("Wide empty grin that never lost a vote," Berryman would later write) transforming itself into America under Joe McCarthy.

To say I was disappointed in Lowell as a teacher is an understatement, although, never having taken a poetry workshop, I had no idea what to expect. But a teacher who is visibly bored by his students and their poems is hard to admire. The students were a marvel: we were two future Pulitzer Prize winners, one Yale winner, one National Book Critics Circle Award winner, three Lamont Prize winners, one American Book Award winner. Some names: Donald Justice, W. D. Snodgrass, Jane Cooper, William Dickey, Robert Dana, Paul Petrie, Melvin Walker LaFollette, Henri Coulette, Donald Petersen, and an extraordinarily gifted woman named Shirley Eliason, who soon turned to the visual arts and became a master. I am sure there were others among the thirteen who were excited by Lowell as a teacher, for Lowell was one to play favorites. No matter how much they wrote like Lowell, some of the poets could do no wrong; in all fairness to Lowell, he praised them even when they wrote like Jarrell. Needless to say, I could write nothing that pleased Lowell, and when at the end of the semester he awarded me a B, I was not surprised. Along with the B he handed me a little card with scribbled notes regarding my poems and then told me I had made more progress than anyone else in the class. "You have come the farthest," he drawled, which no doubt meant I had started from nowhere. "Then why the B?" I asked. "I've already given the A's out," he said. This was at our second and last fifteen-minute conference — which did not irritate me nearly as much as our first, when he accused me of stealing my Freudian insights and vocabulary from Auden. "Mr. Lowell," I had responded (I never got more intimate than Mister and he never encouraged me to do so), "I'm Jewish. I steal Freud directly from Freud; he was one of ours." Mr. Lowell merely sighed.

Lowell was, if anything, considerably worse in the seminar; we expected him to misread our poems — after all, most of them were confused and, with very few exceptions, only partly realized, but to see him bumbling in the face of "real poetry" was discouraging. The day he assured the class that Housman's "Loveliest of Trees, the Cherry Now" was about suicide, Melvin LaFollette leaned over and whispered in my ear, "We know what he's thinking about." His fierce competitiveness was also not pleasant to behold: with the exceptions of Bishop and Jarrell, he seemed to have little use for any practicing American poet, and he once labeled Roethke "more of an old woman than Marianne Moore." He was eager to ridicule many of our recent heroes, poets I for one would have thought him enamored of: Hart Crane and Dylan Thomas. Still, he was Robert Lowell, master of a powerful and fierce voice that all of us respected, and though many of us were disappointed, none of us turned against the man or his poetry. As Don Petersen once put it, "Can you imagine how hard it is to live as Robert Lowell, with that inner life?"

During the final workshop meeting he came very close to doing the unforgivable: he tried to overwhelm us with one of his own poems, an early draft of "The Banker's Daughter," which appeared in a much shorter though still-hideous version six years later in *Life Studies*. Someone, certainly not Lowell, had typed up three and a half single-spaced pages of heroic couplets on ditto masters so that each of us could hold his or her own smeared purple copy of his masterpiece. He intoned the poem in that enervated voice we'd all become used to, a genteel southern accent that suggested the least display of emotion was déclassé. I sat stunned by the performance, but my horror swelled when several of my classmates leaped to praise every forced rhyme and obscure reference. (The subject was Marie de Medici, about whom I knew nothing and cared less.) No one suggested a single cut, not even when Lowell asked if the piece might be a trifle too extended, a bit soft in places. Perish the thought; it was a masterpiece! And thus the final class meeting passed with accolades for the one person present who scarcely needed praise and who certainly had the intelligence and insight to know it for what it was: bootlicking.

His parting words were unqualified praise of his successor, John Berryman, not as poet but as one of the great Shakespearean scholars of the age. And then he added that if we perused the latest issue of the *Partisan* we would discover the Mistress Bradstreet poem, clear evidence that Berryman was coming "into the height of his powers," a favorite phrase of Lowell's and one he rarely employed when speaking of the living. In fairness to Lowell, he was teetering on the brink of the massive nervous breakdown that occurred soon after he left for Cincinnati to occupy the Elliston Chair of Poetry. Rumors of his hospitalization drifted back to Iowa City, and many of us felt guilty for damning him as a total loss.

How long Berryman was in town before he broke his wrist I no longer recall, but I do remember that the first time I saw him he was dressed in his customary blue blazer, the arm encased in a black sling, the effect quite dramatic. As person and teacher, John was an extraordinary contrast to Lowell. To begin with, he did not play favorites: everyone who dared hand him a poem burdened with second-rate writing tasted his wrath, and that meant all of us. He never appeared bored in the writing class; to the contrary, he seemed more nervous in our presence than we in his. Whereas Lowell always sprawled in a chair as though visibly troubled by his height, John almost always stood and often paced as he delivered what sounded like memorized encomiums on the nature of poetry and life. Lowell's voice was never more than faintly audible and always encased in his curiously slothful accent, whereas Berryman articulated very precisely, in what appeared to be an actor's notion of Hotspur's accent. His voice would rise in pitch with his growing excitement until it seemed that soon only dogs would be able to hear him. He tipped slightly forward as though about to lose his balance, and conducted his performance with the forefinger of his right hand. The key word here is "performance," for these were memorable meetings in which the class soon caught his excitement. All of us sensed that something significant was taking place.

Beyond the difference of personal preferences and presentation was a more significant one. Lowell had pushed us toward poetry written in formal meters, rhymed, and hopefully involved with the grief of great families, either current suburban ones or those out of the great storehouse of America's or Europe's past. We got thundering dramatic monologues from Savonarola and John Brown that semester. For Berryman it was open house. He found exciting a poem about a particular drinking fountain in a bus station in Toledo, Ohio. Lowell certainly would have preferred a miraculous spring in that other Toledo — though, now that he was no longer a practicing Catholic, sainthood seemed also to bore him. Berryman was delighted with our curious efforts in the direction of free verse, on which he had some complex notions concerning structure and prosody. He even had the boldness to suggest that contemporary voices could achieve themselves in so unfashionable and dated a form as the Petrarchan sonnet. To put it simply, he was all over the place and seemed delighted with the variety we represented.

Their contrasting styles became more evident during the second meeting of the class. Lowell had welcomed a contingent of hangers-on, several of whom were wealthy townspeople dressed to the nines hugging their copies of *Lord Weary's Castle*. Now and then one would submit a poem: Lowell would say something innocuous about it, let the discussion hang in midair for a moment, then move on to something else. Berryman immediately demanded a poem from one of this tribe. The poem expressed conventional distaste for the medical profession by dealing with the clichés of greed and indifference to suffering. (We later learned it was written by a doctor's wife.) John shook his head violently. "No, no," he said, "it's not that it's not poetry. I wasn't expecting poetry. It's that

it's not true, absolutely untrue, unobserved, the cheapest twaddle."
Then he began a long monologue in which he described the efforts
of a team of doctors to save the life of a friend of his, how they
had struggled through a long night, working feverishly. "They did
not work for money. There was no money in it. They worked to save
a human life because it was a human life and thus precious. They
did not know who the man was, that he was a remarkable spirit.
They knew only that he was too young to die, and so they worked
to save him, and, failing, wept." (It turned out the man was Dylan
Thomas, but Berryman did not mention this at the time.) A de-
cent poet did not play fast and loose with the facts of this world,
he or she did not accept television's notion of reality. I had never
before observed such enormous cannons fired upon such a tiny
target. The writer left the room in shock, and those of us who had
doubts about our work — I would guess all of us — left the room
shaken.

We returned the next Monday to discover that Berryman had
moved the class to a smaller and more intimate room containing
one large seminar table around which we all sat. He was in an an-
tic mood, bubbling with enthusiasm and delighted with our pres-
ence. He knew something we did not know: all but the hard-core
masochists had dropped, leaving him with only the lucky thirteen.
"We are down to the serious ones," he announced, and seemed
pleased with the situation; he never again turned his powerful
weapons on such tiny life rafts. In truth, once we'd discovered what
he'd accomplished, we too were pleased not to have to share his at-
tention with writers we knew were only horsing around.

Now came the hard task for him of determining what we knew
and what we didn't know. At least half of us were trying to write
in rhyme and meter, and a few of us were doing it with remark-
able skill. It was at this meeting that he asked each of us to turn in
a Petrarchan sonnet so that he might have some idea how far we'd
come on the road to grace and mastery in the old forms. (The logis-
tics were simple: we turned in our work on the Friday before our
Monday meeting, and John selected the work to be dittoed and
discussed in class.) He presented us with two models, both recited
from memory.

THE SIRENS *by John Manifold*

Odysseus heard the sirens; they were singing
Music by Wolf and Weinberger and Morley
About a region where the swans go winging,
Vines are in color, girls are growing surely

Into nubility, and pylons bringing
Leisure and power to farms that live securely
Without a landlord. Still, his eyes were stinging
With salt and seablink, and the ropes hurt sorely.

Odysseus saw the sirens; they were charming,
Blonde, with snub breasts and little neat posteriors,
But could not take his mind off the alarming
Weather report, his mutineers in irons,
The radio failing; it was bloody serious.
In twenty minutes he forgot the sirens.

Recited in Berryman's breathless style, it sounded like something
he might have written; he had an uncanny knack of making a great
deal of poetry sound like something he might have written. And
who was John Manifold? An obscure Australian poet who fought in
World War II, someone we should discover if we were serious, as he
was, about poetry. The second sonnet was Robinson's "Many Are
Called," which begins "The Lord Apollo, who has never died . . ."
After reciting it, John went back to a passage in the octave:

And though melodious multitudes have tried
In ecstasy, in anguish, and in vain,
With invocation sacred and profane
To lure him, even the loudest are outside.

"Who are those multitudes?" he almost shouted. Petrie, a great
lover of Robinson, answered, "The poets." "Exactly, Mr. Petrie, the
poets. Certainly the poets in this room." It was perfectly clear he
did not exclude himself.

Much to my horror, my Petrarchan sonnet was selected for dis-
cussion on that third meeting. (I believe the poem no longer exists;
I had the good luck never to have had it accepted for publication.)

Actually, it was not that bad: it was about food, which had been an obsession of mine for several months; I was running out of money and so ate very little and very badly. To be more precise, the poem was about my mother's last Thanksgiving feast, which I had returned home to participate in; since my mother was a first-rate office manager and a tenth-rate cook, the event had been a disaster. John discussed four poems that day. The first was not a Petrarchan sonnet, and as far as he could determine had no subject or any phrasing worth remembering. The second did have a subject, but John went to the board to scan its meter. "This is NOT iambic," he said. After getting through four lines, he turned and headed directly toward the cowering poet, suspended the page over his head, and finally let it fall. "This is metrical chaos. Pray you avoid it, sir." I was next. Much to my relief, John affirmed that, yes, this was a Petrarchan sonnet; it was iambic and it did possess a fine subject — the hideous nature of the American ritual meal become a farce. He paused. "But, Levine, it is not up to its most inspired moments— it has accepted three mediocre rhymes, it is padded where the imagination fails. If it is to become a poem, the author must attack again and bring the entirety up to the level of its few fine moments." In effect John was giving us a lesson in how poems are revised: one listened to one's own voice when it was "hot" (a word he liked) and let the "hot" writing redirect one toward a radical revision. "No hanging back," he once said. "One must be ruthless with one's own writing or someone else will be." (I tried but failed to improve the poem. Even at twenty-six, I had not learned to trust the imagination.)

It was clear that, among those poems considered, mine had finished second best, and for this I was enormously relieved. What follows is the best, exactly in the form we saw it on that late February Monday in 1953:

SONNET *by Donald Justice*

The wall surrounding them they never saw;
The angels, often. Angels were as common
As birds or butterflies, but looked more human.
As long as the wings were furled, they felt no awe.

Beasts, too, were friendly. They could find no flaw
In all of Eden: this was the first omen.
The second was the dream which woke the woman:
She dreamed she saw the lion sharpen his claw.
As for the fruit, it had no taste at all.
They had been warned of what was bound to happen;
They had been told of something called the world;
They had been told and told about the wall.
They saw it now; the gate was standing open.
As they advanced, the giant wings unfurled.

After reading the poem aloud, John returned to one line: "As for the fruit, it had no taste at all." "Say that better in a thousand words," he said, "and you're a genius." He went on: "One makes an assignment like this partly in jest, partly in utter seriousness, to bring out the metal in some of you and to demonstrate to others how much you still need to learn. No matter what one's motives are, no teacher has the right to expect to receive something like this: a true poem." Class dismissed.

A week later a telling incident occurred. The class considered a sonnet by one of its more gifted members, a rather confused and confusing poem which Berryman thrashed even though one member of the class found it the equal of the Justice poem from the previous week. The tortured syntax suggested Berryman's own "Nervous Songs," but he saw little virtue in the poem and felt it was more in the tradition of Swinburne than any contemporary poem should be, writing that tried to bully its readers with rhetoric rather than move them with the living language of the imagination. "Write good prose diction in a usual prose order," he said, "unless you've got a damn good reason for doing otherwise." (It was clear he must have felt he had a damn good reason for doing otherwise when he wrote "Bradstreet.") After class, as we ambled back to the student union for coffee and more poetry talk, the same student who had defended the poem informed Berryman that the author had recently had a sheaf of poems accepted by *Botteghe Oscure*, then the best-paying and most prestigious literary magazine in the world. Berryman froze on the sidewalk and then turned angrily on the student and shouted, "Utterly irrelevant, old sport, utterly irrelevant!" He assured the man that absolute "shit" appeared in the so-called "best" publications, while much of the finest poetry being written went begging. (No doubt his own difficult early career had taught him that.) "You're stupid to have raised the subject, stupid or jejune." He paused a moment. "I'll give you the benefit of the doubt: jejune." John smiled, and the incident passed. He was incredibly serious about poetry, and one of us had learned that the hard way. In her gossipy *Poets in Their Youth*, Eileen Simpson would have us believe that all poets in "the Berryman circle" ached to be the elected legislators of the world and suffered deeply because they were not among the famous and powerful. Everything I saw during that semester contradicted that view: the reward for writing a true poem was the reward of writing a true poem, and there was none higher.

In spite of his extraordinary sense of humor, the key to Berryman's success as a teacher was his seriousness. This was the spring of the Army-McCarthy hearings, the greatest television soap opera before the discovery of Watergate. John, as an addicted reader of the *New York Times*, once began a class by holding up the front page so the class might see the latest revelation in the ongoing drama. "These fools will rule for a while and be replaced by other fools and crooks. This," and he opened a volume of Keats to the "Ode to a Nightingale," "will be with us for as long as our language endures." These were among the darkest days of the Cold War, and yet John was able to convince us — merely because he believed it so deeply — that nothing could be more important for us, for the nation, for humankind, than our becoming the finest poets we could become. And there was no doubt as to how we must begin to accomplish the task; we must become familiar with the best that had been written, we must feel it in our pulse.

"Levine, you're a scholar," he once roared out at me in class. "Tell us how you would go about assembling a bibliography on the poetry of Charles Churchill." A scholar I was not, and John knew it, but he had a point: that poets had to know these things. The ignorant but inspired poet was a total fiction, a cousin to Hollywood's notion of the genius painter who boozes, chases girls, and eventually kills himself by falling off a scaffold in the Sistine Chapel. "Friends," John was saying, "it's hard work, and the hard work will test the sincerity of your desire to be poets." He rarely mentioned inspiration, perhaps because he assumed that most of us had been writing long enough to have learned that it came to those who worked as best they could through the barren periods, and this was — he once told me — a barren period for him. So we knew how to begin the task of becoming a poet: study and work. And how did it end? Here John was just as clear: it never ended. Speaking of the final poems of Dylan Thomas, he made it clear they were merely imitations of the great work of his early and middle period. "You should always be trying to write a poem you are unable to write, a poem you lack the technique, the language, the courage to achieve. Otherwise you're merely imitating yourself, going nowhere, because that's always the easiest." And suddenly he burst into a recitation of "The Refusal to Mourn the Death by Fire of a Child in London," ending:

Deep with the first dead lies London's daughter,
Robed in the long friends,
The grains beyond age, the dark veins of her mother,
Secret by the unmourning water
Of the riding Thames.
After the first death, there is no other.

"Can you imagine possessing that power and then squandering it?" he asked. "During our lifetime that man wrote a poem that will never be bettered."

No doubt his amazing gift for ribaldry allowed him to devastate our poems without crushing our spirits, that and the recognition on his part that he too could write very badly at times. He made it clear to us from the outset that he had often failed as a poet and for a variety of reasons: lack of talent, pure laziness ("Let's face it," he once said to me, "life is mainly wasted time."), and stupid choices. "There are so many ways to ruin a poem," he said, "it's quite amazing good ones ever get written." On certain days he loved playing the clown. One Monday he looked up from the class list sent to him by the registrar and asked Paul Petrie why he was getting twice as much credit for the course as anyone else. Paul said he wasn't sure. "Perhaps," said John, "you're getting extra units in physical education and home economics. I'd like you to arrive twenty minutes early and do fifty laps around the room and then erase the blackboard. You might also do a few push-ups or work on your technique of mixing drinks." He then discovered my name was not on the roll. (The truth was, lacking sufficient funds, I had not registered.) He asked me if I thought the registrar was anti-Semitic. No, I said, just sloppy. "You realize," he said, "that until your name appears on this list you do not exist. Tell me," he added, "does anyone else see this Levine fellow? Sometimes I have delusions." As the weeks passed my name continued not to appear on the roster, and John continued to make a joke out of it. "Levine, should I go see the registrar and remedy this hideous state of affairs?" I assured him it was unnecessary, that it was just a meaningless slipup, and I wasn't taking it personally. "You're quite sure it's not anti-Semitism, Levine? These are dark times." Indeed they were for many Americans, but for the young poets in this workshop they were nothing if not glory days.

"Levine," he said another day, "when was the last time you read your Shakespeare?" "Last week," I said. "And what?" "*Measure for Measure.*" "Fine. I've noticed you consistently complain about the quantity of adjectives in the poems of your classmates." This was true. "Is it the number that matters or the quality?" I failed to answer. "Remember your Blake: 'Bring out number, weight, & measure in a year of dearth.'" I nodded. "'Thy turfy mountains where live nibbling sheep.' Two nouns, two adjectives. Any complaints, Levine?" I had none. "Who wrote the line?" "Shakespeare," I said. "What play?" Again I was silent. His long face darkened with sadness. LaFollette answered, "*The Tempest.*" "Levine do not return to this class until you have reread *The Tempest.* I assume you've read it at least once." I had. "'Fresher than May, sweeter / Than her gold buttons on the boughs. . . .' Recognize it?" I did not. "There is great poetry hiding where you least suspect it — there, for example, buried in that hideous speech from *The Two Noble Kinsmen*, Act III, Scene 1." Much scratching of pens as the class bowed to their notebooks. "We must find our touchstones where we can."

Knowing I had gone to Wayne University in Detroit, where John had once taught, he asked me if I'd studied with the resident Shakespeare scholar, Leo Kirschbaum, whom I had found a brilliant teacher. "Amazing fellow, Dr. Kirschbaum; single-handedly he set back Lear scholarship two decades." Little wonder I'd failed to recognize the line from *The Tempest.* While he was on the subject of Shakespeare, he required the entire class to reread *Macbeth* by the next meeting. " 'And yet dark night strangles the traveling lamp.' Hear how the line first strangles and then releases itself. Read the play carefully, every line, let it heighten your awareness of the extraordinary possibilities for dense imagery. You should know that Shakespeare had less than two weeks to complete the play. Why was that, Mr. Justice?" Don, well on his way to his doctorate, explained that the ascendancy to the English throne of James VI of Scotland called for a play in praise of James's Scotch ancestry. Berryman nodded. "Took him no time at all to write it, and yet it would take half the computers in the world a year to trace the development of the imagery that a single human imagination created and displayed in a play of unrivaled power." So much for the School of Engineering. We were never to forget that men and women of the greatest intellect and imagination had for centuries turned toward poetry to fulfill their private and civic needs.

Certain classes were devoted to special subjects relating to poetic practices — prosody, for example. For two hours John lectured on the development of this study and how amazingly fragmented and useless the literature was. People of great learning and sensitivity had come to preposterous conclusions, nothing in print was reliable. It was our duty to master this literature and discover what was useful and what was nonsense. "A man as learned as George Saintsbury, a man who had read and absorbed so much that in old age he took to studying doctoral dissertations from American universities just to keep busy, a man of that breadth of knowledge, gave us a three-volume study of prosodic practices in British and American poetry, and on almost every significant point he is wrong." Still, he urged us to read the work, for if nothing else it was a brilliant anthology of the diversity and richness of poetry in English. We, the hungry students, demanded to know to whom he went for "the scoop," another of his expressions. He laughed, and pointed to his ear. There was no such book, and as in everything else we were thrown on our own. We would develop a prosody that would allow us to write the poetry we needed to write, or we wouldn't, in which case that poetry would never be written. And in order to do it right, we had to learn from those poets who had already done it, for, as John made clear, those who best understood prosody — Shakespeare, Milton, Keats, Blake, Hopkins, Frost, Roethke — had better things to do than write handbooks for our guidance.

"Let us say you are appalled by the society in which you live — God knows it is appalling — and you want to create a poetry that speaks to the disgusting human conditions around you. You want to be the prophet Amos of the present age. To which poet would you turn for aid?" Silence from the class. "You want to evoke your rage, your righteous indignation, in numbers that will express the depthless power of your convictions. To whom do your turn?" A voice from the class: "Robert Lowell." "Good choice, but there is danger here, correct?" The voice: "Yes, I already sound too much like Lowell. I'm doing my best to avoid him." Berryman: "Indeed you are. When I first saw your poems I thought you'd borrowed Cal's old portable Smith-Corona. Why not go to Cal's source, the poet upon whom he based the movement and the syntax of his own work? And who would that be?" Another voice from the class: "Pope." "No, no, you're blinded by his use of the couplet. Milton, our great Milton." Affirmative nods from the class; how could we not know something so obvious? John quoted "On the Late Massacre in Piedmont," using his forefinger to mark the ends of the lines so we heard how powerful the enjambment was. "Bring the diction three hundred years toward this moment and you have one of Cal's early sonnets." More nodding of heads. "And the key to such rhythmic power is . . . ?" Silence. "Speed, achieved by means of complex syntax and radical enjambment. Speed translates always into rhythmic power, and speed is unobtainable in a heavily end-stopped line."

Then he turned to me. "For the power you so dearly aspire to, Levine, you must turn to the master, Milton, the most powerful poet in the language, though you might do well to avoid the Latin vocabulary. Have you studied Latin?" Levine: "No." "You might consider doing so; that way you'll know what to avoid when you're stealing from Milton. Do you have another favorite among your contemporaries?" Levine: "Dylan Thomas." Berryman: "It doesn't show, Levine, it doesn't show; you've done a superb job of masking that particular debt. How have you managed that?" Levine: "I didn't. I wrote through my Dylan Thomas phase and quit. It was impossible for me to write under his influence and not sound exactly like him except terrible." Berryman: "Levine, you've hit upon a truth. Certain poets are so much themselves they should not be imitated: they leave you no room to be yourself, and Thomas was surely one of them, as was Hart Crane, who probably ruined the careers of more young poets than anything except booze. Levine, you might go to the source of Dylan's own lyrical mysticism, and who would that be?" Silence. "Mr. Justice?" Justice: "Blake." "Exactly, you might go to Blake, who is so impossibly lyrical and inventive no one in the world had the talent to sound like him." In an unusually hushed voice he recited all of Blake's early "Mad Song," ending:

I turn my back to the east,
From whence comforts have increas'd;
For light doth seize my brain
With frantic pain.

"Better to learn from a poet who does not intoxicate you," said Berryman, "better to immerse yourself in Hardy, whom no American wants now to sound like. A great poet seldom read." After class Henri Coulette said to me that he'd passed over Blake's "Mad Song" a dozen times and never heard it until John incanted it.

No one escaped unscathed. John advised Petrie to set aside his Shelley and Elinor Wylie and leap into modernism. Coulette was told to loosen up his strict iambics, to try to capture the quality of living speech. Strangely, he underappreciated the formal elegance of William Dickey's work. Neither Petersen nor Jane Cooper was productive that semester; Jane later said she was put off by John's sarcasm. Shirley Eliason's work he found wonderfully dense and mysterious;

he wanted more. "Write everything that occurs to you," he told us all; "you're young enough to still be searching for your voice. You certainly don't want to find it before you find your subject, and you're still young enough to accept failure." LaFollette seemed the greatest enigma to him. "Yes, yes, you have a genuine lyrical gift," he said one day in class, "but who encouraged you to never make sense, always to be opaque?" LaFollette eagerly revealed that he'd just finished a year's work with Roethke. "Yes," said John, "I can see the influence of Roethke, but Ted's best early work is remarkably straightforward on one level. Of course there is always the shadow of something more formidable, darker. Did Cal encourage this sort of obscurity?" LaFollette revealed he had also studied with Richard Eberhart. John's mouth fell open as he stood speechless for several seconds. "You let Dick Eberhart read your poems, and you are here to tell the tale. Amazing!"

He always wanted more work from Robert Dana, though, when Dana finally gave him a poem of ninety-eight lines, he mused over it for a time and finally noted two good images. His parting words were, "If you're going to write something this long why don't you try making it poetry?" Meeting after meeting produced the same advice: "Write everything that occurs to you; it's the only way to discover where your voice will come from. And never be in a hurry. Writing poetry is not like running the four hundred meters. Coulette, do you remember what Archie Williams said his strategy was for running the four hundred meters?" (Coulette, the resident sports maven, did not know. Williams had won the gold at the '36 Berlin Olympics.) John went on: "Archie said, 'My strategy is simple; I run the first two hundred meters as fast as I can to get ahead of everyone, and I run the second two hundred meters as fast as I can to stay there.' Now, that is NOT the way we write poetry, we are not in a race with anyone, but all of us are getting on in years and we'd better get moving." In other words, go as fast as you can but don't be in a hurry; we had a lifetime to master this thing, and with our gifts it would take a lifetime.

Even Justice got mauled. John found his "Beyond the Hunting Woods" a bit too refined, a bit too professionally southern. Those dogs at the end of the poem, Belle and Ginger, all they needed were a few mint juleps. And Levine? Levine got his. According to John, Levine's best poem that semester was "Friday Night in the Delicatessen," in which a Jewish mother laments the fact that her sons are growing away from her, becoming Americans, becoming — you should forgive the expression — *goyim*. At one point she describes them with "hands for fights and alcohol." "Hands for fights, yes," said John, "but hands for alcohol? No. We drink alcohol, Levine, as I know you've learned — we absorb it through the digestive system. The fact we hold a glass of whiskey in our hands is not enough. The parallel structure is false, but this is an amazingly ambitious poem." (I lived on that word, "ambitious," for weeks, even after a friend said, "He forgot to add, 'Ambition should be made of sterner stuff.'") Again I had finished second best. This poem was written to fulfill John's assignment for an ode, and the clear winner was "A Flat One," by De Snodgrass, a poem of enormous power that depicted the slow and agonizing death of a World War I veteran, and the vet's relationship with a hospital orderly who must kill to keep him alive. Even in this earlier "static semi-Symboliste version" (Snodgrass's description), it was a startling poem. (Although Lowell is generally credited for being the mentor behind the poems of *Heart's Needle* ["A Flat One" actually appears in De's second book, *After Experience*], De now claims that Lowell discouraged the writing of those poems, and quite forcefully. "Snodgrass, you have a mind," he'd said to him. "You mustn't write this kind of tear-jerking stuff." Berryman never found the poems sentimental; he tried to move De's writing further from traditional metrics toward something — as De put it — "more like his own experiments at the time . . . more like regular speech . . . less like the poetry being written at the time.")

A later class also began with a demonstration from the front page of the *New York Times*. "Allow me to demonstrate a fundamental principle of the use of language, which is simply this: if you do not master it, it will master you. Allow me to quote Senator McCarthy speaking of his two cronies, Cohn and Shine." Roy Cohn and David Shine were two assistants — investigators, he called them — of the senator for whom he had gained extraordinary privileges which allowed Shine, for example, an ordinary enlisted man in the army, to avoid any of the more onerous or dangerous work of a soldier. "The senator said the following: 'I stand behind them to the hilt.' We now know what Mr. McCarthy thinks we do not know, that he is about to stab them in the back, abandon them both as political liabilities." John was of course correct; within a few days the deed was done. "Because he is an habitual liar, Mr. McCarthy has blinded himself to the ability of language to reveal us even when we're taking pains not to be revealed. Exactly the same thing holds true with poetic form; if we do not control it, it will control us." He went on: "I do not mean to suggest that each time we enter the arena of the poem we must know exactly where we're headed. We have all learned that is preposterous, for the imagination leads us where it will, and we must be prepared to follow, but — and this is the crucial point—should we lack the ability to command the poetic form, even if that form is formlessness, toward which our writing travels, we shall be mastered by that form and what we shall reveal is our ineptitude." He then turned to a student poem in formal meters and rhymed couplets and painstakingly analyzed it from the point of view of how the need to rhyme and to keep the meter had produced odd and unconvincing movements in the poem's narrative, as well as needless prepositional phrases and awkward enjambments. "A poem of real fiber, a rhymed poem, will find its rhymes on subjects, objects, and especially verbs, the key words of its content." He then quoted a poem of Hardy's which ended:

So, they are not underground,
But as nerves and veins abound
In the growths of upper air,
And they feel the sun and rain,
And the energy again
That made them what they were!

Again with his forefinger he scored the key words, and finally repeated that final line, " 'That made them what they were!'— my friends, what they were! That is the artist in command, that is triumph!"

Once again he seemed a walking anthology of poetic jewels, and once again we learned how exacting this thing with the poetry was.

Later, in Kenney's tavern, where many of us assembled after class, one poet recalled that Ignacio Sanchez Mejias, the matador elegized in García Lorca's great poem, had once remarked, "This thing with the bulls is serious," and thus we produced a catch phrase for John's class: "This thing with the poems is serious."

What became increasingly clear as the weeks passed was that, although John was willing on occasion to socialize with us, he was not one of us; he was the teacher, and we were the students. He had not the least doubt about his identity, and he was always willing to take the heat, to be disliked if need be. In private he once remarked to me that teaching something as difficult as poetry writing was not a popularity contest. "Even a class as remarkable as this one," he said, "will produce terrible poems, and I am the one who is obliged to say so." He sensed that the students had themselves developed a wonderful fellowship and took joy when any one of them produced something fine. Whether or not he took credit for any of this I do not know. To this day I can recall Bill Dickey studying a Justice poem almost with awe. "Do you see those rhymes?" he said to me. "I'll bet this is the first time they've been used in all our poetry!" I shall never forget Don Petersen's welcoming me up the mountain of poetry — at that time Don seemed to believe he was the guardian of the mountain. He told me in his curiously gruff and tender voice that a particular poem of mine was in fact a poem, and though the class — including John — had not taken to it, it was evidence that I had become a poet. His words were welcomed and genuine. I can recall my own thrill on seeing a particular poem by Jane Cooper in which her portrayal of a nocturnal hedgehog came so vividly to life I shuddered. I expressed my wonder openly and knew she heard it. One day both Henri Coulette and Robert Dana took me aside to tell me they could scarcely believe how far I'd come in a single year. We were all taking pride and joy in each other's accomplishments.

This fellowship was a delicate and lovely thing, a quality that always distinguishes the best creative writing classes. We were learning how much farther we could go together than we could singly, alone, unknown, unread in an America that had never much cared for poetry. I don't honestly know how large a role John played in the creation of this atmosphere, but I do know it had not existed during Lowell's tenure; his favoritism, his intimacy with some students and visible boredom with others, tended to divide us into two hostile factions, the ins and the outs. In John's class we were all in and we were all out, we were equals, and instead of sinking we swam together. In spite of John's willingness to be disliked, he clearly was not disliked. Of course he was a marvelous companion, and on those evenings he sought company we were all eager to supply it, but we never forgot that, come Monday afternoon, the camaraderie would be forgotten and he would get to the serious business of evaluating and if need be decimating poems.

Sometimes his seriousness could be more than a little intimidating. On one occasion over drinks, before going to dinner with a group of student writers and faculty, John began to muse over a remarkable poem by the Welshman Alun Lewis, "Song: On seeing dead bodies floating off the Cape." Berryman believed that Lewis was one of the great undiscovered talents of the era. He quoted a portion of the poem, an interior monologue by a woman who has had a vision of her lover's death at sea; then his memory failed him, and he apologized to the group. It so happened one of the poets present knew the poem and took up the recitation:

The flying fish like kingfishers
Skim the sea's bewildered crests,
The whales blow steaming fountains,
The seagulls have no nests
Where my lover sways and rests.

His memory primed, John completed the poem, which ends with the woman lamenting the "nearness that is waiting in" her bed, "the gradual self-effacement of the dead." After a moment's silence John remarked, "The dead do not efface themselves; we, the living, betray their memories." John seemed lost in his reverie on the life and early death in war of the poet when another poet present, an enormous man who worked in town as a bartender and bouncer, began to praise one of John's own war poems which had appeared in *The Dispossessed*. Suddenly awakened, John shouted in the man's face, "We are talking about great poetry, do you get it, old sport, great poetry, and not the twaddle you have in mind. I do not appreciate bootlicking." A silence followed, and the moment passed. This thing with the poetry was indeed serious.

That semester Berryman conducted the most extraordinary seminar on other writers I've ever been a part of; again, for lack of funds, I was not registered, but I missed only a single class and that when the obligation to make some money took me elsewhere. The students were assigned a single long paper of considerable scope, the subject agreed upon by teacher and poet — for all the registered students were from the workshop. The papers themselves were never presented in class, but not because Berryman found them inadequate. Indeed he raved about their quality. The reason was simply that John felt he had news to bring us on the subject of poetry in English from Whitman to the present. The highlight of the semester was his presentation of the whole of "Song of Myself," which included the most memorable and impassioned reading of a poem I have ever in my life heard, along with the most complex and rewarding analysis of Whitman's design, prosody, and imagery ever presented. When he'd finished the reading, he stood in silence a moment and then from memory presented the final section again, concluding:

I bequeath myself to the dirt to grow from the grass I love,
If you want me again look for me under your boot-soles.

You will hardly know who I am or what I mean,
But I shall be good health to you nevertheless,
And filter and fibre your blood.

Failing to fetch me at first keep encouraged,
Missing me one place search another,
I stop somewhere waiting for you.

He stood for a moment in silence, the book trembling in his hand, and then in a quiet voice said, "Do you know what that proves? That proves that most people can't write poetry!"

When the semester began I was the only nonenrolled student

attending, but so extraordinary were his performances that the news spread, and by the time he gave his final Whitman lecture the room was jammed to the bursting point. Crane, Stevens, Bishop, Roethke, Eliot, Auden, Dylan Thomas, and Hardy were also subjects of his lectures. These were not talks he gave off the top of his head. Far from it. He entered the room each night shaking with anticipation and armed with a pack of note cards, which he rarely consulted. In private he confessed to me that he prepared for days for these sessions. He went away from them in a state bordering on total collapse. It would be impossible to overestimate the effect on us of these lectures, for this was an era during which Whitman was out, removed adroitly by Eliot and Pound, and kept there by the Ironists and the New Critics, who were then the makers of poetic taste. In 1954 in Iowa no one dreamed that within a few years Williams would be rescued from hell, the Beats would surface, and Whitman would become the good gray father of us all. (John himself later claimed the Beats didn't know how to read Whitman and mistook his brilliant rhythmic effects for prose. "They don't write poems," is the way he put it.) I cannot speak for the entire class, but I know that Petrie, Jane Cooper, Dana, Coulette, Justice, Snodgrass, and I were convinced that "Song of Myself" was the most powerful and visionary poetic statement ever made in this country. Those lectures not only changed our poetry, they changed our entire vision of what it meant to write poetry in America, what it meant to be American, to be human. "There is that lot of me and all so luscious," I suddenly sang to myself, and I believed it, and thanks to John and father Walt I still believe it. Whitman had laid out the plan for what our poetry would do, and so large was the plan there was room for all of us to take our part, as, for example, Roethke was doing, that poet who according to John "thought like a flower."

It seems unlikely now that Berryman should have performed that task, for was he not an eastern intellectual poet and part-time New Critic himself, a protégé of Mark Van Doren and R. P. Blackmur? Like so much that concerns Berryman, the answer is ambiguous. His reviews often sounded very much like what the New Critics were turning out, except they were far wittier and often more savage; in savagery only Yvor Winters could measure up to him.

Who else would be bold enough to invent a poem that a poet might have written — nay, should have written — as John did in a review of Patchen, and then define Patchen's weaknesses on the basis of the poem Berryman and not Patchen had written? But unlike Winters and the rest of the New Critics, he was unashamedly Romantic at the same time as he was distrustful of the "cult of sincerity." He was, as in so many things, his own man and in a very real sense a loner.

Before we parted that semester he performed two more services for me. The day before he left for New York City — he was going east to teach at Harvard that summer — we had a long conversation on what a poet should look like. The Oscar Williams anthology, one of the most popular of that day, included photographs of most of the poets at the back of the book; John and A. E. Housman were the only exceptions — they were represented by drawings. John's was very amateurish and looked nothing like him. I asked him why he'd used it instead of a photograph. He claimed he wanted neither but Oscar had insisted, and he'd taken the lesser of the two evils. He thought either was a distraction, though the drawing did make it clear he was ugly enough to be a poet. I didn't catch his meaning and asked him to explain. "No poet worth his salt is going to be handsome; if he or she is beautiful there's no need to create the beautiful. Beautiful people are special; they don't experience life like the rest of us." He was obviously dead serious, and then he added, "Don't worry about it, Levine, you're ugly enough to be a great poet."

The next day, at the airport, he was in an unusually manic mood. "Think of it, Levine, in a few hours I shall be mine own John Poins." Not knowing Wyatt's poem written from exile in rural England to Poins in London, I asked him what he meant.

I am not he, such eloquence to boast
To make the crow in singing as the swan,
Nor call the lion of coward beasts the most,
That cannot take a mouse as the cat can . . .

He quoted from memory. "Wyatt, Levine, Wyatt, his rough numbers would be perfect for your verse, you crude bastard." ("Crude bastard" was his highest form of compliment.) Before boarding he invited me to send him four or five poems in a year or so, and he'd be sure to get back to me to tell me how I was doing. Having seen an enormous carton of unopened mail in his apartment, I doubted he'd ever answer, but nonetheless a year and a half later I sent him four poems. His response was prompt and to the point, with X's to mark the lines and passages he thought a disaster and checks where he found me "hot," along with specific suggestions for revision; there was not a single line unremarked upon. There was also a brief letter telling me things were going well in Minneapolis and that he was delighted to know I was fooling editors with my "lousy poems." He looked forward to seeing me one day. There was not the least doubt about what he was in fact saying: our days as student and teacher had come to an end. We could not exchange poems as equals in poetry because we were not equals and might never be, and yet I had come too far to require a teacher. I felt the same way. I'd had one great poetry writing teacher, I had studied with him diligently for fifteen weeks. From now on I had to travel the road to poetry alone or with my peers. This was his final lesson, and it may have been the most important in my development.

As the years pass his voice remains with me, its haunting and unique cadences sounding in my ear, most often when I reread my own work. I can still hear him saying, "Levine, this will never do," as he rouses me again and again from my self-satisfaction and lethargy to attack a poem and attack again until I make it the best poem I am capable of. His voice is there too when I teach, urging me to say the truth no matter how painful a situation I may create, to say it with precision and in good spirits, never in rancor, and always to remember Blake's words (a couplet John loved to quote): "A truth that's told with bad intent / Beats all the Lies you can invent." For all my teaching years, now over thirty, he has been a model for me. No matter what you hear or read about his drinking, his madness, his unreliability as a person, I am here to tell you that in the winter and spring of 1954, living in isolation and loneliness in one of the bleakest towns of our difficult Midwest, John Berryman never failed his obligations as a teacher. I don't mean merely that he met every class and stayed awake, I mean that he brought to our writing and the writing of the past such a sense of dedication and wonder that he wakened a dozen rising poets from their winter slumbers so that they might themselves dedicate their lives to poetry. He was the most brilliant, intense, articulate man I've ever met, at times even the kindest and most gentle, and for some reason he brought to our writing a depth of insight and care we did not know existed. At a time when he was struggling with his own self-doubts and failings, he awakened us to our singular gifts as people and writers. He gave all he had to us and asked no special thanks. He did it for the love of poetry.

Improvisations on Donald Justice

I. JUMP HOG OR DIE

Only critics, as Don himself once observed, should be fulsome in their praise. Still, I would like to make a few observations. There was, I felt, always a concentration, always a kind of fierce intensity in his demeanor — a seriousness that spoke to the seriousness of his calling. This was thirty years ago, in the autumn of 1961, my first encounter with Don in the workshop. As far as I know, in such matters — poetry and teaching — such a disposition persists. It was something in him I admired greatly.

The Iowa Writers' Workshop, as everyone must know by now, was run in those days out of Paul Engle's back pocket, and was housed in some leftover Quonset huts: left over from the post–World War II influx of students on the GI Bill. As is usual in such cases, the students went on and the huts remained — married student housing on one side of the Iowa River, art and writing classes on the other. Don and Paul were the only teachers in those days, joined by Mark Strand in my second year when he was brought up from the student ranks. Since Paul was often forced to be on the road looking for dough, Don became, more or less, the poetry workshop. And that was a good thing, at least for me, someone in need of much instruction and direction, someone, literally, just off the boat, a troop ship from Italy. Not all the instruction was found in the workshop, however. A good bit was after hours and interspersed.

Monday afternoons, workshop over, a group would walk from the Quonset hut to the Student Union. To the Ping-Pong room. Don, Mark, Marvin Bell, Bill Brady, Al Lee, Wm Brown, myself, and sometimes others. This was when I first got the notion that Don's fierce intensity was not limited to things ethereal. Did we play vigorous Ping-Pong, or what? Mark was a good player; I was all right, a journeyman; Bill Brady was all right. But Don was very good. I couldn't beat him. Mark may have a couple times; and Marvin, who was also a good player. But Don was both tough and tenacious, a trait I later saw on the softball field, at the poker table, at the game board (we're talking horse-racing games and war games here), anywhere. For myself, once I discovered poetry, nothing else *really* mattered. I'd tend to drift off if the game at hand wasn't going my way. I lost, in effect, my killer instinct if, in fact, I ever had one. Not Don. *Everything* mattered. It was *all* important. Perhaps not equally, but it all had to be done full bore. It was a quality of participation I envied greatly, but was unable to emulate. But I did play. We all played. But Don *played*. Such intensity. Such an unreturnable service!

As I say, this concentration was much in evidence in his teaching as well. I shall never forget my first conference with Don to go over my poems. It was, in fact, my first conference with *anyone* about my poems, and I was anxious, to say the least. The subject matter of our conversation — Don's conversation — escapes me now. Some ineptitude I was trying to suggest was a poem. Something, no doubt, about goddesses and the Aegean Sea. But Don, as was his manner, was taking it seriously, very seriously. Certainly more seriously than I, having already seen in a couple of workshop sessions what the level of performance was, a level far above what I was doing. In any case, Don was patiently going over the poem. At the same time, a fly was going over it too. And over us, circling our heads, circling the page, circling Don's face as he kept his concentration ardently on the poem and on what he was saying. I, of course, was mesmerized by the fly as it got closer and closer to Don's face, and, abruptly, as Don inhaled to say something, flew into his mouth. His mouth! Don gulped. Bye fly. He actually swallowed the damn thing, so intent was he on the poem at hand. "Did I swallow that fly?" he asked, astonished. I allowed as to how he had. "Jesus," he said. Amazing! Then he actually went back to the poem. From that moment, he had me in the palm of his hand.

Stories. Many stories. Some repeatable, some not. Nights at Kenney's Tavern. The Famous Pig Roast at Nick Crome's farm when Don organized a high-jumping contest over the pig still on the pit, the coals still glowing. Couples straying impassioned in the burgeoning spring leaves and long grasses of the adjoining fields. Hatchet-throwing competition. Later, knife-throwing contests in Al Lee's apartment, the knives and the distances getting larger and longer. Competition. Much competition. It had a wonderful effect on one's poems. The push to get them written. The desire to get them written right for the proper praise from the proper people.

Don was in the early stages of the *Night Light* poems then. I was in the early stages of learning *The Summer Anniversaries*, almost by heart. I learned what meter was about from his poems. The first successful poem I wrote at Iowa (it took me seven months) was an imitation of the meters and structure in "Landscape with Little Figures." He was a teacher in the best possible ways — he opened you to what was possible and was impeccable in his own work. Surely, as he might say himself, a winning combination.

That was 1961–1963. I went away for two years with my M.F.A. degree to the capitals of Europe. When I came back for a second (shorter-lived) go-round in 1965, Mark had gone to New York City and Marvin was teaching. And Don. This was a good time for his poems. He wrote many, especially in syllabics. And since he was writing in syllabics, we were writing in syllabics. The old order was starting to break apart and a new, looser order was looming.

As always in Iowa City, it was a good time to be there. I remember one night I saw him going from town back down to the Quonset huts, to his office, and asked where he was off to. "I've got an idea for a poem," he said. It turned out a few days later to be "The Missing Person." Nelson Algren was in residence that year. Marathon high-stakes poker games. Classes on Stevens and Williams. "Variations for Two Pianos," "The Man Closing Up." I still can't read *Night Light* without an almost unbearable nostalgia. For the things we did, for the poems that were written, for who we were, for our gloriously happy and unhappy selves. There was never a better teacher. There were never better poems to learn from. He is the Thin Man. Such rich refusals!

II. HOMAGE TO THE THIN MAN

The Thin Man

I indulge myself
In rich refusals.
Nothing suffices.

I hone myself to
This edge. Asleep, I
Am a horizon.

I don't know much about southern poetry as a genre, but there are a couple of southern poets whose work I have admired and learned from. Perhaps not learned as much as I should have, but have learned a little from, nevertheless. Those poets are John Crowe Ransom and Donald Justice. I have admired things, and admired them greatly, in other poets, especially Robert Penn Warren and James Dickey, both of whom have a narrative power and seduction I find, at times, almost irresistible. But the progenitors to whom I keep coming back, and to whose work my heart continues to lie open, are Ransom and Justice. And of the two, it's Justice I'd like to say a few words about, Ransom having already his place in history, thank you very much, and deservedly so, while Justice seems to me, if not exactly overlooked or neglected (he has won the Pulitzer Prize for his *Selected Poems* and the Bollingen Prize for "lifetime achievement"), certainly a contemporary master whose public ink is nowhere near his poetic achievement.

Poets are like restaurants — as soon as they are successful, they are imitated. Really good poets are like really good restaurants — they are inimitable, though one is continuously nourished there.

We don't say enough about our teachers. Writers are afraid to talk about their teachers, either out of ego, or the anxiety of influence, or both. They are afraid to admit whom they've read, whose writing had changed their lives, as they all wish to have exited the head of Zeus on their own steam. Good luck. We are all a product of who we read and who told us what. All of us, every man-jack and woman-jill.

Justice's poetic production, like Larkin's — the contemporary poet whose career his most resembles, and whose stature he should most share — has been relatively small, four books plus a couple of selected volumes. Still, it's only small compared to, say, Pound or Williams, not to Hopkins or Crane or Bishop, for instance. Moderate production, major results. Like Larkin's, Justice's work is studded with minor masterpieces, several of which (for instance, the villanelle "Variations for Two Pianos," the sestina "Here in Katmandu," "The Thin Man" in syllabics, "Sonatina in Yellow," "Counting the Mad") are permanent examples of the form or nonce form. Very few of us can claim to have written a clutch of classics. Justice could, though he probably wouldn't. For Justice and James Merrill are the two unequivocal masters of formal verse in our time. Others are accomplished, indeed, even more wide ranging. But Justice and Merrill are the *maestri*. One has gotten his just due, the other not.

One of the reasons Justice's reputation has not yet kept pace with the excellence of his work, I think, is because he was, for so many years, considered *the* teacher of poetry writing in this country who taught at *the* program of creative writing, the University of Iowa. Those of Justice's generation whose reputations did flourish — Merrill, for example, Merwin, Ginsberg, Creeley, Ashbery — for years had no permanent academic position. Merwin and Merrill still don't, though the others have recently sought academic sanctuary. Also, Justice has a Ph.D., another impediment to being a "real" poet. Such nonsense. Look at the work instead, the tensile strength and experience of the language, the expansion of the tradition, the invention in formal structures and meters. Teachers. Think of the great painters of past centuries. All teachers with their workshops and apprentices. Are they any less painters of brilliance? I think not. One of the great heroes for the counterculture, Ezra Pound, longed all his life for an academic appointment. Please, no more idle talk about "professor poets." Let's look at the work.

Is it better to be a "little master" than a big failure? Perhaps yes, perhaps no. Some, like the aforementioned Pound, and Hart Crane, are both at the same time. Others in both camps are neither. A golden bird in the hand. . . .

What a teacher can supply: clarity of line and clarity of vision, patience for what's good and impatience with what's bad, quality and quantity in the metric tools of the trade and quality and quantity in the history of the discipline, the knowledge that one is always a servant of the language and never more. If the teacher's poems are exemplary themselves, it's a powerful show-and-tell.

Not only are Justice's poems exemplary, his entire enterprise has been. He has been an alp of integrity to two generations of young poets. His work has not only withstood the mistrals and siroccos of fashion and trendiness, it has also withstood their seductive subtle breezes as well, and has remained true to its constant demand — write clearly, write well. He has written poems, beautiful poems, in all meters and many forms. He has written plays, stories, and essays. So far as I know, he has never written a novel, but I dare say he has contemplated more than one over the years. Distilled, his writing could serve as a hornbook for any aspiring poet. And, as Walter Benjamin said, "An author who teaches writers nothing, teaches no one."

Every poem that Donald Justice ever wrote is a learning experience for the young poet — and the not-so-young poet, too, I might add. There is a problem being either solved, worked on, or worked on and abandoned in each poem that has survived. That these solutions are so liquid and effortless seemingly only speaks, of course, to the mastery that went into them. Pick any poem, at random, in the *Selected Poems* or *A Donald Justice Reader* and you will see what I mean — theorems are being worked out, equations are being solved, the abstract is being made palpable, the invisible forces are being brought to light. This is the emotion, these cadences, that endures, as Pound would have it.

He is the contemporary master of the adverb (most notably, perhaps, "perhaps"), both when evident and, especially, when suppressed, though he has said he considers the conjunction the most beautiful part of speech.

Another interesting thing about teachers who are good writers — not only do you get their own take on everything, you also get the people who informed them. And if, as I say, the teacher is an exemplary writer himself, you get these influences condensed and distilled, essences, as it were. Justice's debts to and allegiances with Auden and Stevens have been acknowledged (almost every poet born during the 1920s was influenced by Stevens and Auden). Less well known, but more pervasive in a transparent way, is the light thrown on his work by Rafael Alberti and, especially, Rilke, the early Rilke of *The Book of Pictures* and *New Poems*. The nostalgia, sadness, melancholia, and sense of a world lost and a time lost (especially of childhood and adolescence) in both these poets shine like a sunrise, or sunset, over many of Justice's poems, brightening and clarifying, darkening and adumbrating them, outlining their own singularity and substance.

That's about what I wanted to say. Dante put his teacher, Brunetto Latini, in hell, though not because of his teaching. I would put mine, Donald Justice, merely before your eyes, which I hope is not the same place. Reader, read his poems, they *are* addressed to you.

R. V. Cassill

Even back in 1947, when I first knew him, R. V. Cassill seemed to have read all the fiction in the world. That is my first memory of him — talking about fiction. He was an Iowa boy, and ex-GI, and I knew him as both graduate student and teacher at the same time over the next two years in the Writers' Workshop in Iowa City. He and Flannery O'Connor were the only published writers in the workshop then, and I sat in awe of them both: Flannery, who said nothing; and Verlin who said everything. He had an Atlantic First under his belt, and he was writing *Eagle on the Coin*, his first novel.

He was so serious, so opinionated, so intensely alive, and almost so unfailingly right in his criticism of the stories that were presented in those years. In profile, his dark handsome head was that of the buffalo. Sitting in class, I used to take out my buffalo nickel, which I carried as a good luck piece, to admire the likeness. I thought he was the only one among us who knew where he was going.

He was learning his craft as a writer in those early years, but he was a born teacher from the beginning, using his enormous understanding of literature to inspire his students. He pulled no punches, but I never heard him put a student writer down, no matter how bad. His criticism was always tempered by kindness, you went away from it knowing you would write better. Once he told me, after a rather grueling analysis of what was wrong with my story, that I was beginning to write like Willa Cather.

When he came to the workshop as a student, he wore old clothes, old army fatigues and GI boots with mud on them — before it was fashionable to dress that way. He was building his house that spring, from his own architectural design — building it board by board, digging the foundation, pouring the cement, laying the roof, putting in the furnace ducts and the electrical wiring. He designed louvers beneath the windows to let in the Iowa breeze in summer, and across the top of the roof he built a row of clerestory windows to let in light. You could build a house in 1949 for a couple of thousand dollars — money he didn't have until Random House gave him an advance for the novel he was working on. He did everything down to the toilet paper holder which he whittled out of wood. The house still stands east of Iowa City, lived in, a testimony to his workmanship of that period of his life thirty years ago.

When he came to the workshop as a teacher and critic, he dressed up in his only suit, not a suit really, but it passed for one; a brown tweedish short jacket with pants that belonged to another time, another place. They didn't quite match the jacket. He wore a white shirt with a slightly rumpled black tie, almost a string tie, and his GI shoes. I don't think he had any other shoes. As the discussion got lively, which it always did, he would loosen his tie and the ends would swing apart as he talked and moved about. The slight disarray that caused to his clothing didn't detract from the sense of presence he always had. If anything, it added to his vibrancy. He was impressive, either in old clothes or what was his Sunday best.

He could stay up all night drinking and arguing about politics and literature and still be at his typewriter in the early morning. He was neither a day nor a night person, accommodating himself to any hour, but early morning was his best time to write. He had a schedule and he kept it. Besides working on the novel, he was finishing up his M.F.A. degree and writing short stories for his thesis. "Larchmoor Is Not the World," "The Land of the Sleeping Beauty," "This Hand, These Talons," others — all appeared first in the pale purple ink of the hectograph machine that was used to run off copies for the Writers' Workshop.

He did his writing in the mornings, his teaching and house building in the afternoons, and his politicking in the evenings or whenever. He was working for Henry Wallace in 1948 and went to the Progressive Party convention in Philadelphia that year. In the pause of the cacophony of all that, he sometimes painted, his second art: delicate watercolors of the Iowa countryside and oil paintings of his friends. After his house was finally finished, he had no furniture for the rooms, but there were pictures for the walls. I have one of his watercolors — a field of wheat gently blowing in the summer wind seen from his window.

It's a great pleasure to recall the Verlin Cassill of the late 1940s when he was launching his literary career. He never knew I compared him to my buffalo nickel back then, but I am glad to have him read of it now. I have no doubt he'll get hold of one of those nickels to see for himself. He was interested in knowing everyone and everything around him, and I know he still is. A friend gave me a copy of his *Norton Anthology of Short Fiction* a year ago, and I often find myself more engrossed in his notes than in the stories. Who but Verlin would know that Kay Boyle's story is about D. H. Lawrence's dying. Or that a "good tuck-in" in Conrad's *Heart of Darkness* is British slang for "a good meal?"

For some reason, Iowa traditionally has not been kind to its own. When he defected to the east, the state lost one of its best. The landscape has been incomplete since.

Ray B. West, Jr.

Ray was acting head of the workshop in my two Iowa City years. Paul, who'd corresponded with me about coming, was off — at Harvard, at the Harriman estate in New York, at — God knows where. When he did show up in Iowa City, Zeuslike, gift-bringing (*Life* would be doing a story on the workshop, Random House would publish an anthology of workshop writers, he would be editing the O. Henry Prize short stories — some gifts were delivered, some weren't), the metabolism rate changed. Things were faster, the publication world was closer, your internal telephone became long distance, you were part of the Now-world.

Ray's world was different. *Now* was the slow labor of art or the scrupulous weighing and measuring required for a good issue of the *Western Review*. *Now* was the fragile extension of a long *Then*, a rare addition to a longer *To Be*. Ray loved the possibilities in your stories, loved help making them be what they could be. Paul also loved your stories but saw them as part of the mosaic his vision and brilliant administrative gift brought into being, the best new American poems and stories coming out of the midwestern heartland where he'd been born and raised.

Ray saw this as well, and it was undoubtedly part of the reason he'd joined Paul in Iowa City despite the clash of their personalities, temperaments, and ambitions. Paul was galvanic. Even sitting barefoot on a porch eating a hot dog, he was aware that the moment was part of other moments, an interval between accomplishments, a picture for an issue of *Life* or the *Chicago Tribune*. Ray, though not the image of ease, radiated it. He wasn't in a hurry. His laughs were slow, sometimes puzzled as if surprised at themselves. Paul's were explosions of delight.

If you looked quickly, Paul should have looked like Ray; Ray, Paul. Ray's look was almost bohemian — thick, wavy, swept back black hair — graying a bit in 1952, and, like a way station for it, a rich mustache. His eyes were large, brown, eye-glassed. He was slender, about 5'7", walked on the balls of his feet. Paul had thin, straight light brown hair parted in the middle and, if you looked quickly, bland features; but the nose and chin were sharp, the small eyes alert, rapid. A probing, nervously good-humored face; but the humor was his own, not yours. Ray's face was longer, darker, easier; the small, good teeth under the rich mustache were ready for smiles, but these were shared, they took off from what you said more than what he was thinking about it. You relaxed with Ray, were on your toes with Paul.

Ray had a literary magazine and single-handedly had kept it going in different places under different names. (The best known before *Western Review* was the *Rocky Mountain Review*.) Paul wanted it as an outlet for the young workshop writers' work. Ray wanted to keep it as it was, a place for the best poems and stories submitted from all over. He had published some of the world's best writers in it. Though delighted to discover and publish new writers, he did not want to rush them into its pages. When they did make it there, they'd be printed beside Pound and Tate and would know it really counted. Everything Ray knew and was told him that this took time.

Like so many of the young writers recruited — with his exceptional enthusiasm and generosity — by Paul, I came to Iowa City unsure of the place and my reason for being in it. My dear old friends from Chapel Hill, Don and Jean Justice, had somewhat prepared me, and had prepared Paul for me, but the first hot days staying in their small apartment under the landlord's collection of Baconiana on a street of lonely looking frame houses were difficult for me and so for them. "Two Iowan Baudelaires / Sweating out tetrameters" began a poem which Don and I, sweating, tried to write. I sat in on Joseph Baker's intelligent classes on Victorian literature and thought I was too old at twenty-four to go back to school. I'd been working for three years in Europe. My wife was pregnant and we had a one-year-old son. Though the job Paul got me at his alma mater, Coe College, would, with a tuition scholarship and such goodies as cheap student housing and the Engle family cradle, enable us to make it through the doctorate without borrowing (I'd saved $3,000 working for the Occupation Army in Germany), I didn't think my spiritual bank account would hold up. One day I went down the hill to the workshop office and met Ray. He didn't offer the extraordinary personal, boosting welcome Paul did; he just quietly made you know this was a place where literature counted and if this was what you were about, it was where you could or even should be.

I'd never experienced anything like the workshop. There were about twenty-five of us in the large group. Ray presided, Verlin Cassill and Mike (Hansford) Martin were the two assistants. There were good students in the class, many as old or older than I. Some of them were intellectual wild men and women; the instructors had to deal with some very far-out criticism. (Verlin supplied some of that, though he was usually wise and helpful. It was a special summer for him, too. He met the pretty twin swimmers one of whom became his wife.) Of one of my stories, a bald, Genghis-mustached North Carolinian said, "A Harvard instructor wouldn't let peach juice roll down his chin into his shirt." Ray dealt with such criticism patiently, good-naturedly; but firmly. He kept after the heart of the stories, then liked to place them in the tradition, a Hemingway or Andersonlike story. One story of mine bounced off Goethe's *Werther.* Ray saw that and liked it. He wanted us to feel we were part of something larger. He didn't parade his learning, but it was clear how deeply a part of him it was. When he praised a story or part of it, you felt that literature itself was approving what you'd done. Mostly, though, there was much to improve. One could always improve a story.

In the group sessions, Ray wanted everyone to speak, and he would easily alter his opinion after a speaker — student or instructor, it was democratic — convinced him that he'd missed, or said he'd missed, the point. (I sometimes thought he purposely misread something in order to give us confidence in our judgments, though some of us needed no boosting here.)

In our one-to-one sessions, sitting three feet from him in the small workshop office with the plywood walls and pictures of James and Whitman tacked up beside covers of recent *Western Review*s, Ray leaned over the pages of the story he'd marked up and, in his rich, quiet voice, spelled out what he thought about it. Even when I disagreed, I always respected his opinion. His was not a competing ego, he was a teacher who didn't seem to be riddled with introspective doubt. He wasn't competing with you, he wasn't posing over you, yet there was never any doubt that his experience and sensitivity made him a judge whose opinion counted very much.

Working with—rather than for—him on the *Western Review* was a wonderful experience. Herb Wilner, Don Justice, Don Petersen, Mike Martin, David Jenkins, Bill Dickey (the remarkably efficient and agreeable secretary), and several others read the submitted essays, poems, and stories, wrote comments, debated their merits, and then went over them with Ray. It was a lesson in the conversion of individual talent into not exactly tradition but into—how awesome it seemed—publication. When my own workshop story "The Sorrows of Captain Schreiber" was accepted and printed in the *Review*, I didn't feel the favoritism but the seriousness of the whole process. One was in a magazine which Ray had for all those years made into something that really counted. He would not have lowered his standards for anyone. So I believed, and believe now.

I didn't socialize with Ray. I don't know who did, perhaps Herb Wilner whose slow humor and strength (a bit more tormented than Ray's) was akin to his. (Later they would teach together at San Francisco State.) Indeed, I knew very little about him. We were so busy with coursework, writing, teaching, studying for the doctoral exams, watching the Army-McCarthy hearings at the union, playing bridge, poker, charades, and, every decent afternoon at four, croquet by the river, there wasn't time to socialize with quiet people like Ray. And I suppose we thought that he, like us, was busy writing.

What about his own work? Full of my own and that of my friends, I didn't think much about it, but one day our small group of five or six prose writers listened while he read a chapter of a novel on which he was working. I thought it very good and loved hearing him read it. It meant an enormous amount to him and thus to us. As far as I know, it was never published. Perhaps it was never finished, but I think it was offered and rejected a few times, and that Ray, thinking he hadn't brought off something that was as good as he wanted it to be, withdrew it. I have no idea now what it was about except that it was western, Mormon, Utah, and said more about Ray than anything else. Did he tell us that there was a section about his proselytizing year in Germany? Maybe so.

The differences between him and Paul overflowed into a break a couple of years after I left Iowa City in 1954. Ray asked me to do what I could to preserve the threatened *Western Review* and I had a heated exchange about it with president Virgil Hancher (an Oxford friend of Paul's).

Ray lost the battle and moved to San Francisco State. I saw him out there in 1964. I drove to his lovely cedar house in Marin County. He'd put on weight and looked, I thought, sleek as a seal, happy too. He, his charming wife, Lou, and I had sandwiches around their swimming pool. He said swimming was very important to him now. It was far from Utah, far from Iowa City. The magazine deadlines were over, even the world of letters seemed remote. He was fifty-eight.

Yesterday, knowing I was to write this, I took out his book of essays, *The Writer in the Room*, and last night read through his learned, thoughtful, confident, but unpretentious accounts of Emerson, Whitman, James, Twain, Crane, Faulkner, Katherine Porter, Pound, and Hemingway. I hadn't put into words back then what I think I sensed and now feel strongly, that Ray was a conscientiously American literary consciousness whose working life, teaching, editing, and writing articulated that consciousness and its obligations for others. A Henry James sentence he quotes in one of the essays suggests what may be the heart of his code and vocation, the essence of the tenacity, kindness, and gentleness which makes him a permanent part of so many grateful students, collaborators, and writers: "It appears to me that no one can ever have made a seriously artistic attempt without becoming conscious of an immense increase — a kind of revelation — of freedom."

Marguerite Young

Trying on a Style

She was not even sure that she herself existed, that it was not all a stupendous joke played upon her, this seeming passage of life, this needless expansion of the firmament. . . .
—Miss MacIntosh, My Darling

Ah, Marguerite. Marguerite Young. *Miss MacIntosh, My Darling.*

Iowa City, fall 1956. I have set out from New Haven, Connecticut, in a '48 Chevy coupe for Iowa City (Ohio? Idaho?) having been accepted by Paul Engle into the graduate fiction and poetry workshops. (On the Mississippi bridge, my battery died. A symbol of something to come? We were all symbol chasers those days. Something of me would die in Iowa? What?)

First fiction workshop meeting. Over forty young writers (what do we call ourselves? apprentices?), mostly male (aspiring, perspiring in the barracks), on a humid late August afternoon, 1956; high body odor quotient; not enough chairs to go round, we sat on a window alcove, the floor, a church pew. Dripping. Three "mentors" (what do we call them — writers, authors, professors?) around a desk in front, one of them a lady in a cape and black tam. Wearing a woolen cape in spite of the ninety degrees. We who expect to be Joyces, Lawrences, Hemingways, Faulkners, Jameses, are being asked to sign on for the semester with the writer of our choice: Ray West, Marguerite Young. Perhaps Calvin Kentfield? Curt Harnack? Hortense Calisher?

I signed on with Marguerite. (I think of it even now, forty years later as "signing on.") She looked every bit the literary artist.

I'd seen a photo of Joyce wearing a cape. I'd come to Iowa, a Stephen Dedalus in the making. If I was to have a mentor here, it would have to be an artist. Marguerite looked like the genuine article. (Of course you were, Miss MacIntosh, from What Cheer, Iowa!) I handed her my story "Goats," which had won a literary award at Southern Connecticut State. Marguerite looked at me out of merry, hazel eyes, small and direct. "Goats," she said in a small, slightly amused voice. "Wonderful title." I had the impression she was joking slightly, though careful not to embarrass me.

I took her in as best I could without embarrassing *her*. Her face was puffy and pasty. I figured she must write at night. (Insomnia, Marguerite?) I thought of Alice in Wonderland. I didn't dare let her see it in my face. She was an author, after all. Her presence was in her cape. I did not wish her to be more present than she was. I had not expected any literary presence like this at Iowa. I didn't know what to expect. (What was a "writers' workshop" anyway?) Whatever writer's ego I had developed back in New Haven was quickly dying here. Calvin Kentfield, the only professional writer I'd met before coming to Iowa, said, "Know how to get there?" I didn't. But I learned.

I was now in the fiction workshop, with Marguerite as my mentor. Where do we go from here? The second or third meeting of the assembled fiction workshop (where did all those people come from? How did they get here?) "Goats" was massacred, my poor prize story. Marguerite did her best to bring up positive points against a barrage of attacks from the "young writers." (The vibrant symbolism of the goats!) My name was on the piece. I was the goat. The "critics" said my poor mock folk tale was lacking in realism. The sex too obviously Freudian. Marguerite tried to defend my story from the realists. She said, firmly, "It's quite original. The symbols are treated in a very sophisticated manner." I listened for a while from the back of the room, and then I felt sick. I lit out, down to the river, west of the barracks where I vomited my guts out and then enviously watched the swallows catching insects and massing along the railing of the bridge, above their mud nests, preparing for their trip south. I was no Stephen Dedalus who would "forge in the smithy of his soul, the uncreated conscience of [his] race."

After a while, a shadow moved over me, and I turned around. It was Marguerite. I hadn't noticed before—she wore her hair in bangs. Her face was ancient, but the bangs gave her a young girl look. She made a half gesture as if to help me up. Rings on her fingers, bells on her toes. . . . I stood up. "Sorry. I had to leave." "So I noticed." Again I had the feeling she was amused. We started walking. She talked quietly. I mustn't take what people said back there in the barracks to heart. She asked if "Goats" was based on fact. "No. I really don't know where it came from." "Good," she said. "Now, I want you to do something. Take the first three or four pages and try to write it all in one long sentence, letting your imagination feel free to fill in any details and images that come up. Don't censor yourself. No matter how absurd. Don't censor yourself." I was only paying half attention. On my mind, only to get to Kenney's and drown my failure as a writer in a pitcher of beer. (Iowa was partly "dry" in 1956; a few years later you could buy hard liquor in taverns.)

Marguerite talked on and on as we walked the banks of the river. She asked what I was reading and hoped I was reading poetry. "I'm in the poetry workshop," I said. "Good for you." I began to feel better. She left me soon after, after I'd promised to really commit myself to "Goats." I was beginning to hate the piece. I watched Marguerite disappear into the Student Union, a figure from Poe in the Iowa dusk. I went back to my apartment and started putting the story into long sentences and suppressing my censor.

Now "Goats" grew longer and longer as the sentences grew longer and longer, until finally I began to imagine what used to be a short story as a novel. (Every piece of prose Marguerite touched, grew and grew. *Miss MacIntosh, My Darling* is over 1,200 pages in twelve point type, though chaptered out.) Later, when I submitted a fair-sized block of manuscript to Marguerite, she invited me to her apartment for a conference. I went with a deep sense of being honored.

She had prepared tea and biscuits. On a sideboard, I noticed a plaster of paris replica in living color of some battle scene or other from the Civil War. (Gettysburg?) A stuffed raven was mounted on a hill looking down on the scene. I wanted to ask about it. But I'd come to discuss my manuscript, my new style, the long uncensored sentences. (There is a sense of Big Death hovering over all of *Miss MacIntosh*.)

When we were settled, she told me how impressed she was with the revision; she had decided to send a section of "Goats," with a covering letter, to *Botteghe Oscure*. "The Princess will love it." I tried not to betray my ignorance. "It's really coming along beautifully," Marguerite said. I had never heard the word "beautifully" spoken so beautifully. I forgot about the Civil War diorama or whatever it was. I began to leap ahead a bit. I had just heard something that had me thinking I was going to be a published author. (*Botteghe Oscure* was a literary magazine published in Rome during the fifties, by the Princess Caetani. Marguerite had already published in the magazine.)

I continued to work on "Goats," letting the language and the images and the rhythms flow. Details and action and plot seemed to invent themselves. The princess liked what we'd submitted, but found the piece a little long. I was disappointed, but getting "toughened up" by the workshop experience, and beginning to work on "Goats" for its own sake. I was having a romp letting my imagination go and not worrying too much about realism.

From time to time, I'd run into Marguerite and her flowing cape around campus. One midnight, at the Greasy Spoon, I saw her with a coterie, observing the passengers getting off the midnight bus and coming in the back door and taking booths or sitting at the counter to eat. (A large section of the opening of *Miss MacIntosh* consists of meditations in a bus on a midnight ride, particularly on the aged bus driver.) The coterie was silent, observing, as if Marguerite had set them an exercise in observing. I would have liked it if she had invited me to sit with her. But I knew I did not belong in the coterie ritual. There was a fine line between mentor and apprentice. Later, I met her in the student union sitting with a simian-looking hulk of a man, whom she introduced as professor somebody or other. For some reason, I felt jealous. Marguerite made you feel special, aesthetically. This professor didn't seem to be her type. Later, I discovered he was a logical positivist. What on earth was Marguerite doing in the company of a logical positivist philosophy professor? Teaching him the joys of the imagination? A romance? I had been thinking of Marguerite as a kind of nun. Of the imagination.

And so I wrote on. And on. And one day it dawned on me that I might be writing for Marguerite's approval. That realization came as the vista of "Goats" seemed to be unfolding without any end in sight, and I wanted to get on to something new.

About this time, I began to realize the style I was writing in was not mine. Not my voice. And I had to set out and find my own way of making fictions. Marguerite had helped me try on a style and not be afraid to. She used to say, "Oh, the subject matter doesn't matter!" Marguerite opened up my imagination and my language. I got the sense of using a fuller language for an imagination of plenitude. And a sense of the freedom of imagination, and letting go with it. And that's still one of my rare delights.

Vance Bourjaily

Vance came to the University of Iowa Writers' Workshop in 1957 and left in 1979. I came in 1957 and left in 1968. The crucial years for me as a student of Vance's were the first three or four, from 1958 to 1961. No doubt the contexts of his teaching at Iowa changed. That's a story some of his later students may tell — Gail Godwin, John Irving, or Lucy Rosenthal. But in those early years when I studied with Vance, the fiction workshop at Iowa was two things, rather fiercely — male and formalist.

I think there was an element of tension between those leit-motifs, for maleness suggested a certain deliberate development of self, whereas formalism suggested an effacement of the self in favor of the well wrought story. Technique, craft, and form were our watchwords. Yes, but being physically located in Iowa in the domain of the intensely Iowan Paul Engle — what did that mean? I think it meant being close to the soil, to animals, to raw weather, to lots of good people who cared more about the elemental than about letters.

That was a feeling I got from Vance, that he felt better if he had thick country shoes on or boots with some mud on the soles or some cow shit, that he liked a house with a certain quantity of dog hairs from Bix or Moondog, that he wanted to own some land, and a pond, and fish and shoot game. But there was nothing show-off or phoney about it. And there was certainly no hint of the oppressive. Vance was not saying to us, *be like me, write like me*. He was only saying that for him the composition of a self and of a text go hand in hand. That defined a position. It gave you a sort of star fix to navigate by as you came to your own decision about personality, life history, and writing. And that was good because the dogma — the Eliot thing about the artist being only a catalyst, about art being the escape from personality — could get pretty heavy in the 1950s.

On the one hand Vance was very much a formalist. In workshop he talked a lot about technique, about what worked and what didn't. In his own writing he liked to set himself technical problems, judging that the solving of such problems could lead to high literary art. He had certain technical axioms that he challenged us with. *In a really successful tense dramatic scene the combatants never talk about exactly the real issue between them.* He would insist that we read our stuff aloud. If you couldn't read it convincingly, then it wasn't right. There had to be a powerful consonance between sound and sense. If the style created its own autonomous engine, then it was mere virtuosity. If on the other hand it submitted itself to dogged narration and exposition, then it had been sold for a pot of message.

But in other ways Vance was an antiformalist. Lubbock's quasi-Jamesian rules of point of view and other purities he held to be mostly wrong-headed. You could get away with anything if you could make it work, and that included multiple points of view, radical changes in voice, narrative sprawl, etc. Also, what you said mattered in a world larger than books. It was finally indefensible to say that theme is just another formal element accounting for the coherence of fiction. Fiction was inherently rhetorical and political. And that, in those formalist days, was true heresy.

And Vance was interested in genesis, another formalist fallacy. What I remember in this connection is mostly comical. He wanted a typewriter he could mount on the wall and pound out his fiction with boxing gloves. This may have come from his friend Norman Mailer. He noted that writers talk about the flow of writing, the coming of good things. Milk and semen. Vance kept it light, but I saw a serious side to this. You couldn't just be an Aristotelian "maker." You had to tap your unconscious. Sex and aggression may have more to do with writing than we think. Style as plumage, as mating dance.

This heady and maybe deliberately contradictory mixture was all to the good. It allowed Vance to sympathize with and work with a variety of writers. It took him in the direction of encouragement. It took him away from censure and even the slightest unconscious hint that he expected imitation, personal or artistic.

There's an old adage: praise in public, censure in private. In workshop sessions Vance always discovered admirable qualities in a piece of writing, no matter how woefully it might fail in other aspects. I remember a day when a very heavy Germanic story was being discussed in class. The writer had truly out-Manned the great Thomas in long and ponderous sentences. For the student apostles of the well made story and clean prose criticizing this piece was like shooting fish in a barrel. But Vance put a quick stop to the carnage, not by defending the story where it was weak but by setting us an exegetical task: what did the story mean, what was the writer trying to accomplish? The conversation changed dramatically. Suddenly the thing was terrifically interesting. Taking my cue from Vance, I have always striven to get students to criticize fiction on its own terms, not according to some generalized canons of taste. (Vance would later teach a seminar on Mann, and I often wondered if that day's talk might have influenced him in that decision.) Vance never censured at all, in public or private. But in one-on-one conferences with students he could find a way to help the writer see what was wrong. Bill Murray, who worked on his prize-winning novel *Where Down the Blind Are Driven* with Vance, remembers it this way:

> I thought I'd finished a novel once. He invited me out to North Liberty, where he was living then. We sat in the living room with the manuscript on the table. Tina brought beer. For a couple of hours he went over my novel page by page, until I thought it was a piece of shit. When he finished he said, "Pretty good piece of work. You ought to send it out." I was drained, but I knew I had a lesson from a master. I just wanted to get home and get back to work on the manuscript.

In my case Vance had a much harder job to do. I thought I was a novelist at the time, when in fact I needed to be writing short stories. Consequently, there was nothing Vance could do to help me pull those long misshapen manuscripts out of the fire. What he could do was keep on teaching me the smaller things — how to change lumpish exposition into dramatic dialogue, how to modulate my prose so the whole bloody thing wasn't pitched at an unsustainable register of high southern rhetoric, that kind of thing.

So that was Vance's generosity and his gift — to figure out where the writer was at a given moment and offer help at the appropriate level.

A colleague of mine, a teacher of writing, often sits in the middle of a class and writes on a sheet that is projected onto a screen — does the whole thing, sucks his pencil, doodles, scratches out, produces illegible marginalia, suddenly hits his stride for several very fluid sentences, etc. Obviously he wants his students to see the kind of messy process writing often is. Vance never did just that, but he would often share a little piece of his own writing and recount the endless transformations he'd had to work through in order to get it into its present form, analyzing the roots of the difficulty, the misconceptions or technical miscues that lay behind the mistaken drafts. In this way he generously assured us that such misdirections were normal and not necessarily unrecoverable, though he also told the story of his second ruinous unpublishable novel.

And, of course, there were his published fictions for us to read — works of great interest, full of instruction for the novice writer. Three had a powerful effect on me, but not in close correlation with my admiration for them. *The Violated* I admired most — for its amazing reach, the number of strands it wove together, the constant resonance of the performance of *Hamlet* that gives it its center, its close observation of post–World War II manners and obsessions, the awful redolence of war, and much else. But it seemed to me a book so beyond my compass that I could not then make much use of it in my writing, except to acknowledge the continuing power of American naturalism and realism. In short, it was a book that described a place I might never be — though it probably was for others, perhaps Tom Williams, a place of immediate aspiration. In *The Confessions of a Spent Youth* Vance taught me that if you will only be gritty enough you can be downright Dickensian in your profound sympathy with your own human creations. Of all the stories in that book "The Poozle Dreamers" demonstrates this best for me. But finally the chapter from *Now Playing at Canterbury* entitled "The Fastest Jeep in the World" remains my favorite Bourjaily writing, though he has done some fine things since. In that narrative he achieves tremendous drive and tempo and at the same time delivers the incredible fascination and horror that attach themselves to a true *femme fatale*. And here Vance taught me that storytelling, realism, and myth can all inhabit the same fiction, and that was a lesson I truly could put to use in my own writing.

But maybe the most important lesson that Vance taught in his own writing was simply the necessity of constant dedication and immersion. When you were with Vance you knew that writing was not a sometime thing.

Many will say that writing cannot really be taught. Either the tyro has it or doesn't. ("You can't make a silk purse out of a sow's ear" was Paul Engle's way of putting it, but he didn't act as though he fully believed it, working hard to make a poet out of anybody who wanted to give it a shot.) This, of course, is a specific version of the ancient nature-versus-nurture dichotomy, and so it's a fractional truth. But to the extent that writing can be taught, only a fraction of that teaching is likely to take place in the classroom. The rest takes place wherever the students meet each other or wherever students and faculty gather. One of the great strengths of the Iowa Writers' Workshop in the days I spent there was the generosity of the faculty in spending time with students outside of class, not just in formal conferences but in bars, at parties, around poker tables, hunting or fishing.

The poker table was for me the most memorable of these sites. There were changes in the players over time, of course, but those of my days were principally Vance, Don Justice, Kim Merker, Peter Everwine, Bill Murray, and later Mark Strand, Phil Roth, and Kurt

Vonnegut. Why would a poker game help a writer? Obviously not because of some arcane analogy between gaming and writing. In fact poker was not the substance of our intercourse. It was the occasion. The substance — as evidenced in odd scraps of conversation, little quoting matches, comic allusions, and the like — was writing, and the camaraderie of being together as writers. Words, words, words, and frankly an enormous lot of b-s, but writing comes out of words and comes out of the ability to imagine oneself seriously as a writer. Vance was enormously appreciative of the chatter, and a deft contributor himself. Though my writing was going badly, I was with other writers. Ergo I was a writer. Vance helped me to see that I wouldn't have been at that table unless I was a writer. If I failed then, it wouldn't be forever.

Maybe the most memorable nongambling extracurricular activity I had with Vance was helping him one day entertain Sir Charles P. Snow, just then at the height of his powers, probably past the middle of the *Strangers and Brothers* series. Well, what was the appropriate thing to do with a British knight in Iowa? Why take him out in a muddy field with a dog and a student writer and shoot skeet and talk about literature and science and such stuff between shots? (Sir Charles declined to shoot but admired our ability to shatter the sky-borne clay.) And then later, of course, give him some wine the Amish made out of rhubarb — called something like *Peischtingel.* This latter was maybe taking the local color thing a little too far, for it was clear from his novels that Sir Charles at Cambridge drank good stuff — Montrachet, Gevrey-Chambertin, that kind of thing. He nevertheless remained knightly, noting only that while the substance was interesting, it probably should not be called wine. The next day Vance brought him to class for a discussion of a story by Tom Williams about a buck that invaded a general store somewhere in Maine or New Hampshire and tore the place all to hell — sort of a New England version of Faulkner's "Spotted Horses." Sir Charles professed to admire the story and, indeed, the whole workshop idea, only noting that he thought it would be perhaps more useful for more advanced writers.

Was there a hint of mischievousness in Vance's hosting of Sir Charles? I don't know for sure, but I certainly felt that I'd been let in on something pretty grand and richly comic at the same time.

Vance's tutelage of me could not always have been terrifically easy or satisfying. I was pretty naive — straight out of the navy, a believer in the great Pax Americana, ignorant of the social and political contexts of my writing, not a shred of understanding about the publishing world and the rapidly changing audience for the novel. Still, Vance persevered with me and directed my dissertation, a novel-length manuscript. He said at the time, in the gentlest way possible, that he thought perhaps I had not understood my own intentions perfectly. I thought that an odd thing to say then, but he was right. I didn't understand the piece. I came to see that later.

The year after I left Iowa a collection of mine won the Associated Writing Program's short fiction prize. Vance wrote me a lovely letter: I had discovered my rightful subjects, my own voice. Perhaps so, at last, after his monumental sufferance with me, though he wrote not a word of that. It is a great mystery how any of us make these discoveries. But I certainly wouldn't have pushed on through those wretched thickets of formless ersatz southern prose and kept on writing if I hadn't had Vance as mentor and friend — unless I had found somebody very much like him, and that seems unlikely. Odd but common how a time, a place, and a person will stand in memory as something absolutely inevitable, something totally outside the ordinary contingencies of life.

Kurt Vonnegut

Waltzing with the Black Crayon

---

*Paul Engle should get a posthumous medal from the Coast
Guard for all the lives he saved.*
—*Kurt Vonnegut at the memorial service for the
  founder of the Iowa Writers' Workshop*

I

My side of this story begins in London in the summer of 1966
when my English husband of less than one year was running an
experiment on me in our Chelsea garden. We were sitting in the
shade of a mulberry tree so ancient its branches had to be propped
up with stakes. Hoping to root out the source of my unhappiness,
Ian was asking me the same question over and over again.

Ian was a medical doctor who had switched to psychotherapy.
An independent sort, he took inspiration from unorthodox sources.
The present inquisition that I was willingly undergoing was one he
had borrowed from scientology. The auditor asked the client the
same question until the latter answered the truth. For this process
the scientologists used something called an E-meter, a poor cousin
to the lie detector, devised from two seven-ounce V-8 juice cans
stripped of their labels and wired to a galvanometer. When the
client clutching the cans finally spoke the truth, the needle on the
meter stopped jerking around and floated freely. The client was
supposed to feel a floating sense of relief as well.

We weren't using the apparatus. Ian said he could read me as
accurately as any V-8 juice cans could. He kept asking the agreed-
upon question, pushing the truth to the surface. It was like having
a well-intentioned person firmly squeezing a pimple.

Then suddenly I answered truly, the pimple burst, I felt a surge of release, and we agreed that the experiment had been a success. It had indeed. Within the month I had left England. Three months later I was living in a shabby-genteel hotel on Manhattan's East Side, walking to work every morning to my fact-checking job at the *Saturday Evening Post*. In between phone calls to the Farmers Federation ("I'm in the research department at the *Saturday Evening Post*; can you tell me whether a cow has four or six udders?") or the Air Force ("Colonel, is it true that the Delta Dagger can be off the ground in three seconds?"), I typed furtively on a lengthening story about a newly married couple's wretched vacation in Majorca with the doctor-husband's disturbed child. In the *Post*'s morgue, I read a back issue feature on the Iowa Writers' Workshop, where people like Flannery O'Connor had flowered into their potential. At night I lay in my bumpy bed at the Pickwick Arms and read library books chosen to keep up my courage (*Invisible Man*, all of Henry Miller, and a caustically funny fabulist of the current state of the planet Earth named Kurt Vonnegut, Jr.). I was intrigued by the "Junior" and wondered what the father was like; I also wondered about the woman I shared a bathroom with. She wept a lot and her bowels were all to pieces. I never did see her. I came to think of her as a doppelganger who had sense enough to be appalled and terrified by what I had done.

"Why can't you be a writer?" my husband had asked, about forty times in a row, under the mulberry tree in our garden in Chelsea.

"Because I'm afraid I might fail," I admitted at last. And forthwith left him, and stepped off onto empty space.

My life during that Manhattan autumn wore all the outward signs of foolishness and failure. I was twenty-nine years old, with a second defaulted marriage behind me, not one penny in the bank, and a single completed short story about an English vicar who sees God, writes a book, and goes on an American book tour (this was for a writing assignment at the London City Literary Institute, where I had met my second husband). And not even a bathroom to myself.

Yet, below the grid of this quotidian reality on which I marched back and forth between Pickwick Arms and *Saturday Evening Post*, I felt frequent bracing updrafts from an ulterior psychic stream pulsing stubbornly along toward its own destination. My old energy had returned, that elated focus I had experienced in my early twenties when I had boarded a freighter for Europe because that's where I presumed Americans had to go in order to turn into writers.

Surprises happened daily in New York. Many of them bore the quality of augury or plot. Even when they were awful ones, they took on the heightened significance of character-building episodes in a narrative. My passport, along with my wallet, was stolen from my office at the *Post*. I reported the theft to the police, but did nothing about getting a new passport. A kindly civilized man took me out to a fine dinner, then gave me a tour of his office and suddenly threw himself on me. I could have pushed him aside, or simply run for the elevator, but instead heard an aria of crisp, vile epithets issue eloquently from my mouth. He looked aghast and fled from *me*.

An uncle in Alabama died and left me $5,000, meant to be a friendly slap because I had neglected him (my cousin got two digits more than I). Then a friend I met in Europe wrote me out of the blue, announcing that she was now in Iowa City, enrolled in the Writers' Workshop: why didn't I come out, too? I quit my job, checked out of the Pickwick Arms, and boarded an airplane that flew right into the middle of an Iowa snowstorm and dropped me into more white empty space than I had even seen in my life. Naturally, the airline had lost all my luggage.

II

Iowa was one of the most exciting influences of my life. And it was an accident, like everything else in the Sixties . . .
— *Kurt Vonnegut reminiscing with Gail Godwin on*
    December 11, 1997, at his home on East 48th St. in Manhattan.

"You ask what I would have done if I hadn't gone to Iowa," mused Vonnegut. "Died of boredom, I guess. I was *elated* when George Starbuck called me from Iowa in August of 1965. Robert

Lowell had backed out at the last minute, and they needed another teacher in the workshop. Paul Engle didn't know my work, most people thought I was a science-fiction writer, but George was my friend. And the job came with a salary. For that I would have joined the paratroopers. Up until then I had been stuck in a house on Cape Cod with six kids. Iowa in contrast was a party. Everybody in the workshop was so interesting. There was a war on, and we had draft dodgers, and, no offense meant, we even had women who'd been married and divorced. By the way, what ever happened to that disturbed little boy in your first novel?"

"You mean the real person?" I said.

"Sure, the real person."

"Oh, he grew up and went to Oxford, and . . ."

Kurt started to laugh.

"Wait a minute, I'm not finished. He got a double first in math and philosophy."

"Then he didn't have a screw loose, after all."

"No, I think he was just mad as hell."

"The only surprise was," Kurt went on with his reminiscing, "that when I got out to Iowa, I learned I was also expected to teach a course in fiction. I had majored in chemistry at Cornell and anthropology at the University of Chicago. Well, I decided I was supposed to teach technique, so I picked some books and then the class and I set out to discover together how the trick was done. We did *Dubliners, Treasure Island, Invisible Man,* and, let's see, *Madame Bovary,* and *Alice in Wonderland,* and some Chekhov stories.

"The first thing I told my students about writing was: you've got to take care of your reader. The average age of you guys was about twenty-eight. You'd been developed socially and you knew how to dance. All I tried to do was impress upon you that you had to be a good date as a writer. You had to be reader-friendly. The last story in *Dubliners,* 'The Dead,' is *not* reader-friendly. In the first two pages, you've met nine people. *You must not do this!*

"And you've got to give your reader familiar props along the way. In *Alice in Wonderland,* remember, when she's falling down the hole there are all these familiar, comforting objects along the sides: cupboards and bookshelves, and maps. Orange marmalade . . .

"Another thing we discovered about technique: If you want to write a book about politics, don't introduce a love-element, or it will take over the story and the story *ends* when the couple gets together. If your purpose is something else — as it was for Ralph Ellison — you're better off without the love element. And he was.

"Another rule I tried to impress upon you: *MAKE YOUR CHARACTER WANT SOMETHING*. There was a nun in one of my workshop sections who wrote a wonderful story about this nun who goes through an entire day with a piece of dental floss stuck in her teeth. (Laughter.) All you guys were reaching around in your mouths while we were discussing that story. The character in that story *wanted* something!

"Then there was this Hungarian student. I think he was there the year before you arrived. He had gotten out during the revolution and come over here and gone to an American university. He kept turning in these tepid stories about love affairs in American dormitories. I finally told him in a conference, 'Look, these are too tame. Try something a little more dramatic.' He went away and came back with a story that was pure dynamite, about this Hungarian nobleman in World War II who goes around in his van rescuing the wounded from the battlefields. Well, he's just rescued a soldier who's had both legs blown off and he's carrying him back to the van when the Germans come over the hill in retreat. They take his van and supplies and leave him there in the middle of nowhere with a double amputee in his arms. It was an absolutely *riveting* story. The trouble was, it was written by someone else. After that, he vanished from the workshop.

"Of course I had students who refused to take my advice. Remember Ronnie ———? She turned in a story whose first sentence was, 'Listen, you dumb motherfuckers.' I said, 'Listen, Ronnie, you just can't *do* that.' But she did.

"Once the Iowa legislature tried to close us down because a student — not Ronnie — had used 'fuck' in a story. But they couldn't touch us. We had private money supporting the workshop. The citizens of Iowa weren't paying anything for us. That was Paul Engle's doing. He was a hell of a good money-raiser. His father had been a horse trader, and when Paul was a boy he was the one who stuck the ginger up the horses' behinds just before they were shown."

III

I write with a big black crayon, you know, grasped in a grubby, kindergarten fist. You're more of an impressionist. If you want to kind of try what I do, take life seriously but none of the people in it. The people are fools and I say so the instant they're onstage. I don't let them prove it slowly.
— *letter from Kurt Vonnegut, West Barnstable, Massachusetts, to Gail Godwin, still in Iowa City, November 25, 1967.*

When I arrived in January of 1967 in the snowstorm, Kurt Vonnegut was beginning the last semester of his second and final teaching year in the workshop. He already had one foot out the door. He had won a Guggenheim and would soon be on his way to Germany to refresh his memory for his novel-in-progress about being an American prisoner of war during the firebombing of Dresden, *Slaughterhouse Five*. I had wanted the creator of Eliot Rosewater and none other to read my (now novella-length) story about the wretched couple and the disturbed little boy driving each other crazy in Majorca, but there was a brief bout of despair: Vonnegut had become so in demand that his workshop section was overflowing. Sorry, but you'll have to choose someone else.

Then, at the last minute, Vonnegut generously agreed to take on an extra section because I was not the only one in despair.

The sections met once a week, and we critiqued one another's mimeographed work. Jane Barnes, whose forte was social satire, turned in a devilishly funny story called "Coming of Age in Washington, D.C." She wore big swooping hats to the English building and was engaged to another Vonnegut student, John Casey. She had an enviable collection of rejection letters from none other than Roger Angell at the *New Yorker*. Inspired by her example, I was soon amassing a similar collection of letters from Angell myself.

("Dear Miss Godwin, I am sorry to disappoint you again, but you are getting better and better...") Several years later, Jane, who was by then married to John Casey, published an impressive fictional autobiography of Lenin's wife, *I, Krupskaya.*

In the spring of 1967, John Casey was another stimulant to my ambition. He had a novel *under option* by a major publisher. He would sometimes read his friends enticing little snatches from this work-in-progress, sophisticated exchanges between East Coast college kids. I don't know what became of that book, but he later published a dream of a novel set in Iowa, *An American Romance,* and went on to win the 1989 National Book Award for his novel *Spartina,* whose world is a far cry from the college venue of witty smoothies.

Another Vonnegut student was John Irving, already married and with a small son. At Irving's twenty-fifth birthday party, he played his guests a tape of the music for the film score of his first novel, *Setting Free the Bears.* He hadn't finished the novel, no publisher or film person had laid eyes on it, but John had chosen the music he wanted. ("It was from Carl Orff's *Carmina Burana,*" John Irving recalled thirty years later. "I often did that, picked the music for the film before I finished the book. Call it my mayhem confidence.")

"I knew John Irving would make it big," said Kurt as we reminisced. "He was always just so preposterously *funny!* And John Casey, you know, we gave him that American Academy grant for a three-year stipend, and the three years are up and he's just turned in an eleven-hundred-page novel. I have this little device on my telephone that measures the state of people's happiness, and John sounded really *up.* And you, you've become a big shot."

"I don't feel like a big shot. Writing gets harder and harder."

"It's supposed to," Kurt said.

("Can you remember what it was like, working on *Setting Free the Bears* with Kurt at the workshop?" I asked John Irving.

"Oh, for instance, he told me that I was interested in a certain young woman's underwear to an excess of what my readers would be," said John.

"And did you take his advice?"

"Not to the degree that I probably should have," Irving wryly admitted. "But he also said I wrote with so much enthusiasm. He told me, 'Never lose that enthusiasm about your work. So many writers are *unenthusiastic.*'")

The forty-five-year-old Vonnegut of my own conferences, his gangly length tilted back in a swivel chair, desert boots on the metal desk, cigarette and ashtray never out of sight, looked much as he does now at seventy-five, except for the white mustache and a few extra rumples in the face. In those one-to-one sessions, he was loose and easy as a Zen master. He had read my novella-length story, later to become *The Perfectionists*, about the ill-matched couple and the disturbed little boy driving one another berserk on a Spanish island, and had written comments in light pencil in the margins: "Lovely." "First-rate." Or: "No: sandbagging flashback!"

"I'm thinking of expanding it into a novel," I said during one conference. "What do you think?"

"I think it's just great as it is," Vonnegut said.

In our next conference I told him I had decided to go ahead and turn it into a novel anyway.

"Great idea," he exclaimed enthusiastically.

"You were different," I told Kurt Vonnegut in our reminiscing session in December of 1997, the end of the twentieth century in our faces, a whole new millennium about to roll over. I had just delivered my tenth novel to my publisher. He was winding down his book tour for *Time-Quake*, a narrative summary, with autobiographical digressions, about an unfinished novel that he got tired of writing, in which we were forced to relive an entire decade all over again, making the same mistakes. Vonnegut had announced that *Time-Quake* would be his final novel.

"All my books are in print, and I have nothing else to say. There are lots of talented young artists out there, let them have their chance."

I protested.

"Oh, well," he conceded, with a strange smile. "If you must know, I have one more novel in me. You want to hear it? It's about my affair with O. J. Simpson. I met him in a locker room once in Buffalo and asked him to sign my football, not realizing that this was a code for propositioning someone. . . ."

I had fallen for it, as other protesters before me surely had done.

"I think of you as a prophet like Jonah," I told Vonnegut. "You say woe to the planet and draw dire scenarios, and people see their awful, ridiculous selves, and so God relents and decides to keep things going a little longer."

(John Irving tells me there's a current bumper sticker with the globe on a spit, roasting over a fire, with a Vonnegut quote underneath: "WE COULD HAVE SAVED IT BUT WE WERE TOO DARN CHEAP AND LAZY.")

"Well, the whale has certainly spit me up in some odd places," Kurt acknowledged.

"When we were your students, you let us work it out for ourselves," I told him. "Yet your being there for us did the trick. After you left Iowa, the teachers I had were — they had their own agendas."

(One of them explained to me he couldn't read my 250-page manuscript of *The Perfectionists* until duck hunting season was over. After he read it, on a flight to California, he had to admit he was lukewarm. I tried to pin him down to specifics, but he was vague. "Do you think I'll ever make it?" I finally demanded at the end of our conference. "Gee, Gail. How old are you?" "Thirty," I said. He squinted at his watch as though consulting an oracle. "Well, I don't know," he said, "I published my first novel at twenty-four.")

My teacher after that was a dynamic little magician who played writing games with us in class ("Today, we're going to be an Irish monk in the seventh century who has just unearthed an ancient manuscript that turns out to be written by . . . SCHEHEREZADE! Are you ready?")

I loved his classes, but on December 11, 1968, the day after my new agent, John Hawkins, sold the third draft of *The Perfectionists* to David Segal at Harper & Row, my little magician told me in a private conference that he was happy for me, but also sad. He had been urging me toward more experimental sleights of hand, and warned me that if I persisted in this dogged attention to reality I might end up like . . . well, someone like John Updike.)

"All I did in those private conferences with you guys," recalled Kurt, thirty years later, "was to say, '*Trust me*. What I'm going to do now is open your mouth, very gently, with these two fingers, and then I'm going to reach in — being very careful not to bruise your epiglottis — and catch hold of this little tape inside you and slowly, very carefully and gently, pull it out of you. It's your tape, and it's the only tape like that in the world.'"

(When I quoted Vonnegut's "tape" theory to John Irving and asked John if he would care to sum up the essence of the tape that had come out of Kurt Vonnegut's mouth, he thought a minute and then said: "Irreverence for human beings and institutions. Kindness for individuals.")

IV

Dearest Gail —

I thank you for your kind remarks about Jailbird. *We try to run a class operation here, but fail more often than not. The luckiest thing I ever did was to teach at Iowa for those two years. I picked up a very classy extended family that way. It made you and John and John and some others quality relatives of mine for life. I used to be in this trade all alone. Suddenly I was a member of a really great gang. I never tire of asking you and the rest, "How goes it?" If you are ever in trouble, I will take you in.*

— Kurt Vonnegut in New York City to Gail Godwin in
Woodstock, N.Y., September 14, 1979.

Myths & Texts

The Emergence of the Writers' Workshop

George Cram Cook, the eccentric poet and offbeat teacher — and former member of the Tabard writing club — probably deserves the honor of offering the first creative writing course at Iowa. In the spring of 1896, he offered a "Verse-making Class" in which the students practiced writing heroic couplets, Spenserian stanzas, and other common forms of English poetry, and engaged in discussions of artistic questions. The class was open only to those who had taken Cook's advanced course in prose style. In short, "Verse-making" was a high-level, relatively informal course for those who had already demonstrated skill with words.

With a new title, "Versification," Cook continued the course until he left Iowa in the spring of 1899. But there was no hiatus in the English department's attention to creative writing. In the fall of that year Clarke Fisher Ansley arrived as cochair of the department and immediately assigned himself a two-semester course in advanced composition, which included practice in the short story form. When Ansley became the sole head of the department in 1900–01, he assigned Sam Sloan to teach Cook's former course in poetry writing and a course in the short story. In 1902–03, when Sloan began concentrating on eighteenth- and nineteenth-century English literature, Percival Hunt took over the short story course and held it until he left Iowa for Pittsburgh in 1921. Almost as though he were teaching poetry writing, Hunt insisted on careful attention in narrative writing to structure and to the color and connotations of the individual words.

Hunt's classes, however, did not fully anticipate the workshop format, for they included little student participation. That came when Edwin Ford Piper arrived on campus in 1905 and took over the course entitled "Poetics." In this course Piper had his students evaluate their own work, not only in scheduled classroom discussions but also in Monday afternoon and occasional Saturday morning meetings as well. Ansley varied the pattern somewhat in 1907 when he offered a course in advanced writing in which he met the students in individual conferences and adapted the assignments to their individual needs.

Cook, Ansley, Hunt, Piper, John T. Frederick, and Frank Luther Mott — these were the true fathers of the Iowa creative writing program. Cook was the first to teach a course in the subject, but he stayed at Iowa too short a time to be a strong influence. As head of the department, Ansley not only taught the subject but brought in such talented specialists as Piper in poetry, Hunt and Frederick in fiction, and Sowers in drama (though drama writing never featured strongly in the English department). Piper played an especially important role because not only was he an extraordinarily imaginative writer and teacher, but he worked actively with Dean Carl E. Seashore in persuading the graduate faculty to award graduate credit for accomplishments in creative work and to accept creative accomplishments in lieu of scholarly theses and dissertations. . . .

The point worth repeating is that creative writing was an important part of the English curriculum before Norman Foerster arrived in 1930. But it might not have evolved into the semi-autonomous Writers' Workshop, at least not so quickly as it did, without the strong push that Foerster gave it. The chief reason for Foerster's support of creative writing is clear: he believed that the creative writer must by the nature of his art additionally be a literary critic. As Wilbur L. Schramm put it in his chapter on "Imaginative Writing" in *Literary Scholarship*, a volume edited by Foerster, "a (writer) teaches himself to write by a process of constant self-criticism. If he is a thoughtful writer, he will soon proceed from artistic evaluation to a judgment of ideas as well, for he will perceive the need of both art and wisdom. And thus he will join with his natural ally, the critic, to shift the balance of interest in the graduate study of literature away from history and research, back toward art and philosophy, toward an interest in the true as well as the new. . . ." Thus Foerster looked for more support among those in the department who taught creative writing than he did among those who taught literary history. He was furious when he did not get it. The trouble was that those who headed the work in creative writing when Foerster arrived at Iowa—Piper, Sloan, Mott, and Frederick—were regionalists who were interested in writing that found its wellsprings primarily in the culture of the Midwest. Although they welcomed Foerster's support for imaginative writing, they were less than enthusiastic about, as the regional artist Grant Wood put it, Foerster's "disproportionate emphasis on cultures of the remote past" and his tendency "to remain aristocratically aloof from the life of the people at large." Foerster, in turn, made it clear that he had no high regard for the regionalist. Piper he called a "fifth-rate" poet, and he refused to recognize Piper's service in making creative writing an acceptable academic subject.

Although Piper's graduate writing seminar had been informally called a workshop, it was not until after he died in the spring of 1939 that his course became formally titled "Writers' Workshop, credit arranged." The catalog description read: "Group conferences and individual conferences. Consult Professor Schramm for permission to register. Associate Professor Schramm; Professor Mott; Associate Professor Sower: Mr. Engle; Mr. Knight." No one in 1939 anticipated that the term "workshop" would become internationally employed, or that the Iowa workshop, though remaining within the department, would become a semiautonomous unit whose public reputation would outstrip that of the department itself. Wilbur Schramm continued as director of the workshop until 1943, when he took over the journalism school and Paul Engle became director of the workshop. It was Engle, with his indefatigable drive, entrepreneurial skill, and boyish enthusiasm, who brought the workshop its fame and international attention.

Because there has been confusion about who "founded" the workshop, a brief summary may be in order. For at least one good reason, Edwin Ford Piper deserves the honor of being called the founder because he established the workshop format; but in the catalogs the term was never applied to any of his classes. Wilbur Schramm directed the first seminar formally called the Writers'

Workshop in a university catalog. . . . Furthermore, it was during his period that the term came to signify not a single course but the whole body of courses devoted to creative writing. So with reason Schramm may be called the founder.

By 1961 the Writers' Workshop included undergraduate and graduate workshops in poetry and fiction as well as undergraduate courses called Understanding Poetry and Understanding Fiction, graduate courses called Forms and Theory of Fiction and Fiction Writing, and seminars called Problems in Modern Poetry and Contemporary Authors. Ranking faculty members included Engle, Vance Bourjaily, Donald Justice, and Ray B. West, who had brought with him his *Western Review*. Others who were on the workshop staff before 1961 included Robert Penn Warren, Hansford Martin, Andrew Lytle, R. V. Cassill, Robie Macauley, William Stafford, Robert Lowell, Walter Van Tilburg Clark, Warren Carrier, John Berryman, Thomas Mabry, Marguerite Young, Harvey Swados, George P. Elliot, Curtis Harnack, Hortense Calisher, and Bienvenido Santos.

Flannery O'Connor
in the Writers' Workshop

My first impression of Flannery O'Connor was that she looked too young and too shy to be a writer. We were graduate students at the University of Iowa and members of Paul Engle's Writers' Workshop during the fall and spring semester of 1947 and 1948. On the opening day of class, Flannery was sitting alone in the front row, over against the wall. She was wearing what I was soon to think of as her "uniform" for that year: plain gray skirt and neatly ironed silkish blouse, nylon stockings and penny brown loafers. Her only makeup was a trace of lipstick. Elizabeth Hardwick once described her as "like some quiet, puritanical convent girl from the harsh provinces of Canada," and there was something of the convent about Flannery that day — a certain intentness in the slight girlish figure which set her apart from the rest of us. She seemed out of place in that room composed mostly of veterans returned from World War II. Flannery was only twenty-two years old then, but she could easily have passed for seventeen or eighteen.

I don't believe she was to change very much in the next seventeen years before her death. In the later photographs, showing her on the aluminum crutches that became a permanent part of her life, there remains that same schoolgirl freshness, a young gentleness in her face and expression. Only in the unsmiling eyes of the stern self-portrait is there evidence of the Flannery who wrote blood-curdling fiction.

It was her isolation from the other "writers" in the class that first drew me to her, and soon that semester I moved to the empty seat beside her. We and one other girl, Clyde McCleod (her father had named her Clyde), were the only women in the workshop that year.

Most of the others, the former GIs, were tuned in to New Criticism theories, and many sensitive young writers got shot down by the heavy onslaught of their critical fire. Stories were dissected like so many literary specimens; few stood up under the minute probing. Many years later when Flannery was speaking to a writing class at Hollins College in Virginia, I'm sure she was remembering those workshop sessions at Iowa when she said, "Every time a story of mine appears in a freshman anthology, I have a vision of it, with its little organs laid open, like a frog in a bottle."

Sometime late that first semester I learned that Flannery had received the M.F.A. degree the year before and that she had already published one story. "The Geranium," the title story in her M.F.A. thesis, had appeared in *Accent* in the summer of 1946. And "The Train," also from the thesis, was scheduled to come out in the *Sewanee Review* the next spring. Flannery was staying on at Iowa for another year because Paul Engle had gotten her a grant of money to live on while she worked on her first novel. The one person I had thought to look least like a writer on the opening day of workshop had turned out to be the most promising writer there! From then on, I may have looked forward more to sitting beside Flannery than to the workshop itself which, in those days, was something like going to a good movie. Writers read their own stories, sitting at the front of the room.

Flannery never entered into the workshop discussions. I heard that when she was first in the workshop in 1945, before she had published anything, her stories had not been well received and she had not tried to defend them. The only comment I ever heard her make in class was the next spring. Andrew Lytle was in charge that semester during Paul Engle's absence from campus, and he asked her what she thought of the story we were discussing that day. By then, most of the students knew she was already a published writer; everyone in the room wanted to hear what she would say. In a perfectly deadpan voice, addressing herself to the general emptiness of the front of the room, came her laconic reply: "I'd say the description of the crocodile in there was real good." The irony of Flannery's statement lay in the fact that the crocodile was the best thing in the story, but it had absolutely no meaning in the texture of the story itself. She had said all there was to say — but she would never have offered that much if Mr. Lytle hadn't asked her.

I saw Flannery very little that fall except at the Monday afternoon workshop sessions and occasionally on Sunday noon at the Mad Hatter Tea Room, that used to be up over Bremer's clothing store, where I worked as salad girl. Flannery's boardinghouse didn't serve meals on Sunday, and so she came there. I can remember meeting her only twice on the campus or the street. Once she was going to the library to check out *Dead Souls*. She said Robie Macauley recommended that book as one every writer should read, "so I reckon I'd better do it." (Years later she was to say that she supposed Gogol was an influence.) And the other time she was coming out of Woolworths' Five and Ten Cent Store where she had bought one cake of Palmolive soap. (I've thought about that single purchase since then, and it seems to me it says something about the uncluttered life she always lived. I doubt if Flannery ever bought two of anything at one time, unless it were peacocks or swans or bantam chicks. Her room at Iowa, when I saw it that one time, expressed the same kind of monastic simplicity: the neatly made bed, the typewriter waiting on the desk. There was nothing extraneous in that room except for a box of vanilla wafers beside the typewriter. She nibbled on cookies while she wrote, she said, because she didn't smoke.)

My friendship with Flannery continued the next semester. I would have liked to have gone to the movies with her or had a Coke with her, but it simply didn't occur to me that things like that could ever be a part of her life. I did, however, begin to consider myself her closest friend on the campus. Her favorite place to go in Iowa City was out to the city park. Once, I walked out there with her on an especially bleak February Sunday afternoon to look at the two sad and mangy bears, the raccoons, and the special foreign chickens they had. It seemed a particularly desultory thing to be doing, and I was puzzled at how completely absorbed and interested Flannery was that day looking at these things which I knew she'd looked at many times before. She was still working on the novel then, of course (which was to be *Wise Blood*), although she never talked about it, and I knew nothing at that time about the zoo and park scenes in that book until I read it a few years later. But, I also realize now, her fondness for the zoo went beyond the fact that she may have been getting "material" for her work. Years later, in letters to me, she was to recall the city park as almost the only asset Iowa City had to offer. The flowing letter begins with a comment on Iowa City housing and is dated December 28, 1952. She wrote:

> I remember those boarding houses in Iowa City very well and all the cold rooms I looked at. My landlady, Mrs. Guzeman (at 115 E. Bloomington Street), was not very fond of me because I stayed at home and required heat to be on — at least ON. It was never UP that I remember. When it was on you could smell it and I got to where I warmed up a little every time I smelled it. One of these days I would like to see Iowa City again, but only for the zoo where those game bantams were and the bears donated by the Iowa City Lions Club. I am raising peafowl myself. They are beautiful; and contrary and expensive but I justify the expense on the grounds that I don't smoke or drink liquor or chew tobacco or have any bad habits that cost money. . . . One of these days I hope they'll be all over the place. . . .

That spring in the workshop I heard Flannery read for the first time. It was a chapter from the novel she was working on and had made into a short story for the occasion (although it turned out to be for all time, since no trace of it ever turned up in either of her novels). She called the story "The Woman on the Stairs," and it was under this title that it was published the following year in the August 1949 *Tomorrow*. Although the story has since been described as perhaps the most purely comic of any of her stories, the odyssey of Ruby Hill on the stairs, this woman "shaped nearly like a funeral urn," proclaims the sorry human state which underlies most of her characters who suppose that they are in control of life and are calling all the shots.

In many of the stories Flannery was to write later, she permits a moment of vision to descend on the main character — very like the Joycean epiphany — in which he may see himself clearly for the first time. The moment of insight, when her characters see themselves as sinning beings, comes from the working of grace for them.

It is achieved through things which cannot be predicted. It is something mysterious which cannot be elucidated. Grace comes to the Grandmother of *A Good Man Is Hard to Find* in her recognition of the Misfit as her own child. It comes to Mr. Head of *The Artificial Nigger* through the artificial nigger, and to Mrs. Turpin of *Revelation* in the pigpen. But it does not come to Ruby Hill as she sits at the top of the stairs looking "down into the dark hole, down to the very bottom where she had started up so long ago," for she hears only the leery echo of her own empty words. Ruby Hill then may be one of Flannery O'Connor's truly damned characters, and the story, although exemplifying elements of the purely comic, becomes tragical in the sense that the character is denied any glimpse of self-understanding, and therefore salvation. She sits at the top of the stairs literally full of nothing, feeling the roll in her stomach "as if it were not in her stomach. It was as if it were out somewhere in nothing, out nowhere, resting and waiting with plenty of time."

But few, if any, of us knew that afternoon in the workshop when Flannery read this story that it was about original sin, that her vision embraced the early Christian concept of man's loss of innocence with rejection of his first parents from the Garden, that she really did believe in evil and damnation and redemption. We knew none of these things, and I, for one, did not even know that day — and not until several years later — that Flannery O'Connor was a Roman Catholic.

Why then were we so strangely moved by her reading that afternoon which I suppose was the most memorable Monday the workshop has ever had, before or since? As I remember her voice now, its slight southern drawl enhancing the country idiom she was just beginning to perfect and was always to use, both in her characters' dialogue and as a kind of indirect discourse, and giving a humorous reinforcement to the irony in that story, I realize that her stories are always intensely oral in the highest sense of the storytelling art. It is a great loss that no recordings were made of Flannery reading her fiction. But, of course, her voice alone could not account for the feeling we had that afternoon that we were in the presence of a significant writer.

I think now it was because her lonely fiction magnifies the drab and the colorless, and we were stirred to a recognition of ourselves in the human predicament. Flannery considered herself a realist above all else. Her characters, no matter how freakish and bizarre they may seem on the surface, or how commonplace and white trashy — no matter how unsettling — speak home dark truths and, if anything, become almost too lifelike. As Ruby Hill climbs the dark steep stairs, fighting off the knowledge of her pregnancy which she equates with death, so do we all in some lonely moment of our lives struggle with that old paradox that life begets death. We, too, live in the funeral "urns" of our bodies.

After Flannery finished reading the story, we sat there until Andrew Lytle gave meaning to our silence by saying workshop was over for the day. For once, there was not going to be any critical dissecting. Flannery disappeared out the door to go back to her room upstairs at Mrs. Guzeman's. Most of the others took off for the Brown Derby on Dubuque Street, which was the writers' hangout that semester. The workshop afternoon was over. That he had said nothing about Flannery's story was a tribute to her genius. But I and Clyde McCleod wanted there to be something more — some more tangible token of our admiration. We went around Iowa City on that late spring afternoon, walking into people's yards as if they were public domain, to gather arms full of flowering branches, taking only the most beautiful, and we carried them up to Flannery.

Chicken à la King

My wife and I came to the writing program at the University of Iowa in 1949. After a semester in a farmhouse in Coralville we were invited to live with Paul and Mary Engle in the house on Friendly Avenue, with my wife as a part-time babysitter for Sara and Munchie Engle and an assistant to Mary Engle in the entertaining of visiting literary firemen.

Paul and Mary were very used to and very kind to low-self-esteem M.A.'s. They had a dacha at Stone City, not far from Iowa City, a crumbling baronial pile on a hill in an amphitheater of abandoned rock quarries, without running water and with the usual Iowa four-holer out back. We often spent weekends there.

To visit the Engles at Stone City came John Crowe Ransom, editor of the *Kenyon Review*, an eminent poet and critic, and a fine old southern gentleman. It seemed to me that Robert E. Lee must have resembled Mr. Ransom, gentle in his demeanor, formal in dress, and steely in intelligence. In those days the southern mafia controlled the American literary establishment.

We were seated in lawn chairs on the lawn that sloped down to the river at Stone City, drinking the mint juleps Paul had constructed for the occasion. Sara Engle ambled up beside Mr. Ransom's lawn chair, maybe eight years old, cradling her doll to her skinny chest.

"And what is the dolly's name?" asked Mr. Ransom politely.

"This is the Royal baby," Sara said. "Sucking on the Royal tit."

The weekend was not over for Mr. Ransom. We all returned to Iowa City for a grand dinner party, to which the A-list of departmental and university honchos had been invited, with Mr. Ransom as guest of honor. Chicken à la king was the entree, and my wife and Mary Engle labored all afternoon over the makings. Mary had a Band-Aid on her finger for some minor cut, and it was discovered that the Band-Aid had become part of the chicken à la king. She and my wife went into serious overdrive mucking through the chicken looking for the Band-Aid. The children were recruited to the search. It became a grand and rather hysterical game, scooping up handfuls of chicken and sauce and pouring them through fingers, futilely. There was a forlorn hope that the Band-Aid had disappeared elsewhere.

At dinner my wife was seated next to the sage of Kenyon College. She was aghast to see, when the plates were being cleared, that despite the platoon of other academics at the table, it was on Mr. Ransom's plate that the little wad of Band-Aid had appeared.

Snapshots of Paul

Memories of Paul approach the quality of snapshots in a family album. He seems always to be traveling like a favorite uncle touring the world. Capturing a view of the man is more like sorting through postcards he has sent from one country or another.

1949, Spring. The *Des Moines Register and Tribune* publishes yet another article about the innovative Iowa Writers' Workshop. *Life* magazine follows suit with a story and a photo spread. One picture of students lounging on the grass around their instructor under a mammoth oak on the campus is particularly enticing. Writers and poets-to-be, they look to my high school girl eyes very much the chosen few, the bright and promising, the lucky ones who get to listen to and be heard by instructors who have actually published. And all for the cost of tuition to SUI — $50 a year in those days for in-state students. Paul was the Pied Piper who led them. After seeing the articles there was never any question about my going to the workshop. In spite of some long discussions with my wary father, I was headed to Iowa City, not Ames.

1949, Autumn. The Quonset huts by the river. Although as a freshman I found myself in a lesser writing class, my sights were always on the workshop. One day I found the courage to stop in when Paul happened to be behind the desk. Our talk was warm but brief as he was preparing to leave for a meeting up the hill. Still he took the time to make a telephone call and find me my first job in Iowa City, one I needed to help pay my expenses. It was a menial one but I was grateful for it. After that I always felt that Paul "knew who I was" and was "keeping an eye" on me. The way a good uncle does, gracefully.

1950. Paul finds me another job, this time tending his children. Paul, Mary, and the girls live in one of the unusual houses built, I believe, by a Mr. Black, east of town. There were several similar ones side by side, fieldstone fronts, built on various levels, imaginative and, it was said, very poorly built. Days spent there lent a romantic touch to my mundane student life in the dormitory. Visitors looking for either Mary or Paul occasionally added to the exotic mix. Included were various visiting firemen scheduled to speak at the workshop. Roethke and Auden are two I remember. Another, a tenor, kept me entertained with arias while I worked. Those days and that job happily showed me a far more exciting world than I would otherwise have known. After all, those were the days of locked dormitories and curfews. I had Paul to thank for it.

1952. The fiction workshop. My twin sister enters a story in a contest run by a little magazine published somewhere in the south. Since Paul has only been marginally involved in the meetings we have had to discuss our writing I am surprised to learn that he even knows about it. But he does. He singles her out for congratulations during a class session, and I feel it includes me too. We are both pleased and stunned. It is as if Paul is everywhere at once, knows everyone and everything.

1958. 49th and Fifth Avenue, New York. Paul is heading west, I'm heading east. In the middle of that thoroughfare we surprise each other. I've been living in the city since graduation (except for nine months in Europe where I married) and feel the city belongs to me. Nothing should surprise me and seldom does. But finding Paul in the middle of Fifth Avenue did. He seems on top of the world, striding into some lion's den of corporate America no doubt to ask for funds for the workshop. A quick squeeze. "How's the family? I'm meeting someone at General Electric for lunch."

"Can you come to dinner, Verlin and I would love to see you."

"I'll call later." And he's gone.

I didn't have a chance to tell him that I'd had a story accepted for publication. But somehow he knew. I received a congratulatory note from him later.

1960. We're renting Paul and Mary's house on Bayard Street for the summer while they are in Stone City. The Engles bought the house from a well-known doctor at University Hospital. There had been a scandal. The doctor's wife committed suicide in the master bedroom. I went to sleep every night remembering the story. By now we have three small, very active children and the house is both enormous and pretty fancy by our Greenwich Village standards. I spend much of the summer trying to keep the damage to a minimum. Our daughter, Erica, gets hold of some lipstick and decides to redecorate the imported French wallpaper. Verlin spends the summer attempting to erase the artwork.

Paul appears on workshop days on this errand or that, quickly in and out of his office in the chicken coop behind the house. These flashtrips bring me some trepidation; I'm worried about what the children have got into by now. Paul notices but never says anything about the mischief. He smiles, chats, and watches the kids trying tricks on the huge trampoline the Engles have left in the yard.

1962. The Memorial Union. A sit-down luncheon for 250 guests. Paul is hosting the gathering of several New York editors, Bennett Cerf among others. After introducing the featured guests on the podium he continues by naming everyone, table by table, person by person, around that enormous room until he has finally introduced every single soul by first and last name. It is only one example of his unusual memory that we all witnessed over the years but it was the one that impressed me most.

1964. Our farmhouse east of town on Route 6. Paul visits to talk to Verlin about "the workshop situation" as it became known to us. He had been invited many times for student-faculty parties but I am only remembering this visit. Serious. Soulful. Unhappy to see us leave.

1969. Cabot Street, Providence. A blizzard has hit in the early morning hours. Paul was expected, but we seriously think we will get a call saying he's decided to stay in New York or New Haven. Instead, I look out the living room window to see Paul trudging through the snow, having walked all the way from the downtown train station. He stays overnight, and we have a delightful visit catching up on gossip about Iowa City and hearing about his travels abroad.

1976. Iowa City. I've come through town with our daughter, Erica (the one with the artistic talent mentioned earlier), who is looking at colleges. Paul and Hualing greet us with all of the reminiscences of the earlier days, reminders of the people, students, faculty, foreign students, of our time at the workshop, making it difficult for Erica to consider any other school. I am reminded of my first meeting with Paul. I wonder but do not ask if he remembers that brief encounter. He has been instrumental in my college selection, my course selection, my education, and, by default, my marriage. Many serious and important choices in life. Full circle, I have brought Erica to meet him now that she is an adult. While she eventually chose to go to Michigan rather than Iowa, she did write a novel and won a Hopwood award for it. I have a feeling we didn't even need to tell Paul when that happened — he already knew.

How many people Paul has touched in such crucial ways is probably impossible to tell. But I feel flattered and grateful that I was among them.

Dylan Thomas at Iowa

I had never met Dylan Thomas. I had read his poems and knew him only through the Augustus John portrait that appeared in the New Directions volumes of his work. As I waited that early spring afternoon, in 1951, on the platform of the Santa Fe station in Iowa City, I wondered, as did my companions Robert Lowell and Robie Macauley, how I would know him. Dylan was coming to read at the University of Iowa that evening, and, because the Iowa state high school basketball tournament was being held in town that week and all the hotels were booked up, he was to stay with me in the handsome but old-fashioned house on Kirkwood Avenue that I rented from the widow of a former mathematics professor.

The plans for that first day were the usual ones for any visiting celebrity. We would go directly from the station to the Lowells' apartment for drinks, then to the Jefferson Hotel for dinner, then to the reading in the Senate Chamber of the Old Capitol Building, a simple, attractive stone structure that had housed the first terri- torial administration of Iowa in the mid-nineteenth century. After the reading, Dylan would be taken to the rooms of the local press club for beer and an informal meeting with members of the Writ- ers' Workshop, then home to sleep in a bedroom from which we had evicted our elder daughter.

These plans weighed a little heavily on me, because John Fred- erick Nims had called me the night before from Notre Dame to say that Dylan had just left there. He had arrived, John said, in terrible shape. The boys in Chicago had been feeding him boilermakers, and he had a tremendous hangover. "Keep him on beer," he ad- vised. "Dylan loves beer and gets along well on it." I consulted Lowell because the first drinking would be done at his place. "Non-sense!" he said. "Let him drink what he pleases." Lowell had told me a day or two earlier he hoped Dylan could be provoked into creating some scandalous fuss that would enliven the city. That was before we had learned that Dylan would not be in Iowa City just overnight, as was customary with most such visitors, but would stay for just one day short of two weeks.

John Malcolm Brinnin, who was sponsoring Dylan on his tour, had written me after I had agreed to house Dylan, saying that Dylan's teeth were in very bad shape. He had two weeks free after the Iowa stop, and Brinnin hoped I could find a local dentist to look at them, perhaps repair them, at least patch them up a bit. I felt sure that we could get some dental work done at the Iowa School of Dentistry and told Brinnin so, but my wife was more than a little dismayed to hear that the guest she had accepted for an overnight stay was now expecting to remain for two weeks. . . .

When the train from Chicago slowed for its brief stop in Iowa City, I scanned all the doorways without seeing anyone remotely resembling the portrait by Augustus John. Fortunately, when it stopped, few passengers got off. Dylan was immediately recognizable. He didn't resemble anyone I could conceivably have envisioned, but he was the only passenger who stood, duffel bag in hands, with a slightly bewildered look on his face. Although he was then only thirty-six, he resembled more my wife's Yorkshire-born grandfather than he did the famous portrait. He was shorter than he had appeared when he was the youth in the picture. His body had rounded out and his features had thickened. He wore a brown tweed suit with an almost orange cast, somewhat faded and rumpled. He had obviously been drinking on the train, but the unsteadiness was in his body, not his eyes, which were blue and clear. As I approached, his full lips twisted into a shy grin.

"So this is Iowa?"

I am not sure these were his exact words, but they were something as innocuous as this, said with a lightly ironic detachment that one could respond to as one wished.

I introduced Lowell and Macauley to him. Cal was more than six feet in height, somewhat ungainly in his movements and halting in speech, with piercing dark eyes, a quick ironic wit, and a quick smile. He was the only one of us known to Dylan by name. Robie was not quite as tall as Lowell, but leaner and with a more youthful face. He was also quiet and soft spoken, almost self-effacing.

We all climbed into my postwar Hudson for the ride to the Lowells' apartment. Cal sat beside me in the front, but twisted about talking to Dylan as I drove. Dylan clutched the blue denim bag between his knees (he had refused when I offered to store it in the trunk), and Robie sat hunched in the opposite corner. Dylan praised Cal's poetry, even recited a few lines from one poem; Cal said he was highly honored.

I can't remember much of what went on at the brief party at the Lowells' place. What I do remember well is that Dylan refused the hard liquor, saying he preferred beer, thus seeming to confirm Nims's statement over the telephone and assisting me in the decision to have only beer available. He seemed nervous about the reading. When the time neared for us to leave for dinner, he said he would like to wash and change some of his clothes, which he did in the Lowells' small kitchen, seeming to prefer that to the bathroom. He changed only his shirt and added a necktie. The shirt was of a rich blue linen, obviously very expensive, and he said he had stolen it from the Andrew Drexel Biddle residence in Washington when he was staying there. He had opened a drawer, he said, and there were all those shirts — hundreds of them. He needed a shirt, and they had so many. He had taken two. With the blue shirt, he wore a white necktie, and the crumpled tan tweed suit.

When we arrived at the Jefferson Hotel, the usually quiet dining room was crowded with basketball fans. Luckily, we had reserved a table in a slightly out-of-the-way corner and could, by raising our voices, talk in comparative privacy. Dylan did most of the talking, because he was the only one who ordered nothing to eat. Mostly it was light talk with an undercurrent of nervousness that I attributed to the forthcoming reading. He consumed three bottles of beer during our meal, growing livelier as his nervousness increased until even our waiter was joining in the laughter. He said nothing memorable. Rather, it was his way of picking up a phrase, usually one by Cal Lowell, turning it slightly, then using the new phrase to supply a discourse on, let us say, the objective correlative, applying it to the New York subway system, the Iowa basketball fan, or even to one of us.

Whenever he made a joke at our expense, he would raise his sandy eyebrows and peer beneath them at the person involved, as though studying the effect he produced.

He seemed at the moment incapable of taking anything seriously, and this puzzled me, even alarmed me a little, because his poetry seemed to me so intensely serious. I hoped he would take the reading seriously.

As it turned out, there was no need for alarm. He grew serious as soon as we began the two-block walk from the hotel to Old Capitol. I was walking beside him, and as we entered the shadow of one of the gray stone buildings along the way, he commented without irony about his dislike of the academic atmosphere. He had no friends among the academics in England, he told me. He couldn't stand their bloody nit-picking. I attempted halfheartedly to defend the American universities, pointing out that more and more of them were opening their doors to writers and artists, and the very presence of poets on the staff was bound to change the nature of the discipline, if not the whole university. He nodded, but I doubt that he heard me. Like any performer, he was beginning to concentrate on the task ahead.

The Senate Chamber was full when we arrived, and there was applause as he approached the platform. He and Lowell took their seats on the dais. Lowell was to make the introduction. The rest of us sat down in seats reserved for us in the front row. The room became quiet. Lowell stood, and his introduction was given in the halting, almost mumbling manner in which he always spoke, effective in that it seemed sincere and unstudied. It was brief. We all knew why we were here, he said, to hear an important poet, perhaps the most important poet of our time — a poet who had altered the modern trend, who seemed to have sprung from a different tradition than most poets today, who had revived what seemed to be the romantic sensibility at its best.

Dylan arose and was received with another round of applause. He launched right into the reading. His manner could not have been more different from Lowell's. His tone was full-bodied, his style elocutionary. His syllables penetrated the far corners of the hall, each word distinct from the next, so that it seemed to hover a moment in the air like the flare of a rocket before giving way to the one that followed. He held the book in his left hand almost at arm's length, gesturing with the other. He did not, at first, read from his own work, but from the works of the great English poets. He showed no sign of his earlier drunkenness. Only one thing out of the way caught my attention. A pitcher and a glass of water stood beside him on the lectern. Occasionally, he would pause, pick up the glass, carry it halfway to his mouth, then his eyes would catch sight of the clear liquid, a look of revulsion would flicker on his face, and he would replace the glass without allowing it to touch his lips.

The reading ended with a few — a very few — of his own poems. I recall the particular intensity with which he read the poem addressed to his dying father: "Do Not Go Gentle into that Good Night." The words came crisply, like the crackle of a flame through the opening stanzas, then softened and diminished into the final lines, where they flared for a brief moment like the dying flames of a smoldering fire. It provided a spectacular conclusion to the reading, and he received a standing ovation from his audience.

The rooms of the Iowa City Press Club, where I took Dylan after the lecture to meet the students of the Writers' Workshop, were anything but lavish. They were little more than a loft in an old building adjoining the campus. The club itself had been formed, I think, mainly as a means of getting around the strict Iowa liquor laws, which at that time did not allow any drink stronger than beer to be served publicly. Its furnishings were sparse, composed of a few pieces of old furniture donated by members and a bar constructed of unpainted boards laid across two sawhorses. To this, we had added about a dozen card tables with folding chairs that we had rented from a local furniture store.

Dylan was noticeably more relaxed, now that the reading was over. He had obligingly signed the many copies of his books that had been brought up to him by members of the audience, and, in contrast to his earlier mood, he chatted gaily with me on our return across the campus to the club, where the students and faculty were already getting the party under way. As we entered, he was, much to his obvious pleasure, taken up by a table of girl students, who settled him in one of the folding chairs, and immediately provided him with a large glass of beer from a pitcher sitting on their table.

There were between seventy-five and a hundred people in the room, some of them at the tables, some standing around the bar, others moving about or standing against the outside wall, all in animated conversation, as was usual at such meetings but with many a curious — sometimes an envious — eye directed at the girls' table. I made a point of staying away from it, so that Dylan could mingle freely with the students.

When, after a short while, it seemed to me that the girls were unduly monopolizing the guest, I got up and walked over to the table, thinking he might welcome an excuse to move about. I arrived there just as one of the girls was complaining that there was no way to make a living writing poetry.

"Mr. Thomas?" she asked, "What would you advise a girl to do who wants to write poetry? To make a living, I mean?"

Dylan's advice startled me.

"Get out on the street," he told her.

It took a few seconds for this somewhat foreign expression to sink in; then there was a suppressed giggle from one of the students. The others remained silent. I thought this not the best time to interrupt. I joined a group of students who were standing, talking near the far wall and that included two of our best students.

One of them, not one of the best, said: "Don't you think you ought to rescue him from them?" indicating Dylan and the girls at the table near the door.

I glanced again at the table. The students' heads were again bent in bemused concentration on something Dylan was saying.

"He seems to be enjoying himself," I said.

"Yeah! But that's not the point — "

"I know," I cut in, "why don't you just go over and join them?"

"I will," he replied.

He motioned for the others to follow, and two of them did, but not the two best. Just as they reached the table, the girls broke into shrieks of delight. Dylan leaned back in his chair, a cigarette dangling from his lips. He was relaxed and beaming.

I had thought to go over and get him, bring him to meet the two students I was standing with, but now I couldn't bring myself to do it. I was afraid it would spoil the atmosphere if Dylan thought it his duty to talk to certain people. I hadn't yet learned Dylan's propensity for remaining anyplace where he was comfortable and enjoying himself, how painful it was for him to move into a new situation.

As it turned out, others soon followed the example of the three students, and before long half the room had surrounded the table where Dylan was holding forth. Imperceptibly, his chair inched back from the table, and he was addressing the whole group, cigarette still dangling and wobbling ashes on his tie and vest as he spoke. When he removed it, which he did only to take a long swallow from his beer glass, he would do so by plucking it from his mouth with three fingers of his left hand, palming it, so the smoke curled out between the fingers just below the knuckles.

We had agreed to vacate the hall by one o'clock, but when that hour arrived, Dylan was still not easy to dislodge. He appeared not to welcome interruption. Even as we left, he paused on the long steps to the street, propping himself against the banister to tell another story. Outside, across from the deserted campus, he stopped again to agree to Cal Lowell's proposal that he visit the poetry workshop on Tuesday afternoon.

It was at least two o'clock by the time we reached my house. I didn't trouble to drive the car down the alley to my garage, but left it parked in front on the street. Dylan seemed less drunk now than before the reading, even though he had been drinking beer steadily for four hours at the club.

Inside, I asked him if he would like another beer before bed, and he accepted.

My wife went upstairs to check the children and to see that Dylan had all that was necessary in his room. Dylan followed me to the kitchen, where I got two bottles of beer from the icebox (it was an icebox, not an electric refrigerator). We sat at the kitchen table, where I complimented him on his reading, and he expressed satisfaction with the way the evening had gone. I told him the next day was free. The Macauleys had said something about coming by for drinks in the afternoon, but nothing definite had been decided. For Wednesday I had made arrangements to call at the dental college for an examination of his teeth. No time had been set, but it should be in the morning, because I had to teach in the afternoon.

"Ah, yes," he said, "the bloody mouth."

I got the impression he had forgotten all about his reason for staying over. He lifted the beer bottle to his mouth, put it down, wiped his mouth with the back of his hand.

" 'Tis m'fuckin' curse."

This was said in broader dialect than he had used since his arrival, except in stories.

My wife entered the room then, and Dylan started, almost guiltily. My wife paid no attention, and he relaxed. It was the first time I was to notice how the quality of his language changed to meet the occasion. Not that obscene language was not natural to him. It was — when he was in male company or when he was angry or wanted willfully to shock someone he disliked. At other times, he could be exceedingly proper. Never once did he use profanity before our children. Instead he told them about his own children and their dog, "a great shaggy beast of a dog," as he described it. To me he told a different story. He loved his daughter, he said, but his newborn son he detested. He was jealous of him, he maintained, "the little bugger, suckin' away there at his mummy's tits."

My wife told him that his room was ready. We moved out of the kitchen. She explained that since there was only one bathroom, we would wait until after he had used it. As we stood at the foot of the stairs, Dylan a few steps above us, my wife added:

"Now is there anything else you would like?"

"Yes," Dylan replied, pausing.

My wife took a step toward him.

"A nice plump blonde."

As the words penetrated, she stopped abruptly. Dylan laughed, then turned and continued up the stairs. My wife was blonde and the word "plump" could probably have been used to describe her — but not by me.

Very early in the morning or what seemed to me, who had not got to sleep until about 3:30, very early, I was awakened by a strange sound in the room, something like a chant, or like hymns coming from a distant church — except there were no churches in our neighborhood. Listening closely, I thought they were coming through the partition between our room and Dylan's. There was something eerie in the tones, but nothing alarming, so I soon dropped back off to sleep. When I awoke finally, all was quiet. My wife was frying eggs and bacon and I had the *Des Moines Register* spread out on the kitchen table, when Dylan came down the stairs and into the room. What would he like for breakfast? my wife asked him. Nothing, he said, except a glass of milk.

"Really?" I asked. "Nothing more?"

"No," he replied. "I detest eggs."

As he drank the quart of milk I had fetched him from the ice chest, ignoring the glass, drinking directly from the bottle, he told us about the experience he had with ham and eggs (he called it "eggs and gammon"), when he first went to London from Wales. He had rented a room that provided breakfast, and the landlady was very nice. Each morning she would bring him a large breakfast of tea, biscuits, and eggs with ham. At first he tried to eat the eggs. He couldn't bear them. Not wanting to offend so nice a lady, he poured the eggs and meat into an empty bureau drawer. The next morning he did the same. Eventually the drawer was filled to the top. When he could get no more into it, he simply walked away from the room and didn't return.

"I couldn't bear the eggs," he said, "and I couldn't bear to face the nice lady."

Before he had finished drinking the milk, he took a small bottle from his pocket, extracted something from it, popped it into his mouth, and washed it down with the last of his milk.

He must have read my curiosity on my face. He held up the little bottle for us to see.

"My pregnancy pills," he announced grinning.

He had got them from John Nims's wife. She had been pregnant, and the doctor had given them to her for morning sickness. She had thought they might help Dylan.

"Oops!"

Dylan put his hand to his mouth, rushed to the back door, out onto the porch. I had started to laugh, thinking this only an extension of the joke about morning sickness, then we could hear the sound of retching coming from the back porch. He returned in a moment, wiping his mouth with his handkerchief, a large blue bandanna that he stuffed into his trousers pocket.

He was laughing, but his eyes were watering.

"Sorry," he said.

"They don't seem to work," I commented, for want of anything better.

"No, they don't, do they?"

My wife thought he ought to see a doctor, but Dylan shrugged this off saying doctors had only one cure for everything that ailed him — stop drinking. He went to the icebox and helped himself to another bottle of milk.

This was to become a daily procedure: a bottle of milk, a pill, vomiting. If we were staying at home, another bottle of milk. If we were going out, the vomiting would usually begin on the path on the way to the car.

The remainder of the day passed quietly and uneventfully. I told Dylan to help himself to the beer in the icebox, and he did, liberally. I liked beer and drank it along with him.

When mealtime came, Dylan picked at the food put before him, as if out of politeness, but ate very little of it. It was then, with the children present, that he talked most about his own wife and children. His wife was, he told us, a ballet dancer. He also told us about the Boathouse in Wales, where he lived and worked, and, as he talked, I got a distinct impression of homesickness, a wishing he didn't have to stay and go through with the rest of his commitments.

Later in the afternoon, I screwed up my courage and asked him what that sound was I had heard coming from his room early this morning. He looked first puzzled, then a little chagrined, then waggish.

"Oh, you heard that, did you. That was me — singing."

He had awakened early, he said, gone down to the kitchen and opened a bottle of beer. He had taken it back to his room, drank it, and sung Welsh songs until he became sleepy again.

This was to become a morning ritual, and each morning I was to awaken to the muffled sound of such sad songs emanating from the adjoining room.

Sometimes, as it turned out, he would read in the mornings too. I didn't know this until one morning when I went to his room to rouse him. He lay in bed with a book in his hand.

"This is a fine book. Do you know it?" he asked.

"Whose is it?"

I thought it a book he had brought with him.

"Nancy Drew."

The name sounded vaguely familiar — perhaps some little-known British novelist. He held it out for me to see. It was one of my daughter's books, from a shelf near her bed. The Nancy Drew Mysteries for Girls.

"It's really very good," he said.

The visit to the dental school was an exercise in futility. I don't know what I hoped for, perhaps that the dentists would recognize his name and feel honored to repair his teeth, perhaps there would one day be a plaque on the front of the Iowa Dental Building proclaiming the fact that on a certain day the famous poet Dylan Thomas had his teeth renewed in this structure, much as such plaques registered the progress of Mozart across Europe in another day.

What happened was that a student dentist got him into a chair, peered into his mouth, and began almost visibly to tremble. He looked as helpless as if he had peered into the depths of the inferno. He called his professor, who also peered, but looked only solemn, shaking his head and making clucking noises with his tongue. He asked how long Dylan would be in Iowa City.

"About ten days," I told him.

"Impossible," he said. "We would need a month to six weeks."

When we were again out on the street, Dylan seemed strangely relieved.

"Let's go have a beer," he suggested.

I drove Dylan to Joe's Place where we each had a beer; then I left him to go to the business office to pick up the check for his reading. I had a class and some conferences with students in the afternoon. I told him I would call for him at five o'clock, but if he got bored in Joe's Place he could go back to the house. He assured me he would be there at five o'clock.

This was to become our daily routine. I would leave him at Joe's Place on the way to my office. Lowell would pick him up at noon for lunch. Except that Dylan never wanted lunch, and Cal wound up making his own lunch of hot dogs, the only food they served at Joe's. When I picked him up the first day I gave him his check from the university, and he stuffed it nonchalantly into his jacket pocket. The next afternoon when I came by to take him to Lowell's class, the check was still there, but the long white envelope had grown limber and drooped from his pocket.

"For God's sake!" I said. "You're going to lose that. Haven't you a wallet or something you could put it in?"

"Hate the bloody thing," he said. "Forgot all about it. Got to get it off to Brinnin."

We sat at a table while I addressed the crumpled envelope to Brinnin and Dylan scribbled his endorsement on the back of the check. I told him to add: "Pay only to John Malcolm Brinnin for deposit only." He thought this was a brilliant idea.

As it turned out, he had run out of money and had run up a tab at the bar. He had offered to write a check, but the barman had preferred to extend him credit. His rules, he said, precluded cashing second-party checks unless the second party were known to him.

Second-party checks? This puzzled me. Dylan showed me his checkbook. It was filled with blank checks, all signed with Brinnin's signature.

"My God, Dylan!" I said. "Do you realize those checks are just like cash? Anybody could make one out and cash it. What was Brinnin thinking?"

Again Dylan thought it brilliant of me to have figured out something so complicated. He promised to be extremely careful with the checkbook. As soon as we left the bar, I insisted upon walking to the next corner and putting the letter directly into a postbox. If I didn't, I told myself, I would be the only one worrying about it.

Lowell's class was held in what we called the Writers' Workshop Building. It was a barracks built during the war to house cadets who had come to the university to study.

When we arrived, the students had already assembled, about thirty-five of them, seated in classroom chairs about the perimeter of the room. Cal seated Dylan in a chair at the far end, then gave him a short introduction. When he had finished, Dylan grinned boyishly, and asked him what he was supposed to do. Cal, a little flustered, waved his arms in the air.

"Anything," he said, "just anything."

The students laughed. Among them were poets who were later to make rather impressive reputations, like De Snodgrass, who was to win the Pulitzer Prize, and Bill Stafford, who would be granted the National Book Award; like Bob Shelley, whom I thought the most talented, who would kill himself within a few weeks.

Dylan explained that he was no critic, he didn't really know how to talk about poetry, the way critics did. He asked Lowell if he had an anthology. One of the students handed him a collection of British and American poetry. Dylan began leafing through the pages. He would read some of the poems he liked best, he told us.

His performance, completely spontaneous, constituted a superb act of criticism. Invariably, he chose the best of the poems in the volume. Next, he told why he liked them. Occasionally he would pause and tell why he didn't like something, so was not going to read it.

Again the reading was, as it had been the first night, exceptional. Yet, as he read on, I began to get the feeling that he was not uniformly good with all poems. He read them all the same, round-bodied, fluent, intense. Not all poems accommodated themselves to that manner. One of them, John Crowe Ransom's "Captain Carpenter," recounts the misfortunes of his encounters, one by one, until finally "the red vitals of his heart" are plucked away. It is satiric ballad, written in a mock-heroic style, so there is temptation to give it a full, straightforward reading. I had heard Ransom read the poem, and he had stressed the irony by giving it a quiet, dry reading.

After the performance, while we were riding home, I asked Dylan if he had ever heard Ransom's reading. He hadn't, so after our arrival, I played it for him on a recording I had from the Library of Congress. He listened for a few stanzas, then burst out: "Sweet Jesus! The man doesn't know how to read his own poem."

On most of the evenings, as was customary in Iowa City with a visiting dignitary, we were invited out, if not for dinner, at least for drinks. Usually it was to the home of a faculty member or the apartment of a graduate student. All had heard about the telephone call from John Nims, so only beer was served. Dylan was, naturally, the center of attention, and, though nervous at meeting new people, he thoroughly enjoyed parties. They all seemed to wind up with him telling stories, stories of his childhood in Wales and his early days in London, telling of his radio experiences during the war and his filmmaking experiences after. He seemed to avoid literary talk, although the names of writers would inevitably enter into some of his tales. He told of a snowball fight he had with a group of Russian generals on the grounds of a castle in Austria — how they rolled about in the snow like a hassle of schoolchildren.

One night on returning home, he asked if anything were scheduled for the following evening. I said there wasn't. He told us he would like to take us to dinner somewhere. We were to select the place.

The next day started out as usual. Dylan got up early and had his beer, went back to bed and sang his sad songs. He got up later and had a glass of milk, took his pill and another beer, vomited them up on the way to the car. I dropped him off at Joe's Place, where Lowell was to meet him at lunchtime, then went to meet my students.

When I called back for him a few minutes after five, he was not there. The bartender said he had left about an hour earlier. I drove home, thinking he might finally have tired of Joe's Place and gone on ahead of me. He hadn't. I called the Lowells, but they had not seen him. My wife was upstairs dressing to go out with him to dinner. She had arranged for the children to stay with some of their friends. When she came down, he still had not arrived. The doorbell rang. Ah, I thought, there he is now, but he wasn't. Instead, there were two students, Keith Botsford and John Hunt, and they had brought with them Seymour Lawrence, then a publisher's traveler, who just happened to be in Iowa City, to meet Dylan. I told him we expected him at any moment, but that there wouldn't be much time, as we were already late for an appointment. My sense of hospitality was tempered by my growing impatience. The visitors stayed about thirty minutes, then left.

Dylan didn't arrive until 9:30. He was obviously very drunk. He didn't say anything about dinner, and neither did we. My wife went back upstairs and changed her clothes again, came down and prepared some cold food. Dylan dropped into a chair and went immediately to sleep.

Dylan awoke about 11:30, went directly to the icebox for a beer, then sat down at the table. He seemed less drunk now than sleepy. He apologized for not meeting me earlier at Joe's Place. He had met a woman, he told us, who had invited him to her place to read her poetry. She had given him Scotch, keeping his glass full while she read her poetry to him. He couldn't remember her name, all he could tell us was that she lived somewhere over by the river. The poetry, he said, was perfectly dreadful, but the Scotch was good. He had drunk, he guessed, about twelve glasses.

He didn't say anything about the dinner we had missed until the next day, when he suddenly remembered and was so filled with remorse that we couldn't stay angry with him.

As far as I know, Dylan had hard liquor only twice during his stay with us, and he scarcely seemed to notice as long as the beer held out, but both times he did have it something outrageous occurred. The second time was at the home of the English department chairman, Baldwin Maxwell. Georgia Maxwell, when she telephoned the invitation to my wife, had said she couldn't possibly serve only beer to the friends she was inviting, so my wife had asked her please to have beer on hand along with the other drinks. This she agreed to do.

The party was composed of faculty members from the arts, writers and painters mostly, and members of the faculty of medicine, who were particular friends of the Maxwells. Dylan, as guest of honor, was quickly surrounded by the doctors and their wives.

When the drinks arrived, martinis, manhattans, and beer on a silver tray passed by Dr. Maxwell, I was standing talking to Jim Lechay, the painter, about ten feet from where Dylan was standing. As the tray was placed before him, Dylan paused. He may even have given a quick glance in my direction. At any rate, there was definite hesitation, then he reached out and took one of the martinis. I had the feeling that if I had made a gesture or said a single word, he would have chosen the beer. Perhaps I didn't make a move because I, by this time, had become thoroughly sick of beer myself. It was almost with relief that I saw him take the martini. When the tray reached me, I too took a martini.

After my second or third martini, I found myself standing before the table, picking at bits of food as I drank and talked to an Italo-American sculptor, Humbert Albrizzio, from the art department. Suddenly Dylan was standing beside us. He looked very sober, and he bowed almost formally.

"We must go," he said. "I have insulted one of the guests."

Before I could imagine what kind of remark to make to so unexpected an announcement, Albrizzio, who was as short as Dylan, with a fringe of dark hair about his domed baldness, clapped Dylan on the back enthusiastically.

"What? You've insulted one of the guests? Wonderful! Wonderful!"

Dylan's soberness vanished immediately. Humbert went on:

"I think we better have another drink on that."

The two of them linked arms and marched back in the direction of the living room. Georgia Maxwell, who had entered the dining room from the kitchen just in time to overhear them, turned and fled back through the kitchen to snatch away the martini pitcher before they arrived.

Elizabeth, Lowell's wife, told me what had happened in the living room. One of the doctors' wives, a tall woman with a southern accent, had asked Dylan, archly, but with a disarming sweetness:

"Mr. Thomas, how do you-all like your new so-cialized medicine?"

Dylan, responding as usual more to her femininity than to the tone of her voice, began an enthusiastic paean in praise of the welfare state. The woman scarcely listened, but as he went on enumerating the many benefits, her breast began to heave, her face took on a look of agony, and her eyes darkened.

"Why —!" she blurted out. "You don't know what you're talking about!"

Dylan's face changed from amiability to ferocity. He had assumed she wanted a straightforward answer. Now she was telling him, who had lived under the program, that he didn't know what he was talking about.

Elizabeth couldn't remember exactly what Dylan had then said to the woman. She did know that the first words were, "You bloody, fuckin' bitch — " which she said was followed by the most elegantly strung together sequence of obscenities she had ever heard uttered. The doctor's wife collapsed in tears onto her husband's starched white shirtfront. It was then that Dylan had come striding in to me to make his startling announcement.

Thanks to the spontaneous response of Albrizzio, the party did not immediately crash about the heads of the unfortunate hosts. It merely dissolved into two factions. The doctors and their wives continued to occupy the living room, where I could see them through the archway, glasses in hand, undoubtedly conversing in the highly civilized manner of those who are firm in their convictions and know they are beyond reproach. The artistic coterie held forth in the dining room, drinkless, but with the food in their possession, which they gobbled in a loud and disorderly manner. The host and hostess moved back and forth between the two camps trying to appear as though nothing had happened.

Of course they knew something had. For the next several years whenever I had a letter from Baldwin Maxwell it always referred, no matter how irrelevant the context, to some aspect of Dylan's visit. The next year, when both Lowell and I were away in Europe, Dylan returned for another tour of America, but he was not invited to appear at the University of Iowa.

The artists and writers were the first to leave the party, but I can remember that it was a long, probably painful for the Maxwells, leave-taking in the entryway.

Dylan demonstrated one of his "funny laughs." Elizabeth asked Cal to do this. He obliged. Georgia Maxwell said Baldwin had a funny laugh. Dylan looked at him.

"He's doing it now," he said.

I recall a remarkable look of relief on the face of Georgia Maxwell as the door finally closed behind us.

Outside in my car, Lowell suggested that we all go to their apartment for a final drink. This was vetoed by Elizabeth, who at that time was watching carefully over Cal's health, seeing that he didn't drink too much and that he got enough sleep at night. I didn't hear it, but my wife told me afterward that Dylan muttered under his breath: "Don't break your jaw agreeing." In any case, we went home by ourselves and finished the evening off with the usual bottle or two of beer.

Dylan was scheduled to fly the next morning from Cedar Rapids to San Francisco. Dylan knew no one in San Francisco, and I had tried without success to get in touch with Mark Schorer and Wallace Stegner, the only two people I knew in the Bay Area, to see if one of them could meet his plane. I did reach Brewster Ghiselin in Salt Lake City where the plane was to touch down, and asked him if he couldn't contact some of his California friends. He said he would and that he would also be at the plane when it stopped in Salt Lake if I thought that a good idea. I asked Dylan, whom I had shown Brewster's volume of poems, and he said he would like to meet him.

Still, he dreaded the flight from Cedar Rapids. The morning he was to leave, he even forwent the usual beer, and I believe, although I am not sure, that he ate some solid food at breakfast. He did not take his pill. I particularly remember that, because I was hovering about the bathroom waiting to get in, when I heard Dylan's voice coming from the half-open door. "Where are you?" he was saying in an aggravated tone. "Where are you, you blarmin', blasted, bloody little pill?" I looked in, and he was on his hands and knees, groping about for the last of Mrs. Nims's pregnancy pills that he had dropped onto the white tile floor.

I also remember that he didn't vomit anything up that morning. It was an overcast, gray spring day, and as we drove out beyond Iowa City, the hills lay leaden but clear on both sides of the road. Below them, the fields had been turned in neat rectangles of black soil.

"You know," Dylan remarked from his seat beside me, "that's really a rather pretty scene."

He looked at me in mock astonishment and grinned.

"My God!" he exclaimed. "I must be sober."

And he was, and he remained so as we waited around in the almost-empty room for his plane to arrive from Chicago. He was the most quiet I had seen him since his arrival. Quiet, he appeared to droop. You were aware again of the loose-fitting tweed suit, baggy at the knees and elbows. Even the flesh of his face seemed to sag. He made only one joke. When we were standing before the ticket window, he noticed a cutout poster of an advertiser's vision of the American traveler. An antiseptic family of four (husband, wife, and two children) were striding happily into what was called "an air holiday."

Dylan pointed to it and grinned.

"The West family," he said.

By the time the plane's arrival was announced, the gray clouds had settled even closer to the earth and hung in a heavy mass above the field. We said brief good-byes at the gate. Dylan hoisted his blue duffel bag and shuffled preoccupied out to the plane. He paused at the boarding stairs and waved vaguely, then he climbed the steps and disappeared into what seemed to us to be darkness. The door closed, the steps were rolled away. The plane trundled awkwardly to the end of the runway, turned itself slowly about, started again, returned toward us, gathering speed.

I moved out away from the doorway in order to see it leave the ground. I had scarcely done so than it disappeared into the gray overcast, seeming from my vantage to be moving slowly, as though reluctant to leave the earth. I had a vision of Charlie Chaplin moving slowly down the road in the final scene of so many of his movies.

So Began the Happiest Years of My Life

The mass was still in Latin; the Dodgers still in Brooklyn. It was late August, 1952. A man named Paul Engle had offered me a fellowship, and I had said yes, and caught a big plane to Cedar Rapids, and a little plane to Iowa City, where I spent a long afternoon listening to a lone fly on a windowsill in the Jefferson Hotel. It was the shank end of evening now, and I was hungry. Two of the three restaurants were closed for vacation, and the third closed at nine, two minutes before I tried the door. I bought a pack of Chesterfields in Racine's, where an old bald man chalked the day's baseball scores on a blackboard. I drifted down to the river, where a tired moon floated, and bombed that moon with my cigarette. The night confirmed the afternoon: I was a long way from California. I was homesick, heartsick, and too broke to go home. So began the happiest years of my life.

It was customary for most of the poets who passed through the workshop in the 1950s to talk about it afterward as though they had done time on Devil's Island. I can only imagine that all their days in Iowa City were like my first day. I know that my mood changed with the coming to town of the other students. How fine they all seemed, the young men and women in their cashmere and shetland, in their arms the tall chimneys of new books. They brought September with them. Shops and theaters and even restaurants opened their doors. The university, like a camel laden for some great journey, lurched to its feet and got started.

But these images are no more than anyone might remember of a dozen different college towns in the Midwest of the fifties. What made my happiness were the people and books I came to

know. I can't name them all, without sounding like the dazed re-
cipient of an Oscar. Still, I do name these few: Catullus and Horace,
Dr. Johnson and Proust, Dante, Donne, and Baudelaire. They are
still on my shelves, but those shelves could become rubble in a Cali-
fornia earthquake, and it wouldn't matter. These writers walk
around in my memory in the company of the men who introduced
them to me: Gerald Else, John McGalliard, Charles Woods, and
John Berryman.

Paul Engle brought me to Iowa City on the strength of a hand-
ful of poems he — and I think he alone — saw any strength or
touch of talent in. The other young poets in the workshop became
my teachers — not that I let them know that. In some cases, it was
a matter of avoiding the mistakes of others. But mostly it was try-
ing to write up to the level of my fellows. How high that level could
be can be seen in the pages of two remarkable first books, *The Sum-
mer Anniversaries* by Don Justice and *Heart's Needle* by De Snod-
grass. We were lucky, those of us in the workshop of those days,
for our world was an Aristotelian world — there was a there out
there — and it included the idea of a tradition, master to journey-
man to apprentice.

The university, then, did what universities are supposed to do. It
made the idea of itself manifest: *there were these men and women,
and they read these books, and they talked about them, and they
wrote these poems, and they read them to each other.*

If I could climb into a time machine and chance upon my ear-
lier self sitting, say, with a nickel glass of beer at Kenney's, if I could,
I'd buttonhole that young man and say, "Enjoy it, dammit. Never
again will you be surrounded by so many marvelous people. You
and your friends will soon be scattered to the four corners. You will
go home and grow up and be lonely." When I think about it, I'm
not sure there wasn't an old gray-haired bore who said something
like that. I should have bought him a beer. "Irene! Draw one for the
Ancient Mariner."

Fair Days and Fowl

I will never know how that envelope tracked me down, addressed as it was to an office I had vacated years earlier. Call it fate.

The envelope contained a brochure announcing the Iowa Writers' Workshop fiftieth anniversary celebration. Within spitting distance of fifty myself, I found myself flooded with nostalgia not only for my two years at the workshop, but for the youth they represented.

It was March 1986. I was working in New York as editor and publisher of *Physicians' Travel & Meeting Guide*, a magazine I had founded in 1982. In addition to advertising, *PTMG* consisted of travel articles, columns by celebrity editors (Arthur Ashe, Johnny Miller, Mario Andretti), and—its raison d'être—the salient details on thousands of upcoming medical conferences, all cross-indexed by date, location, and subject. Though *PTMG*'s promotional materials described it as "a unique educational resource," I knew that for many of its 300,000 physician-readers it functioned primarily as a compendium of tantalizing, tax-deductible getaways.

The timing of the workshop announcement was fortuitous. Ten months earlier, *PTMG* had been purchased by a huge publishing conglomerate. With *PTMG* now solvent, it occurred to me that there might be a way — albeit a minor one — that I could help the workshop celebrate its fiftieth anniversary.

The brochure stated that Paul Engle would be the jubilee's guest of honor, and though we had never met it seemed appropriate to make my offer directly to him. In a letter composed with what

I hoped was sufficient deference for the man who had been the workshop's guiding spirit for half a century, I proposed establishing a program to send selected workshop students to exotic locales to prepare travel articles for *PTMG*. The magazine would cover all expenses and pay a generous fee for the resulting article which, though it would not be "real" writing — i.e., fiction — would nonetheless provide a budding writer an opportunity to see his or her work in print. I suggested to Mr. Engle that he might wish to announce this new program to the workshop students during the upcoming jubilee.

Less than two weeks later I was flattered to receive a personal reply. Mr. Engle expressed thanks for my "most generous offer" but explained that the semester would be over and thus all the students gone by the time of the workshop festivities. That was unfortunate, he continued, but perhaps there was another way to get the program started in a timely manner.

Mr. Engle then informed me that he and his wife, Hualing (whose impressive credentials he proceeded to summarize), were going to China soon after the workshop celebration, that he had in his lifetime done considerable traveling and, more to the point, considerable travel writing (he directed my attention to the several reprints accompanying his letter). Did I think doctors would be interested in China? If so, he felt sure he could provide a unique perspective for them. As if to prove it, he unleashed a torrent of fascinating Sinological arcana.

"Later," the letter continued, "I'd like to propose an article on the two English Universities, Oxford and Cambridge, which I know, having been three years a Rhodes Scholar at Oxford and rowed on the Thames in the Oxford races and the International Regatta at Henley. Lovely places to learn that odd language and to translate Kant's philosophy for my Oxford examinations and can comment on changes since I heard Hitler speak twice in the 1930's and saw the Nazis at night with torches and riding with folded arms in troop carriers all day, and I saw the bodies on the streets. See enclosed article from *American Heritage* on some experience from that time. Some of my articles have been picked up by *Reader's Digest*. I suppose it's of no interest to you, but I do know Eastern Europe because of my duties with the International Writing Program. I also have a lot of experience and many friends in Japan.

"I do deeply hope it is not tactless of me to write to you in this way."

Following his signature, Mr. Engle squeezed in another paragraph:

"About China — I can also describe having acupuncture, burning, needles. Another possibility is an article on the remarkable variety of landscapes and buildings within the tiny island of England — hop poles in Sussex, mountains in Wales and Scotland, lakes in Yorkshire, bare heaths in Dartmouth southwest, Luleorth Cove in Dorset where I used to swim, where the ship with John Keats on his way to death in Rome was blown in by a storm. I've been in the Philippines, South Korea, Indonesia, India, Pakistan, Taiwan, others."

Thus began our correspondence. When I informed Mr. Engle that our magazine had recently published a major travel feature on China, he turned his considerable energies to selling me on the piece he had proposed about England. His real interest in traveling there, he confided, was to attend the fiftieth reunion of his Oxford class. I wrote back that, given *PTMG*'s highly educated audience, an article on Oxford sounded ideal. (I never revealed to him that facilitating Paul Engle's return to Oxford seemed to me an entirely appropriate "thank you" from an undistinguished but nonetheless grateful workshop alumnus.) Though surprised by his enthusiasm to write for so obscure a publication, I set about making his trip a reality.

As I had feared, the Brits resisted the idea of providing free travel and accommodations for *two* writers. But I persisted, and by the time of the workshop jubilee, plans for the Engles' Oxford journey were starting to gel. I drove the twenty miles from the Cedar Rapids airport to Iowa City alternating between nostalgia for my years at the workshop and mounting anxiety about meeting Paul Engle face to face.

The first event of the jubilee was a picnic along the banks of the

Iowa River fronting the university's art museum. When my wife and I arrived, the evening light was shimmering on the water and the air was filled with the collective buzz of the gathered writers — hundreds of them, it seemed — all undoubtedly talking about their writing, their agents, their editors, their books. As the publisher of a slick magazine designed to help doctors take tax-deductible vacations, I felt like an interloper.

Paul Engle was standing in what might best be described as a receiving line of one, greeting people in the inimitable, hearty voice and precise diction I recognized from our recent telephone conversations. I was not ready to meet him.

I led my wife to the food table where we took up paper plates and helped ourselves to barbecued chicken, salad greens, and ears of fresh corn. I chose an empty table on the shadowy fringe of the festivities.

I glanced over. The line of writers waiting to meet Paul Engle had grown. A few minutes later a perky young woman carrying a notebook sashayed over and introduced herself. She was a reporter from California here to do a feature piece on the anniversary celebration. Had either of us attended the workshop? Could she sit down? Could she ask a few questions? Great!

After efficiently jotting my who-what-where-when-how-and-whys in her notebook, she remarked pleasantly, "You've really made use of your workshop experience."

From somewhere behind me I heard Paul Engle's booming laugh. "Excuse me?" I asked the reporter.

"You're an editor," she said. "You publish magazines. You really make use of what you learned here."

"No. I don't," I told her.

Her brow furrowed. "But you said — "

"I run a travel magazine," I explained. "I came here to write fiction."

She made a face.

"Listen," I said. "I don't mean to denigrate journalism, or travel writing, or anything else. All I meant was that when I was here I was writing fiction, and since I left here I haven't."

"Do you ever regret it?" she asked.

The light was fading. It was getting chilly. All around us writers of all ages were casually consuming golden ears of corn.

"Come on," I said to my wife, standing and taking our soggy paper plates, "let's go say hello to Mr. Engle."

We got in line and shuffled slowly forward. The sun was a red bruise on the horizon. When our turn came I gritted my teeth, put out my hand, and introduced us. Paul Engle's eyes went from twinkly to positively pyrotechnic. His face broke into a huge grin, only to be replaced a moment later by a look of extreme consternation.

"But I don't know you," he declared earnestly.

"That's right," I replied, and almost added, "I haven't written anything." But what I actually said was, "We've never met."

"But you were here at the workshop," he said, his expression pained. "I looked it up. From '63 to '65. How is it possible that we never met?"

The explanation was apparently too obvious for him to grasp. When I was a wet-behind-the-ears student, Paul Engle, though only middle-aged, was already an éminence grise, a figure occasionally glimpsed loping through the Iowa mist, making his rounds — or so I imagined — among the superbly accomplished and justly celebrated.

But before I could reply he had tugged my wife and me into positions on either side of him and had commenced greeting the people next in line.

"Well, hello," he declared in his irrepressibly hearty voice, "so *very* good to see you. Have you met Steve and Gretel Salinger?"

My wife and I became his bookends. Each time I tried to slink off, a powerful paw would pull me back. With little choice but to grin and bear it, I occupied my mind with memories.

In the fifties, Nikita Khrushchev, the gruff, shoe-banging Chairman of the USSR, was invited to visit the United States. President Eisenhower asked him if there was any one place in this great land of ours that he particularly wanted to see. Without hesitation, the communist dictator answered "Iowa." So, after the official meetings in Washington, Khrushchev came to Iowa to inspect the world's most productive farms, to bend down and sift through his thick peasant fingers the richest soil on Earth. And though, to my adolescent mind, Khrushchev's pilgrimage seemed inexplicable, a decade later I found myself making the same journey.

Iowa City was as remote to me as Vladivostok, and nearly as mysterious. I arrived here after four years in Ithaca: not the storied isle of Ulysses, but the upstate New York burg whose justice of the peace had stared at my parking ticket and my Cornell sweatshirt and smirked, "Fifty dollars or fifty days."

"Well, hello! So *very* good to see you. Have you met Steve and Gretel Salinger?"

Iowa City is a revelation. Iowans, I soon discover, are both friendly and unflappable. They actually like college students!

The university has sharp hills, a meandering river, a modern campus overflowing with blondes, and two ramshackle Quonset huts overflowing with talent.

They have come from everywhere, these aspiring writers. So damned many of them! With such distinctive voices! Such fertile imaginations! Turning out so much good work! And elsewhere on the strange oasis of a campus other grad students are producing ceramics, prints, drawings and paintings and . . .

Where have all these talented people come from? What are they all doing in *Iowa*, for God's sake?!

"Well, hello! So *very* good to see you. Have you met Steve and Gretel Salinger? Steve publishes . . . ."

A week into Richard Yates's fiction workshop I submit a new satirical story and, as is the custom, make an appointment to discuss it with him in his office. It is already clear from class that Yates does not like me. He is an Ichabod Crane type — tall and thin, introverted, soft-spoken, Christian. I am a chunky, wise-cracking, New York Jew.

At our private meeting he figuratively but methodically tears my wise-cracking, New York Jew story to shreds. I gather up my red-ink-marked pages and slink out. Back in my basement apartment I read and reread his harsh comments, finally concluding that the bastard is right. I slowly click a fresh piece of paper into my Royal portable and begin work on a serious idea I've had in the back of my mind for some time but have been afraid to tackle.

A week later I submit the new story to Richard Yates. I wait a few days and make an appointment.

When I enter his office he is crumpled in his chair, the picture of gloom. My story lays neatly squared on his otherwise empty desk.

"Look," he says miserably, "I really don't know what to say to you."

I swallow hard. "Sir?"

"This," he says, patting my pages. "Well, it's . . . uh . . . it's . . ." and he sighs . . . "it's pretty damned good."

His words have cost him dearly. The silence is awkward.

"My last story was terrible," I remind him, hoping that will cheer him up.

It doesn't.

Richard Yates forces himself to tolerate me and in time we become almost friends. He drinks too much and makes himself sick, and loneliness stoops his shoulders like saddlebags. But he loves writing and doesn't know how to be dishonest about it. One day he starts a class by holding up a paperback copy of *Catch-22* and ripping out a large chunk. "Look," he cries, tossing loose pages into the air, "I can tear out a hundred pages and I haven't changed anything. What can I say about a book like that? Class dismissed."

"Well, hello! So *very* good of you to have come. Have you met . . . ?"

A seminar in modern fiction. Brian McMahon is discussing *Catcher in the Rye.*

"Tell us, Mr. Salinger," he asks in his melodious brogue, "what do you think of this other Mr. Salinger's writing style?"

I reply that I prefer a more muscular prose, that J. D. Salinger is too delicate for my taste, that it always seems like he is writing with a tweezer. "And," I declare, "you can't pick up anything really important with a tweezer."

"Ah," McMahon says, nodding his head appreciatively. "I see your point, Mr. Salinger. Like a diamond, for instance."

The guest of honor turns to me. "You know, of course," he says with a wink, "that Engle means angel."

R. V. Cassill cocks his head as I question a point he has just made to the class.

"Tell me, Mr. Salinger," he asks with his courtly, poisoned sweetness, "have you read —" and he names a little-known story by F. Scott Fitzgerald.

"Yes, sir, I have." Blind luck.

"I see," he continues, undeterred. "And have you read . . ." and he names an obscure story by Faulkner which, by wild chance, I have read the previous semester.

He nods his large head sagely. "And how about . . ." and here he recites an unfamiliar title in French.

"No, sir," I admit.

"I thought not," he replies. "It has yet to be translated into English. But *had* you read it, Mr. Salinger, you *might* have understood my point. No matter. Let us move on."

"Well, hello! So *very* good to see you. Have you met Steve and Gretel Salinger?"

A group of workshop students is dining together in the student union cafeteria. I make a somewhat vulgar remark to my friend Ellyn who surprises us both by throwing her glass of milk in my face. The cafeteria becomes quiet. I smile and dry off, reminding myself that revenge is a dish best served cold.

The next day, in response to a radio advertisement which seems heaven sent, I mail in a check for $3.95. A week later I receive a notice that a package awaits me at the post office.

The carton seems far too small, but when I get it home and carefully pry loose the lid, there they are, packed together like a giant yellow Easter confection. Live baby chicks. Three blessed hundred of them!

Ellyn is in class. Her apartment is on the ground floor of a sturdy old house that faces Dubuque Street. I slip around to the back, ease open a window, insert the carton and gently shake its contents onto her living room rug. I return to my car, stow the empty carton in the trunk, and, after a brief stop at a feed store, drive home through the Iowa twilight to await her call.

It doesn't take long. Ellyn is apoplectic. Her rug is ruined. The chirping is driving her mad. Yes, she admits, she shrieked when she entered the apartment, and yes, she supposes it is in its own perverse way very funny. But what in hell is she supposed to do now?

"Put out some water," I suggest. "In shallow pans. The poor things must be thirsty."

I return to her apartment. With difficulty we round up the small nimble army, using every available receptacle (getting all the chicks back into their original container proves impossible). Under cover of darkness, we load them into the trunk of my car. I have a plan.

Appropriately, our first stop is the student union cafeteria. I enter, nonchalantly carrying two plain brown paper bags filled with chicks whose anxious chirping is muffled by the Beatles tune blaring from the jukebox. Ellyn follows with two bags of chicken feed. We find an empty table and inconspicuously lower one of each bag to the floor, then move upstairs and casually deposit a second set on an easy chair next to the circular Herky the Hawk rug.

We make good our escape. Crime is exhilarating.

We leave bagfuls everywhere: Hospitals, firehouses, libraries, fraternities, sororities, dorms, private homes.

Most of the chicks end up at the children's hospital where a special enclosure is built for them. As they grow they provide hours of entertainment for youngsters sorely in need of a lift. The criminals are never caught.

"So *very* nice to see you! Have you met the Salingers? Have you tried the chicken?"

Throughout the weekend Paul Engle keeps my wife and me close to him, almost like talismans. At his insistence, during our three days in Iowa City we spend two afternoons and two evenings trailing after him. In the presence of so many genuine luminaries, his attention to one of such low wattage is embarrassing. More than that, it is perplexing. I have been to his home: the issue is not money. Besides, he has already traveled the globe under the far more generous auspices of the Rockefeller Foundation.

One day, months later, the nickel drops. Suddenly I think I understand why Paul Engle wanted to spend so much of what was in effect *his* jubilee with the publisher of an obscure magazine. It occurs to me that the hundreds of people crowding around him that weekend were all paying homage to his past. Only I — who was sending him on assignment overseas — was an emissary from his future. The past was important, but even at seventy-eight Paul Engle was far more excited by the future.

No one can be taught to be a writer, Paul Engle said to me that weekend. What a workshop could do, he believed, was to establish an environment where creative writing was the central activity, where young writers could mix both with their peers and with established professionals. The best we can hope for, Paul Engle told me, is to save a young writer some time, to bring him along a bit faster than he might progress alone.

Perhaps the breadth of the workshop's success comes from the modesty of its ambition, and the clarity of Paul Engle's vision.

Over the years the Writers' Workshop and its graduates have engendered more than their share of both praise and criticism. But one thing should be beyond dispute: In the last half century, the thousands of creative writers who have found security, both psychic and financial, on the faculties of America's colleges and universities can trace the creation of their positions to the program started in the Depression year of 1936 at the University of Iowa.

Six months after the Jubilee Paul and Hualing Engle traveled to Europe and attended his Oxford reunion. They cruised one way on the *QE2* and flew the other on British Airways. The British Tourist Board provided the hotel accommodations. The Engles even found time for a complimentary excursion aboard the fabled *Orient Express*. I had done my job to honor Paul Engle's past. And he — as he had done for so many others before me — had seen to my future.

My weekend in Iowa at Paul Engle's side reignited the passion that had sent me westward twenty-three years earlier. When my contract with *PTMG*'s new owners ended there was no question what I would do. It took seven years, but my novel, *Behold the Fire*, was published by Warner Books in the fall of 1997.

Thanks, Paul.

Afterword

America, . . . I defy you, I challenge, I implore you, . . .
— *Paul Engle*

Paul was a good storyteller. He described an event or a person
with a storyteller's sense of details and twists. And a wicked sense
of humor. I learned a great deal about his life and personality from
the endless stories he told me.

Paul used to say, "I probably shoveled more horse manure than
any other American writer." Paul's father first worked with car-
riage horses, breaking and training them, and then taking a rail-
road car of them to New York City where he demonstrated their
style on the Harlem Speedway, now a paved many-lane road of
speeding cars.

Each morning at 6:00, Paul rode a bicycle to the barn, harnessed
two horses to two telephone company wagons hung with ladders,
coils of wire, lead-melting pots, clips for climbing poles, and cut-
ters. He had to drive one horse with his left hand and lead the
other with his right. There were ten railroad tracks to cross. If an
engine came close and whistled that high steam sound, one horse
reared one way; the second, another. Paul was more terrified of
what his father would do if he let go of the horses, so he hung on,
yelling in imitation of his father's authoritarian voice. Then he
would tie the rigs to poles in the alley behind the telephone com-
pany where workmen would pick them up for the day's work. Later
came the saddle-horse life, three- and five-gaited "show" horses,
controlled, as his father taught him, by a gentle voice and a firm

hand. He taught young girls and old women to ride. The smell of horse manure, he claimed, never left his clothes until he went to Oxford.

He also liked to say, "If you could handle two horses rearing in two opposite directions crossing ten railroad tracks when the train was coming, you could handle the difficulties of creating a writing program in this country."

For many years, Paul delivered the *Cedar Rapids Gazette* on a route beginning at the corner of 4th Ave. and 15th St. SE and going to the city limits. The carrier boys' office was at the edge of the Cedar River, and the boys played along the dirty banks waiting for the afternoon edition, throwing cinder chunks at the long rats, boxing in a corner of the distribution room, later riding a mile to begin the route, at the end of which wolves were howling in the timber. One winter Paul fell through the ice with an overcoat on and would have drowned save that the new First Avenue bridge in Cedar Rapids was being built above, and, suddenly, when he popped up in an airhole, the other kids had timbers to shove to him so that he could crawl along them. Before he reached the pressroom, which was very warm, his clothes turned to ice, and he could barely move inside them. They dried out next to the intense heat of the furnace where used lead rolls were melted. He started out on his deliveries, reached the end of his route two miles away, black night, below zero, and the wolves in cry. Delayed fright came over him, and he shook not with cold but with shock. He began to weep then, and ran all the way home crying in the darkness.

Paul Engle would never have gone to Coe College without Miss Elizabeth Cook, a schoolteacher at Washington High School in Cedar Rapids. She helped him when he was first beginning to read poetry and then later when he began to write it. Paul was her best student. One day he went to her apartment and showed her a letter from the *Saturday Review of Literature*. It said that his poem had been accepted, and it contained a check for $10.00. "Miss Cook, look, I'm in the big money," Paul said.

But when he first went to Coe, he had no money; his family was desperately poor, and his father could not help him. Paul didn't know how he would pay his tuition until the registrar of the college called him in and said, "You've been awarded a scholarship funded by an anonymous contributor." In Paul's last year at Coe (1931), Miss Cook was killed by a car as she was crossing a street. And it wasn't until the registrar of the college called Paul into his office and said, "The last thing that Miss Cook did before she died was to bring me this envelope," that he learned that she was his benefactor. In the envelope were ten-dollar bills which she had saved from her small schoolteacher's salary and with which she had paid Paul's tuition in silence until she died.

Old Gabriel Newburger, hanging on after severe heart attacks on nitroglycerin, willpower, and writing poems about the Ozark farmers he knew from his peddler father, was another of Paul's benefactors. Mr. Newburger owned a department store in Cedar Rapids. Paul visited Gabe every day at his apartment. When Paul received his Rhodes Scholarship, Newburger asked, "What clothes you're going to wear Paul?" "What I have on," Paul said. "No son of mine is going to live with those Englishmen looking the way you do," Gabe said. "Go down to the store and start out naked in the men's department. Get underwear, socks, two suits, shirts, neckties, an overcoat. Charge to me."

Three years later when the old British ship the *Aquitania* brought the Engles back to New York from England, Paul and Mary were waiting in third class when a purser called out Paul's name. He had a special delivery letter from Gabe. The opening sentence read, "If you brought one nickel back from Europe and didn't see everything you could, you are no son of mine." Included was the sum of $25.

Paul met Stephen Vincent Benét in the early thirties when he was a graduate student at the University of Iowa and Benét visited the university, invited by Norman Foerster, then dean of the School of Letters. Paul had just won a fellowship from Columbia University.

It paid him $800, which was big money in those days. Benét seemed to have decided that Paul was a good risk as a young poet. He told Paul, "When you come to New York, call me." It was the beginning of a friendship which lasted until Benét's death in 1943.

In New York, the Benéts used to invite Paul to have dinner with them on holidays or whenever they had visiting writers. In the spring he would go and spade up their backyard in order to plant a few things in it. Once he dug up a dead cat.

Paul also met many wonderful people in their house. Philip Barry, the playwright, who wrote "The Philadelphia Story"; William Butler Yeats; and John Masefield, the Poet Laureate of England. At Columbia, Paul's graduate major was English, but he was also interested in anthropology and studied with Franz Boas and Ruth Benedict, who were among the great scholars in their field at that time.

When Paul showed Stephen Benét the poetry he was writing then, Benét said, "Look, go on. When you get a book-length manuscript, let me take it. I'll get it published." *American Song* was published by Doubleday in 1934 and its young author hailed in the *New York Times Book Review* as "A New Voice in American Poetry."

One Saturday afternoon in 1932, Paul received a telegram saying that he had been nominated as a finalist for the Rhodes Scholarship if he could promise to be in Des Moines by Monday morning. Paul's fellowship money was in the Columbia University bank, locked up until Monday, and he had to be on an evening train west or he couldn't make the deadline. Such banks as, in the bottom of the Depression, were still operating, had closed at noon. Paul's first thought was to call Steve Benét. So, stopping work on a story, Benét went down to the Yale Club and sat there in the lobby cashing checks on anyone he knew who came in until he had the whole amount for Paul's fare out and back. Steve called Paul at 5:00 P.M. Paul walked down from 123rd St. where he lived, across the park, got the money, and was on the westbound train with five minutes to spare.

Paul met Samuel Barlow on a Cunard Liner in 1932 when he made his first trip to England. Sam was a composer, symphonic conductor, and musical patron. He devoted most of his time to music. His opera *Mon Ami Pierrot* was performed in 1934 by L'Opera Comique in Paris, the first time the company staged an American's work. The French government awarded him the Legion of Honor. His Concerto for Magic Lantern and Symphony Orchestra, an adaptation of *Babar, The Little Elephant*, was performed by the Philadelphia Orchestra in 1936, directed by Leopold Stokowski.

Sam was also a liberal activist. His houses at Gramercy Park in New York, Eze in France, and his apartment in Paris were centers for artists and musicians. Paul met him by blind chance on the ship the night just before they reached Europe. Paul had gone to the ship's bar for a drink. There were two gentlemen at a nearby table. After a while, one of them said, "Come and have a drink with us." They talked and talked. Finally, Sam said, "I suppose you write poetry." Paul said, "You've read it?" "No, never heard of you, but you look and talk like somebody who writes poetry," Sam replied.

The Barlows had a music room in their house at Gramercy Park in New York. Sam's wife, Ernesta, a great beauty, discovered an old early-eighteenth-century chateau that had been neglected and was being torn down. They bought some walls from inside the house, shipped them back to New York, and had them built into a room, encasing the brick in the by-then-two-hundred-year-old French oak. Chamber music played in such a room kept its precise measure of vibration, the tiniest wavelength. "It was like sitting inside the music," Paul said.

It was the Barlows who first introduced Paul to opera. However, he arrived at the Metropolitan Opera House wearing his stocking cap, a mackinaw, and very heavy shoes called brogans. An usher in white tie, white gloves, and tails looked first at his ticket, then at his clothes, then led him down a long beautiful corridor, all gilt and carvings, to the closest box to the stage. There sat Sam in his evening clothes and highly polished shoes. He stood up and said, "This is our hostess, Mrs. Vincent Astor." Paul was trying to stuff his stocking cap into his pocket when Mrs. Astor said gallantly, "Your cap looks as if it's very comfortable in this cold weather."

When Paul was at Oxford, he spent the first Christmas with the Barlows at Eze. Their house was built on the foundations of the

Temple of Isis erected by the Romans. Three young Russian musicians came to the Christmas dinner. All of them had left the Soviet Union after the communists took over: Vladimir Horowitz, Gregor Piatigorsky, Nathan Milstein. Horowitz came with Wanda Toscanini, daughter of Arturo Toscanini, whom he was about to marry. They had a very elaborate dinner with a great deal of wine, more wine than the cornfield boy from Iowa was accustomed to. After dinner, they went into the circular drawing room fronting the Mediterranean below. There Sam had a grand piano. Piatigorsky had not brought his cello. Milstein hadn't brought his violin. Nobody had expected to play. But when he saw the grand piano, Horowitz couldn't resist it. He went over and started to play, showing off for his bride-to-be, Wanda Toscanini. Paul was sitting on the floor opposite the piano and fell asleep! Horowitz decided that Paul should wake up and began playing extremely loud chords on the piano, banging down, just as hard as he could, fortissimo. Paul did wake up, and then everybody laughed.

More stories. More kindness. Paul once told me, "All my life, always there were people who did extra kind things for me." He returned their kindness by doing extra kind things to others, especially writers. He understood what it means when you lend a hand to a person at the crossroads in his or her life.

So, one last tale.

At Oxford, Paul encountered another totally different world from the one he had known in Iowa. His tutor, Edmund Blunden, the poet, a shell-shocked survivor of World War I, had been in the first battle of the Somme when he was eighteen years old. It was the greatest catastrophe in British military history up to that time. Fifty-six thousand casualties between sunrise and sunset, every man a volunteer. Edmund and Paul became lifelong friends.

Paul traveled extensively around England and on the Continent, from London to Kharkov, and from Stockholm to Sicily on vacation between Michaelmas, Hilary, and Trinity terms. He visited Stalinist Russia, and Nazi Germany where he lived with a German family and watched the horror unfold from the inside.

Paul spent his first summer vacation at Oxford (1934) in the mountains of Bavaria to learn German on his own. There he met Franz Mueller, whom he later called "the truest European" he ever knew. Franz invited Paul to spend Christmas with his family in Berlin-Friedenau, where Paul went often to a long, narrow book-store near von Kleist Platz. There he discovered, in a very handsome and expensive edition, the poems of Rainer Maria Rilke. One day the owner invited him back down an aisle with a wall on one side and room after small room on the other, until they came to a room without windows or outside walls. The old man said, "You like Rilke? I see you looking at my most beautiful books. Real leather." "Yes," Paul said. The man left, returned, and put all the Rilke books on the table. "Take. If you don't, they will come and burn them." He did not use the word *Nazis*; they were always *They*. Then the old man called out to a closed door. An attractive girl of sixteen brought in tea, and left. Pouring the tea, the old man repeated, "Take them. Take all of the books." "Why?" Paul asked. The man stared at him. "I am a Jew." Then he turned and gestured toward the door the lovely young girl had closed. "I am old. It does not matter. But my daughter, that girl. She must go. Out of Germany. We are the damned Jews. You are American. You are the lucky one. My daughter, Rebekah, get her out. Take her out. Leave me to die. We Jews are very skilled at dying. . . ."

"I will try," Paul said. "I will try."

Once back in Iowa, Paul wrote to friends who could help. He also wrote the old man, but there was no reply.

On December 9, 1934, Paul broadcast his "Talk to America" at the invitation of the National Broadcast Company of England. It concluded,

> . . . You have become the world's comedian, America. You have given it a new jazz-song and a new laughter. But you can't wise-crack your way out of this. You can't see the way on by sticking your head in the sand. Lift it up — to the clear, hard American light — you can see a long way in that clean air.
>
> Here in Europe I think of you, — in Vienna, where the starved faces watch, all day long, the uniforms go by; in Rome I have

stood in the Coliseum and watched another Caesar raise another eagle; in Munich I have seen a private, civilian army pledge itself to Blood and Honor. In the lovely South Tyrol, for a week, trains of soldiers with fixed bayonets, and car-loads of artillery.

And you, America, will you take the lead out of all this? Will you read Henry Thoreau and Nikolai Lenin and Jesus Christ? I speak bluntly and simply to you. There is a world-way and it is for you to show it — the way of production for use, of a job for every man, of peace, and the unity of nations.

This will be your new life, America, and my generation will make it. We will make it through whatever travail and agony come to us, through whatever opposition. If we do not go down into the abysm of the dead and departed past — and we will drag the whole world down with us.

Our art, our poetry, will go with you either way. I defy you, I challenge, I implore you, build our new American life. It will find its expression in our new American art, and our poetry will make a song of it, the richness of Indian words, with the rhythm of our jazz, the lingo of our slang.

Here in Gothic Oxford, there are many of us who carry a vision of that life in our minds, and hear that song in our hearts. It is being written in American today. Put your ear to the ground, give it the continent-long winds. Build a third time, America, and that song will be as loud in your land as the voices of your men can make it.

It was with this sense of mission that Paul came back to America. It was with this vision that Paul took over the Writers' Workshop as the director in 1941 and struggled to develop it from a program of "brilliantly untalented students," as he sometimes said, into the most prominent writing program in the country; it was in this same spirit that he and I later started the International Writing Program and jointly made it the *Voilà une Utopie* for writers all over the world.

Marvin Bell lives in Iowa City and teaches in the Writers' Workshop. He has also been a Woodrow Wilson Visiting Fellow, a Lila Wallace—Reader's Digest Writing Fellow, and served as a faculty member at Goddard College and the Universities of Hawaii and Washington. He has received awards from the Academy of American Poets and the American Academy of Arts and Letters, and has held Guggenheim and NEA fellowships as well as Senior Fulbright appointments to Yugoslavia and Australia. His thirteen books include *The Book of the Dead Man, Ardor,* and *A Marvin Bell Reader* (selected prose and poetry). His first collection, *A Probable Volume of Dreams,* received the Lamont Award.

Robert Bly, poet, translator, and editor, graduated with a B.A. from Harvard, 1950; and an M.A. from the University of Iowa, 1956. He was the originator and editor of *The Fifties,* a literary magazine (which became in turn *The Sixties, Seventies,* and *Eighties*). He was also cochairman of Writers vs. the Vietnam War. Among his many books of poetry are *The Silence in the Snowy Fields, The Light Around the Body* which won the National Book Award in 1968, *The Teeth Mother Naked at Last, This Body Is Made of Camphor and Gopherwood,* and *Selected Poems.* He has translated work by Thomas Tranströmer; *The Selected Poems of Rainer Maria Rilke;* and poems by Neruda, Lorca, Machado, and Jiminez. His most recent prose work is *Iron John.* Bly has received fellowships in literature from the Fulbright, Guggenheim, and Rockefeller foundations, and an award from the National Institute of Arts and Letters.

Vance Bourjaily taught in the workshop from 1957 to 1979. He is the author of twelve and a half books. The last, which accounts for the fraction, was coauthored with his son Philip and is called *Fishing by Mail*. It is possible that Philip, who was born and lives in Iowa City, might argue that the proportion of contributions makes his father the author of 12.3 books. Bourjaily was born in Cleveland, Ohio, and educated at Bowdoin College. Among his best known novels are *The Hound of Earth, The Violated, Confessions of a Spent Youth, The Man Who Knew Kennedy*, and *Now Playing at Canterbury*. He was the editor and cofounder of *Discovery*.

Michael Dennis Browne has taught at the University of Minnesota since 1971. He was born in Walton-on-Thames, Surrey, England, and came to the U.S. in 1965. He received his B.A. at Hull University and later attended Oxford. Among his many books are *The Wife of Winter, The Michael Morley Poems*, and *Selected Poems 1965–1995*. He is the recipient of an NEA Fellowship, a Bush Fellowship, and a Loft-McKnight Award.

Born in 1918 in Ohio, Warren Carrier attended Wabash College, and received his B.A. in 1942 from Miami University of Ohio. He took his M.A. at Harvard in 1948 and his Ph.D. from Occidental College in 1962. Carrier taught Romance Languages at the University of North Carolina, 1942–1944; and at Boston University, 1945–49. He was appointed an assistant professor at the University of Iowa in 1949, and remained for three years. A poet, novelist, and translator, Carrier has authored fifteen books, including five collections of poetry, five novels, a collection of stories, and a book of translations. With Paul Engle, he edited the text *Reading Modern Poetry*. Prior to coming to Iowa he founded and was the original editor of the *Quarterly Review of Literature*.

Kay Cassill has had dual careers as a professional writer and artist. Her fiction, nonfiction, poetry, prints, and photographs have appeared in many publications worldwide. She served as special correspondent for *People Weekly* from its inception until 1986. A graduate of the University of Iowa Writers' Workshop, she subsequently spent four years in the study of printmaking with

Mauricio Lasansky and painting with James Lechay. She has studied at the Academie de la Grande Chaumier (Paris), the New School for Social Research, Brown University, and the University of Rhode Island. She has been a visiting lecturer at Brown University—Pembroke, Wesleyan University, the University of Rhode Island, and Providence College.

R. V. Cassill is the author of twenty-three novels, among them *The Eagle on the Coin*, *Clem Anderson*, *Pretty Leslie*, *The President*, *The Goss Women*, and *The Unknown Soldier*. He is also the author of seven short story collections and a textbook, *Writing Fiction*, and is the editor of both *The Norton Anthology of Short Fiction* and *The Norton Anthology of Contemporary Fiction*. His numerous honors include an Atlantic First Award, a Fulbright Fellowship, an O. Henry Award for the short story, a Guggenheim Fellowship, and an American Academy of Arts and Sciences Award for Exceptional Accomplishment. Cassill taught in the Iowa Writers' Workshop from 1948 to 1952 and from 1960 to 1966, and later at Brown, Purdue, and Columbia. He is also an accomplished painter.

Henri Coulette was born in Los Angeles, California. He received his M.F.A. at the University of Iowa in 1954, and his Ph.D. in 1959. He taught English at Cal State—Los Angeles for almost thirty years. He also taught at Stanford and at the Iowa Writers' Workshop. His books include *The War of the Secret Agents*, which won the Lamont Poetry Award from the Academy of American Poets in 1965, and *The Family Goldschmitt*. His *Collected Poems* were published posthumously in 1990. He was awarded the James D. Phelan Award for Poetry, 1966; and a Guggenheim Fellowship, 1976. Henri Coulette died in South Pasadena in 1988.

Robert Dana attended the Writers' Workshop from 1952–1954. He is the author of twelve books of poetry including *Starting Out for the Difficult World*; *What I Think I Know: New & Selected Poems*; *Yes, Everything*; and *Hello, Stranger*. In 1984 he edited *Against the Grain: Interviews with Maverick American Publishers*. At Cornell College, he revived the *North American Review* in 1964, remaining its editor-in-chief until 1968. He has served as distinguished visiting writer at several American universities and most recently at Stockholm University in Sweden. Dana has been awarded two National Endowment Fellowships for Poetry and won the Delmore Schwartz Memorial Award in 1989.

Hualing Nieh Engle was born in Hupei, China, and moved to Taiwan in 1949. She published nine books of fiction and translations of Faulkner, Fitzgerald, Stephen Crane, and Henry James before she came to the Writers' Workshop as a visiting writer in 1964. She earned her M.F.A. at Iowa in 1966 and cofounded the International Writing Program with Paul Engle in 1967. They married in 1971. They continued to codirect the program until they retired in 1988. She has published twenty-two books, including short stories, novels, and translations. Her novel, *Mulberry and Peach: Two Women of China*, has been translated and published in several languages; the English edition published by Beacon Press won the 1990 American Book Award and will be reissued later this year.

Paul Engle was born in 1908 in Cedar Rapids, Iowa. He received his B.A. from Coe College in 1931 and an M.A. from the University of Iowa in 1932, presenting for his thesis an original book of poems, *Worn Earth*, which won the Yale Younger Poets Prize. It later became the first University of Iowa poetry thesis to be published as a book. Engle was a Rhodes Scholar from 1933 to 1936, at Merton College, Oxford University. He joined the faculty of the University of Iowa in 1937, became director of the Iowa Writers' Workshop in 1941, and remained director until he resigned in 1966. He went on to found the International Writing Program at Iowa with his second wife Hualing Nieh in 1967. When he died in 1991 at O'Hare airport in Chicago, he was on his way to receive from the Polish government its Medal of Merit. Among Paul Engle's many works are *West of Midnight, American Song, American Child, Golden Child* (opera libretto), *A Woman Unashamed, Images of China,* and *A Lucky American Childhood* (biography). One of the founding members of the National Council on the Arts, he was nominated with Hualing Nieh Engle for the 1976 Nobel Peace Prize.

Eugene Garber was born in 1932 in Birmingham, Alabama. He earned his B.A. from Tulane University and holds an M.A.

and Ph.D. from the University of Iowa. He has taught at Iowa, Western Washington State—Bellingham, and at SUNY-Albany where he was director of writing from 1977 until his retirement. Among his honors are a National Endowment Fellowship, and, in 1981, an AWP short fiction award for his collection, *Metaphysical Tales*.

John C. Gerber was born in New Waterford, Ohio, in 1908. He began his formal education in a one-room school in the hills of western Pennsylvania. He took his B.A. at the University of Pittsburgh in 1929, an M.A. in 1932, and a Ph.D. at the University of Chicago in 1941. He began teaching at the University of Chicago in 1938 and joined the English faculty at the University of Iowa in 1944. He was chair of the department of English, 1961—1976; and director of the School of Letters, 1967—1976. After he retired in 1976, he accepted the chair of the English Department at SUNY-Albany where, in 1984, he retired for the second time. He returned to Iowa as coordinator of the Center for Fine Arts, 1984—1986.

Gail Godwin is the author of ten novels, including *A Mother and Two Daughters*, *Violet Clay*, and *The Odd Woman*, all of which were nominated for the National Book Award, and two short story collections, *Dream Children* (many of the stories were written at Iowa) and *Mr. Bedford and the Muses*. *Evensong* (a sequel to *Father Melancholy's Daughter*) will be published this year. She was raised in Asheville, N.C., and earned her B.A. at the University of North Carolina and her M.A. and Ph.D. at the University of Iowa. She has received an American Academy of Arts and Letters Award for Literature.

James B. Hall was born at Jack Oaks Farm not far from Pansy, Ohio. After graduation from Blanchester High School, he attended Miami University of Ohio and the University of Hawaii; after overseas service in World War II he studied literary criticism, literary history, and creative writing at the University of Iowa and earned his Ph.D. in 1953. His work includes two books of poetry, four novels, and four collections of short stories, the most recent, *I Like It Better Now* (1992). He was the founder of the creative writing programs at the University of Oregon and the

University of California–Irvine; and was the founding provost of the Arts College (now Porter-Sesnon) at UC–Santa Cruz.

Oakley Hall served in the Marine Corps from 1939–1945. He is the author of twenty novels, including *Warlock* and *The Downhill Racers*, which were turned into films. He was for twenty years director of the program in writing at the University of California–Irvine and is the general director of the Squaw Valley Community of Writers. He was inducted into the Cowboy Hall of Fame in 1990.

Curtis Harnack served as executive director of Yaddo in Saratoga Springs, N.Y., from 1971 to 1987. Harnack was born in LeMars, Iowa; he earned his B.A. at Grinnell College, where he later taught, and his M.A. from Columbia University. He taught in the Writers' Workshop in 1957 and again in 1959. He has also been a Fulbright professor at the University of Tabriz in Iran. From 1960 to 1971 he was a member of the literature faculty of Sarah Lawrence College. He is the author of a number of nonfiction works, including *We Have All Gone Away*, *Gentlemen on the Prairie*, and *The Attic*.

Michael S. Harper was born in Brooklyn, N.Y., and took his B.A. at California State University–Los Angeles and his M.A. and M.F.A. at the University of Iowa. He is University Professor and professor of English at Brown University, where he has taught since 1970. He has also been a visiting professor at Harvard and Yale, as well as distinguished professor at Colgate University. He held the Elliston chair in poetry at the University of Cincinnati in 1979 and served as American specialist at the International Congress of Africanists in 1977. Among his best known books are *Dear John, Dear Coltrane*; *Images of Kin: New and Selected Poems*; and *History Is Your Own Heartbeat*. He has received awards from the American Academy of Arts and Sciences, the Black Academy of Arts and Letters, and the National Endowment for the Arts.

Donald Justice was born in Miami, Florida, in 1925. He earned his B.A. from the University of Miami in 1945, his M.A. from the University of North Carolina at Chapel Hill in 1947, and his Ph.D. at the University of Iowa in 1954. He taught in the Writers' Workshop from 1957 to 1966 and 1971 to 1982 before moving to the University of Florida. He also taught at the University of Missouri and Syracuse University. Justice's first volume of poems, *The Summer Anniversaries*, was the Lamont Poetry Selection of the Academy of American Poets in 1960. His other work includes *Night Light*; *Departures*; *Selected Poems*, which won the 1980 Pulitzer Prize; *The Sunset Maker: New and Selected Poems* (1995); and *A Donald Justice Reader*. He has received fellowships from the Guggenheim and Rockefeller Foundations and the National Endowment for the Arts. He was cowinner of the Bollingen Prize in 1991 and received a Lannan Literary Award in 1997. He is a chancellor of the Academy of American Poets.

Philip Levine was born in Detroit in 1928. He has his B.A. and M.A. from Wayne State University and an M.F.A. from the University of Iowa. He has taught at many universities, including Cal State–Fresno, Tufts University, Princeton, and NYU. He has been Elliston lecturer in poetry at the University of Cincinnati and Poet-in-Residence at Vassar College. His book *The Names of the Lost* won the Lenore Marshall Award in 1976; *7 Years From Somewhere*, the National Book Critics Circle Award in 1979; *What Work Is*, the National Book Award for poetry, 1991; and *The Simple Truth*, the Pulitzer Prize for poetry, 1995.

Kiyohiro Miura was born in Hokkaido, Japan, in 1930. He attended Tokyo University before coming to the U.S. in 1952. He took his B.A. in American History at San Jose State College in 1955 and his M.F.A. at the University of Iowa in 1958. He is the author of several scholarly books; a collection of short stories, *A Traveler in the Universe*; two collections of essays; and three novels. His novel *My Eldest Son Became a Buddhist Monk* won the Akutagawa Literary Prize in 1988 and was published in English in the U.S. by Charles E. Tuttle Co. in 1996 under the title *He's Leaving Home*. Miura was also honored in 1991 with a Japan Foundation Award.

Novelist and short story writer Bharati Mukherjee has both a Ph.D. in English and comparative literature and an M.F.A. in creative writing from the University of Iowa. She also has an M.A.

from the University of Baroda in English and ancient Indian culture. She is currently professor of English at the University of California–Berkeley. Among her publications are *The Holder of the World*, *Jasmine*, and *The Tiger's Daughter*, and two collections of stories, *Darkness* and *The Middleman and other Stories*, which won the National Book Critics Circle Award for fiction in 1988. She has also been the recipient of an NEA fellowship, a Guggenheim, and a Canada Council Senior Arts Fellowship.

William Cotter Murray was born in County Clare, Ireland, and came to the United States in 1949. He studied at St. Flannan's College and took his B.A. at Southern Connecticut State in 1956. He attended the Writers' Workshop in 1956 and received his M.A. in English in 1961. He taught in the fiction workshop from 1965 to 1969 and in the English department of the University of Iowa from 1958 until his retirement in 1992. He is the author of two novels, the Meredith Award–winning *Michael Joe* and *A Long Way from Home*. His most recent work is the collection of stories, *Irish Fictions*.

Philip F. O'Connor was educated at San Francisco University and San Francisco State College. He took his M.F.A. at the University of Iowa in 1963. He taught for more than thirty years in the creative writing program at Bowling Green University in Ohio. His first collection of stories, *Old Morals, Small Continents, Darker Times*, won the Iowa School of Letters Award in Short Fiction in 1971 and was recently reissued in a third printing. His first novel, *Stealing Home*, was a Book-of-the-Month Club selection and an American Book Award nominee for best first novel. Two other novels, *Defending Civilization* and *Finding Brendan*, were Pulitzer Prize nominees. He has three times been a member of the Pulitzer Prize Fiction Jury and was chair in 1994.

Steven D. Salinger was born in Brooklyn, New York. He has a B.S. from Cornell University, 1963, and an M.F.A. from the University of Iowa, 1965. He lived for seventeen years in St. Thomas and for five years taught English at the College of the Virgin Islands. Subsequently he launched two tourist magazines and founded a jewelry business. Moving to New York in 1982, he established *The Physicians' Travel & Meeting Guide*, a magazine for doctors. Warner Books has just published his first novel, *Behold the Fire.*

W. D. Snodgrass served in the U.S. Navy before coming to the Writers' Workshop in 1946. Before leaving in 1955, he earned a B.A., an M.A., and an M.F.A. He won the Pulitzer Prize in 1960 for his first book of poems, *Heart's Needle*. He has also received an Ingram Merrill Foundation Award, a Poetry Society of America citation, a Guinness Award (U.K.), a Guggenheim Fellowship, and the Centennial Medal of Romania. Among his other works are *After Experience*, *The Fuhrer Bunker*, and *Selected Poems 1957–1987*. He has taught at Cornell University, Wayne State University, the University of Rochester, Syracuse, and the University of Delaware.

Richard Stern attended the Writers' Workshop from 1952 to 1954, when he received his Ph.D. He has taught at the University of Chicago since 1956. His seventeen books include the novels *Golk*, *Other Men's Daughters*, and *Shares, A Novel in Ten Parts*. *Noble Rot: Stories 1949–88* was the 1989 *Chicago Sun-Times* Book of the Year in fiction, and *A Sistermony* won the 1995 Heartland Award for Non-Fiction Book of the Year. In 1985 Stern was given the Award of Merit for the Novel by the American Academy of Arts and Letters.

Lewis Turco founded and was the director of both the Cleveland State University Poetry Center and the Program in Writing Arts at SUNY-Oswego. Turco retired in 1996 after thirty-five years of teaching and is now the proprietor of the antiquarian Mathom Bookshop in Dresden, Maine. He is the 1997 winner with his Italian translator, Joseph Alessia, of the Bordighera Bi-Lingual Poetry Prize for his collection *A Book of Fears*. His books include *The Shifting Web: New and Selected Poems* and *The Public Poet: Five Lectures on the Art and Craft of Poetry*. He attended the Writers' Workshop in 1959–1960, and received his M.A. in 1962.

Constance Urdang was born in New York City and moved to St. Louis in 1960 with her husband, the poet Donald Finkel. Before attending the Iowa Writers' Workshop, she graduated cum laude from Smith College. Urdang's volumes of poetry include *The Picnic in the Cemetery*, *The Lone Woman and Others*, and *Only the World*; among her works of fiction are *Natural History*, *Lucha*, and *American Earthquakes*. Her work won her, among other honors, the Carleton Centennial Award for Prose, a National Endowment for the Arts fellowship, the Delmore Schwartz Memorial Poetry Award, and the Oscar Williams and Gene Derwood Award. She died of lung cancer in 1996.

Kurt Vonnegut was born in Indianapolis, Indiana. From 1940 to 1942, he majored in chemistry and biology at Cornell University. In 1943, he volunteered for military service and became a battalion intelligence scout with the 106th Infantry Division. He was captured by the Germans during the Battle of the Bulge in 1944 and shipped with other American prisoners in boxcars to Dresden where he was later freed by Russian troops. Vonnegut taught in the Iowa Writers' Workshop from 1965 to 1967 while writing *Slaughterhouse Five*. Among his other works are *Mother Night*, *God Bless You, Mr. Rosewater*, *Jailbird*, and *Timequake*; two collections of stories, *Welcome to the Monkey House* and *Happy Birthday, Wanda June*; and three collections of essays. Vonnegut received an Award for Literature from the National Institute and Academy of Arts and Letters in 1970. He is a member of the American Academy of Arts and Letters.

Ray B. West, Jr., was born in Logan, Utah, in 1908 and earned his Ph.D. from the University of Iowa in 1945. After holding appointments at several universities, he returned to Iowa in 1949 to head the fiction writing program at the Writers' Workshop. In 1969, he accepted a professorship at San Francisco State University, where he served as chair of the creative writing department until 1973. West also held visiting professorships at the University of Innsbruck, 1951–1952, and in Ankara, Turkey, 1956–1958. He was the founder and editor of the *Western Review*.

Charles Wright was born in 1935 in Pickwick Dam, Hardin County, Tennessee, and grew up in Tennessee and North Carolina. He attended Davidson College, the University of Iowa, and the University of Rome. From 1957 to 1961 he was in the Army Intelligence Service, stationed in Verona, Italy. From 1966 to 1983, he was a member of the English department of the University of California–Irvine; and since 1983, he has been a professor of English at the University of Virginia. Charles Wright has published over twenty books of poetry, translations, and nonfiction. His most recent works include *The World of Ten Thousand Things*, *Chickamauga*, and *Black Zodiac*. Wright has received a National Endowment for Arts Fellowship, an American Academy of Arts and Letters Award, a PEN Translation Prize, the National Book Award, an Award of Merit from the American Academy of Arts and Letters, and the Tanning Prize. In 1998, Wright's book of poems *Black Zodiac* won both the National Book Critics Circle Award and the Pulitzer Prize.

Jean Wylder attended the Writers' Workshop in 1947. She graduated from the University of Iowa with an M.A. in fine arts and literature and a degree in social work. Wylder was a social worker for the Franciscan Community Health Center in Rock Island, Illinois, and a recognized local educator and social worker in the Quad Cities area. She died in Albuquerque, New Mexico, in 1989.

Wai-lim Yip is a poet, translator, and critic, and has been a professor of comparative literature and creative writing at the University of California—San Diego since 1967. He is the author of more than twenty books of poetry and criticism including *Fugue*, *Crossing*, *The Edge of Waking*, and *The Wild Flower Story* as well as *Ezra Pound's Cathay*, *Modern Chinese Poetry 1930–1950*, and *Chinese Poetics*.

ACKNOWLEDGMENTS

Henri Coulette, "So Began the Happiest Years of My Life," from *Iowa City: The Cradle of Writers* series, edited by Glen Epstein, the *Iowa City Press-Citizen*, copyright © 1981 by Henri Coulette.

Robert Dana, "Far from the Ocean: Robert Lowell at Iowa, 1953," the *North American Review*, September/October 1997, copyright © 1997 by Robert Dana.

Paul Engle, "The Writer and the Place," excerpted from the introduction to *MIDLAND: Twenty-Five Years of Fiction and Poetry Selected from the Writing Workshops of the State University of Iowa*, edited by Paul Engle, Random House, Inc., copyright © 1961 by the State University of Iowa.

John Gerber, "The Emergence of the Writers' Workshop," excerpted from *The Teaching of English at the University of Iowa*, Maecenas Press, copyright © 1995 by John C. Gerber.

Philip Levine, "Mine Own John Berryman," from *The Bread of Time*, copyright © 1993 by Philip Levine. Reprinted by permission of Alfred A. Knopf, Inc.

W. D. Snodgrass, "Mentors, Fomenters, and Tormentors," the *Southern Review*, 1992, copyright © 1992 by W. D. Snodgrass.

Kurt Vonnegut, "New World Symphony," written for Paul Engle's memorial service in 1991, copyright © 1991 by Kurt Vonnegut.

Ray B. West, Jr., "Dylan Thomas at Iowa," excerpted from "Dylan Thomas in the Iowa Writers' Workshop," *San Francisco Fault*, October 1972, copyright © 1972 by Ray B. West, Jr.

Charles Wright, "Improvisations on Donald Justice," *Quarter Notes*, University of Michigan Press, Ann Arbor, copyright © 1993 by Charles Wright.

Jean Wylder, "Flannery O'Connor in the Writers' Workshop," excerpted from "Flannery O'Connor: A Reminiscence and Some Letters," *North American Review*, Spring 1970, copyright © 1970 by Jean Wylder.